INDO-TIBET-CHINA CONFLICT

INDO-TIBET-CHINA CONFLICT

Dinesh Lal

KALPAZ PUBLICATIONS
DELHI-110052

Indo-Tibet-China Conflict

Rs. 750

ISBN: 81-7835-714-3

Published in 2008 in India by
Kalpaz Publications
C-30, Satyawati Nagar,
Delhi-110052
E-mail: kalpaz@hotmail.com
Phone : 9212729499

Laser Type Setting by : Rajeshwar Prasad, Udgam India, Delhi
Printed at : Singhal Print Media, Delhi

Contents

Preface

Tibet is the crucial key in the relations between India and China. Both India and China, today, consider Tibet vital for their national security. Any strong power, established in Tibet, is a direct threat to security of India. It is this factor which will decide the course of history in relations between India and China. Tibetan developments, therefore, find a prominent place in this book. Furthermore both the countries are emerging economic powers. Will they cooperate or rival each other in economic field? This is the question in every one's mind. Beside many other factors such as religion and culture are also the key to Indo-China-Tibet relations.

In this book, we have covered relations between India, China and Tibet keeping Tibet at the centre stage. We have covered history, present scenario and the future of relations between these three countries in a very systematic and organized manner. This book has been written for scholars, students, administrators and as well as the general reader. We have attempted to cover all essential points as well as all facts.

In formulation of this book, the author has freely consulted large number of sources so no authenticity is claimed. Author is especially thankful to all those persons who helped in shaping this book in its final form. Suggestions for further improvement of this book are not only welcome but also greatly appreciated.

1

Introduction

India had made substantial contributions to Chinese culture due to her proximity to her northern Asian neighbours which is separated only by the mountainous range of Himalayas. Exchange of ideas and inventions goes long back between two countries. Spread of Buddhism from India to China created a bond between these two countries. Actually, Buddhism originated in India and was modified by the Chinese especially during the Tang Dynasty when monks brought the scripts back and disseminated the idea with newly-invented block-printing.

The religion of Buddhism manifests itself in many forms today. Chinese Buddhism is very different from Indian versions of the same religion. The difference between India and China is that although the latter country has made many contributions to secular aspects of human civilization, you don't see too many Indians acknowledging or knowing about them.

It would make more sense if both nations try to find common ground and enjoy mutual respect based upon their long history of neighbourly interaction. Forty years have passed since the 1962 war, but it still influences Sino-India relations. The Chinese People's Liberation Army in a bitter and cold battle in the Northeast vanquished the Indian army. India has repaired its relationship with the Chinese to some extent, but those wounds have not been forgotten.

Excuses have been thrown up for the military debacle. India was ill prepared it believed in non-violence it trusted the Chinese. Fingers have been pointed, most famously at then Prime Minister Jawaharlal Nehru, defence minister Krishna Menon, and Lieutenant General B. N. Kaul, who was in charge of the army on India's eastern frontier.

Evidence indicates that in the early years after independence, Jawaharlal Nehru himself privately instructed B. N. Mallik, head of the

Intelligence Bureau, to count China as an enemy. It was under his authorization that armed Indian border guards drove away the Tibetan administrators and occupied Sela by force in 1948, and Tawang and other Chinese territories to the south of the McMahon Line in 1952. But Nehru's government did not end here it sought to decide for itself where India's borders with China should lie and then impose the alignments it had chosen on China.

In 1960, the Nehru government not only refused publicly to negotiate with Premier Zhou Enlai who made a special trip to New Delhi to seek a friendly settlement of boundary issue, but rejected any standstill agreement.

In the following year, it ordered the 'Forward Policy', under which the Indian Army relentlessly attacked the People's Liberation Army's posts along the entire border and killed many Chinese soldiers in an attempt to extrude them out of all the Chinese territory it claimed.

This hostile and provocative policy not only broken up the status quo, but also breached the peace and tranquillity along the entire border. In October 1962, Nehru ordered the army to take the offensive and made a statement about it on the 12th of the same month.

After the war, India claimed that China was occupying about 33,000 square kilometres of its territory in the Aksai Chin region of Ladakh. China claimed that India was occupying 90,000 square kilometres Beijing claims the entire state of Arunachal Pradesh as its territory.

Though the two countries have tried to mend their relations over the decades, several issues remain unresolved; the Dalai Lama and the Tibetan government-in-exile in India, China's non-recognition of Sikkim's merger with India, nuclear tests in 1998 by India and India's allegation that China is arming Pakistan, including the latter's nuclear programme.

In China's policymaking with India, Tibet remains the key for India-China boundary dispute. The Chinese suspects that India favours an independent Tibet and secretly supports Tibetan separatists. Until Tibet is totally pacified, Beijing would not want to give up this bargaining chip that an unsettled boundary vis-à-vis India provides it with. An unsettled border provides China the strategic leverage to keep India uncertain about its intentions, and nervous about its capabilities, while exposing India's vulnerabilities and weaknesses, and ensuring New Delhi's good behaviour on issues of vital concern to China.

Since India controls 90,000 square kilometres of Tibet and the Himalayan region, the Chinese government will not easily give up its territory. Many Chinese thinkers believe that China's comprehensive national power in relation to India is likely to increase over time, and that would enable Beijing to drive a better bargain on the boundary question in the future.

Sino-Indian border issue is linked with sovereignty, territorial integrity, and the respective status of the two countries in the global hierarchy. One Chinese concern is that a border settlement, without major Indian territorial concessions, could potentially augment India's power position and thus impact negatively China's rise. An unsettled boundary suits Chinese interests for the present because China's claims in the western sector are complicated by the Indo-Pakistan dispute over Kashmir, Pakistan's interests in the Sino-Indian territorial dispute, and Beijing's interest in keeping India under strategic pressure on two fronts.

Many Chinese analysts believe that the military balance has shifted in their favour with the completion of the 1,118-kilometres Qinghai-Tibet railway and other military infrastructure projects in Tibet and that negates the need for any territorial concession to India in the eastern sector.

The Indian government has also responded by unveiling plans for economic development and major infrastructure projects like building of 72 roads, three airstrips and many bridges in the border areas along the undefined L.A.C. that would enable the Indian military to swiftly move forces into the region and sustain them logistically in the event of any untoward trouble or emergency.

Issue of Dalai Lama and Tibetan Government in Exile

After the failed uprising in 1959, the Dalai Lama fled Tibet and set up the Government of Tibet in Exile in Dharamsala, India, which is often referred to as Little Lhasa. The Dalai Lama met the Prime Minister Jawaharlal Nehru, to urge India to pressure China into giving Tibet an autonomous government, as relations with China were not proving successful.

Nehru did not want to increase tensions between China and India, so he encouraged the Dalai Lama to work on the Seventeen Point Agreement Tibet had with China. After establishing the exiled government, he re-established the eighty thousand Tibetan refugees who followed him into exile in agricultural settlements. He formed a Tibetan educational system in order to teach the Tibetan children what he believed to be traditional language, history, religion, and culture. The Tibetan Institute of Performing Arts was established in 1959 and the Central Institute of Higher Tibetan Studies became the primary university for Tibetans in India. He supported the refounding of two hundred monasteries and nunneries in an attempt to preserve Tibetan Buddhist teachings and the Tibetan way of life.

Issue of Sikkim

China sent troops to help Sikkim in 1791 and defend Tibet against the Gurkhas. After Nepal's following defeat, the Qing Dynasty established control over Sikkim. Following the advent of the British Raj in neighbouring India, Sikkim allied with them against their common enemy, Nepal. In 1947, a popular vote rejected Sikkim's joining the Indian Union and Prime Minister Jawaharlal Nehru agreed to a special protectorate status for Sikkim. Sikkim was to be a suzerainty of India, in which India look after its external affairs, defence, diplomacy and communication. In 2000, in a major embarrassment for the government of People's Republic of China, the seventeenth Karmapa Urgyen Trinley Dorje, who had been proclaimed a Lama by China, made a dramatic escape from Tibet to the Rumtek Monastery in Sikkim. Chinese officials were in a dilemma on this issue, as any protests to India on the issue would mean an explicit endorsement of India's governance of Sikkim, which the Chinese still regarded as an independent state occupied by India. China finally recognized Sikkim as an Indian state in 2003, which led to a thaw in Sino-Indian relations. In return, India announced its official recognition of Tibet as an integrated part of China.

Issue of Nuclear Tests

Ever since India carried out the Shakti sequence of nuclear tests in May 1998, several letters appeared in various newspapers, magazines and journals including Current Science expressing criticism. These perhaps give the impression that the scientific community as a whole is opposed to the tests. China, which had so far restrained from commenting on the nuclear tests carried out by India reacted sharply warning India of serious penalty. The Chinese foreign ministry in a terse statement said the Chinese government is shocked and strongly condemns the tests, which will have serious effects on peace and stability in South Asia and the world at large. The statement said that allegations by India that, China posed a nuclear threat to India are groundless and is a mere excuse to develop nuclear weapons.

The spiritual head of the Tibetan community the Dalai Lama has on the other hand urged India not to be pressurised by developed nations to halt its nuclear agenda. The winner of the Nobel Peace Prize said in Madison, USA that with the tests, India has proved that it is no longer an underdeveloped nation and it should have the same access to nuclear weapons as developed countries.

In April, Pakistan successfully tested a medium-range missile capable of striking deep inside India. Indian Defence Minister Fernandes pointed that China aided Pakistan to develop the missile. Pakistan and China denied the charge. But in the weeks before the nuclear tests, China was rankled when India's new Defence Minister, George Fernandes, described China as the main threat to India.

The United States did not believe in justifications given by India for its nuclear tests. Ex-prime minister Mr. Vajpayee in his letter to Ex-President Clinton, said that India carried out its tests mainly because of the perceived security threats from China and Pakistan. The Assistant Secretary of State for South Asian Affairs, Mr. Karl Inderfurth told a US Senate Foreign Relations Committee that India had pointed out to unresolved border problems with China and China's ties with Pakistan.

Chinese government said that Progress has been gradually made in the process of nuclear arms decrease, with the Nuclear Non-Proliferation Treaty being prolonged indefinitely and the Comprehensive Test Ban Treaty being reached under such circumstances, India conducting nuclear tests runs against international trends and is detrimental to the peace and stability of the South Asian region.

When India announced the tests, Brajesh Mishra, a top aide to India, said India needed a nuclear deterrent because India faces a very dangerous nuclear environment. India has long said it needed to keep its options open because of neighbours China and Pakistan. Since China conducted its first nuclear weapons test in 1964, China had said its nuclear weapons are for defence only and that it would never be the first to use them.

Issue of China Arming Pakistan

The famous Maoist saying "enemy's enemy is a friend" is the base of Pakistan and China relationship. China is arming Pakistan to put pressure on India. A well armed Pakistan will ease pressure on China's Border with India. American intelligence agencies have claimed that China is constantly aiding Pakistan's effort to build long-range missiles that could carry nuclear weapons deep inside India. Pakistan also gained nuclear capability, presumably with China's help, and conducted a nuclear test of its own.

China is arming Pakistan with advanced missile technology. Recent Pakistan missile tests highlight the close working relationship between Beijing and Islamabad. While Chinese diplomats in the U.N. talk of finding peace with a nuclear Pakistan, the People's Liberation Army is rapidly provided Islamabad with advanced weaponry.

Pakistan demonstrated its newfound missile technology from China by test-firing a new anti-ship missile during recent military exercises. The shore-launched firing of this anti-ship missile was carried out by Pakistan during the large-scale war games. China Precision Machinery Import-Export Corp. (CPMIEC) has been working for two years with its Pakistan counterpart, developing a radar-guided variant of cruise missile.

The Chinese missile proliferation to Pakistan has brought sanctions against some of the specific PLA-owned companies involved. China has previously been sited as the source of missile, nuclear, chemical and biological weapons sales to Iran, Iraq, Sudan, Pakistan, North Korea and Libya. In one case, detailed Chinese blueprints of an atomic bomb were turned over to U.S. intelligence officials by Libya.

REFERENCES

Anderson, Benedict: Imagined Communities: Reflections on the Origin and Spread of Nationalism, London, Verso, 1991.

Andrugtsang, Gompo Tashi: Four Rivers, Six Ranges: Reminiscences of the Resistance Movement in Tibet, Information and Publicity Office of His Holiness the Dalai Lama, 1973.

Ardley, Jane: Resistance, Religion and Politics: the Tibetan Independence Movement in Comparative Perspective, Keele University, 1999.

Arnold, Edwin: Bhagavadgita, New York, Dover Publications, 1899/1993.

Benn, James A: 'Where text meets flesh - burning the body as an apocryphal practice' in History of Religions, 1998.

Besant, Annie and Bhagavan Das: The Bhagavad Gita, Madras, Theosophical Publishing House, 1926.

Bhattacharjee, Arun: A History of Modern India, Liverpool, Lucas Publications, 1988.

Burman, Bina Roy: Religion and Politics in Tibet, New Delhi: Vikas Publishing1979

Carrasco, Pedro: Land and Polity in Tibet, Seattle, University of Washington Press, 1959.

Chandra, Bipan: India's Struggle for Independence 1857-1947, New Delhi, Penguin, 1989.

Conner, Victoria and Robert Barnett: Leaders in Tibet: A Directory, London, Tibet Information Network, 1997.

Craig, Mary: Tears of Blood: A Cry for Tibet, London, HarperCollins, 1992.

French, Patrick: Liberty or Death: India's Journey to Independence and Division, London, Flamingo, 1997.

Gandhi, M.K.: An Autobiography, or The Story of My Experiments with Truth, Ahmedabad, Navajivan Trust, 1927.

International Commission of Jurists: The Question of Tibet and the Rule of Law, Geneva, ICJ, 1959.

Iyer, R. N.: The Moral and Political Thought of Mahatma Gandhi, New York, Oxford University Press, 1973.

Philips, C.H. and Wainwright, M.D.: The Partition of India: Policies and Perspectives 1935-1947, London, George Allen and Unwin Ltd., 1970.

Ray, S: Gandhi, India and the World: An International Symposium, Melbourne, Hawthorn Press, 1970.

Richards, Glyn: The Philosophy of Gandhi, Surrey, Curzon Press, 1991.

Richardson, H. E.: Tibet and its History, London, Oxford University Press, 1962.

The Dalai Lama: My Land and My People: Memoirs of the Dalai Lama of Tibet, New York, Potala Corporation, 1962.

2

History of Indo-China Relations

Introduction

India-China relations have a long history, which was seen both ups and downs during these last six decades. The relations between late fifties and early eighties were sour due to situations leading to the war of 1962, which led to a serious setback in bilateral relations. However, India and China restored ambassadorial relations in 1976. Various heads and other high-level dignitaries of both the countries have visited each other. In 1979, the then External Affairs Minister Atal Bihari Vajpayee made a visit to China, which lead to the renewal of contacts at the highest political level after two decades. Chinese Foriegn Minsiter Huang Hua made a return visit to India in 1981. The visit of PM Rajiv Gandhi to China in December 1988 was a landmark in India-China relations. Premier Li Peng visited India in December 1991. Prime Minister Narasimha Rao visited China in September 1993. President Jiang Zemin's state visit to India in November 1996 was the first by Chinese Head of State.

It guided the way for recommencement of political negotiation at the highest level between the two countries after a period of almost twenty-eight years. During these visit both side agreed to develop and expand bilateral relations in every field. They also agreed to form a Joint Working Group on the Boundary question to seek a fair, reasonable, and mutually acceptable solution.

Besides the Joint Working Group on the border issue and the Joint Economic Group on economic and commercial issues, there are bilateral exchanges in Science and Technology, outer space, mining, audit, defence, personnel, and culture.

During his visit, the two countries agreed to work towards constructive and cooperative relationships while continuing to address outstanding differences.

Four Agreements were signed, of which the most important was one on Confidence Building Measures in the Military field along the LAC in the India-China Border Area was signed along with other agreements. Six MOUs/agreements were signed during the visit on cooperation in tourism, provision of hydrological data by China to India, peaceful uses of outer space, science and technology and phyto-sanitary measures.

Following the talks, the two leaders signed a joint statement and identified a series of common consensus reached by the two governments in the hope to comprehensively expand the friendly agreement on the political guiding principles for resolving the boundary issue between China and India.

In the present scenario, economic relations and border dispute are the two main which guide the Sino Indian relation the former one being the most important. With regard to the economic relations even the Chinese feel that with both economies growing, India's relative advantage in information technology software and china's relative benefit in manufacturing hardware must be combined to produce a new synergy. The economic relations between two countries have developed immensely in the past few decades, the cross border trade has got new impetus when in 1991 both countries agreed to open Lipulekh pass for trade between both the countries. Recently in July 2006 Nathula pass which joins the Tibet and Sikkim has been opened for trade after nearly forty four long years.

Ancient Period

India and China had relatively little political contact before the 1950s. Despite this, both countries have had extensive cultural contact since the first century, especially with the transmission of Buddhism from India to China. China and India have also had some contact before the transmission of Buddhism. References to a people called the Chinas, now believed to be the Chinese, are found in ancient Indian literature. The Indian epic Mahabharata contains references to China, which may have been referring to the Qin state which later became the Qin Dynasty. Chanakya (350-283 BC), the prime minister of the Maurya Empire and a professor at Takshashila University, refers to Chinese silk as cinamsuka (Chinese silk dress) and cinapatta (Chinese silk bundle) in his Arthashastra.

Origin: Historical and cultural ties between China and India had already flourished between the first and 10th centuries AD, thanks to the arrival of Buddhism in China (and then in Japan, Korea and Viet Nam) via the Silk Road, that links India to China. This cultural dimension helped shape Chinese civilization from the Han Dynasty all the way to the Sui and Tang dynasties.

China was linked culturally to India, via Buddhism. Both were already pursuing their wider Asian interests then, as they dominated the philosophical and cultural psyche of Asia. This civilization dialogue between China and India could be seen in three aspects of Chinese civilization: architecture and temple-building, sculpture and paintings and creative arts.

China and India have met and held dialogue with each other for more than a thousand years through Buddhism and the Silk Road. This historical civilization dialogue was then extended to the rest of East or Confucianist Asia.

In the Records of the Grand Historian, Zhang Qian (113 BC) and Sima Qian (145-90 BC) make references to Shendu, which may have been referring to the Indus Valley (the Sindh province in modern Pakistan), originally known as Sindhu in Sanskrit. When Yunnan was annexed by the Han Dynasty in the first century, Chinese authorities reported an Indian Shendu community living there.

Spread of Buddhism from India to China: There is a legend concerning spread of Buddhism to China. Purportedly, Emperor Ming dreamed of a golden deity who was interpreted by his advisors to be Buddha. The Emperor then sent to India for Buddhist texts. However, a much more plausible theory is that Buddhism spread to central Asia from the Indo-Greek Bactrian Kingdoms by the silk trade routes in the second century BC. After China conquered parts of central Asia in the first century BC, there were Buddhists living under Chinese rule. Though Buddhism started out in China as a religion of foreigners, it gradually came to the forefront of Chinese religion. When Buddhism came to China, it had already changed in many ways.

Part of Buddhism's appeal to the Chinese was the new interpretation of a heaven-like Nirvana, the texts and art that Buddhism had inspired. The main appeal, however, was the original Buddhist ideas of the nature of suffering and the escape from suffering. These aspects of Buddhism helped to spread the religion within China. The T'ang Dynasty was a time of great prosperity for Buddhism in China. Though T'ang rulers themselves were Taoists, all religions were tolerated during this period.

It was during this dynasty that Buddhism gained its largest and most varied following in China; from the Tang rulers to the general population, Buddhism had followers in all class groups. This was the period of the greatest exchanges between China and Buddhism. Buddhist painting and sculpture became very highly developed.

New schools of Buddhism developed and flourished during the Tang. Although these new schools branched off of mainstream Buddhism, some followers journeyed to India to return to the roots of Buddhism. Near the end of the Tang Dynasty, emperor Wu-tsung came to power and began a religious persecution in which many Buddhist temples and shrines were destroyed and hundreds of thousands of monastic followers were forced to return to lay life. This persecution marked the end of the prosperity and religious freedom that Buddhism enjoyed during the Tang dynasty.

Despite the loss of many Buddhist documents during the religious persecution of the late T'ang, Chinese sects of Buddhism remained true to their heritage, and were reinforced by new sects that formed at that time. When Buddhism was introduced into China, some of the basic principles appealed to the Chinese, making it popular in that culture. The Chinese modified Indian Buddhism to make forms of Buddhism that were distinctly Chinese. Two very popular new schools were Pure Land and Ch'an. Ch'an or Zen Buddhism developed in China as a more mystical form of Buddhism that concentrated mostly on meditation and reflection. Zen Buddhism is based on the original teachings of Buddha, Hinayana and Mahayana, and also on the culture of China. Zen followers focus on meditation on the teachings of the Buddha, and concentration to improve the mind. The Pure Land tradition of Buddhism concentrated on devotion. The common population mostly followed Pure Land, which is thought to be the reason behind some secret organizations and rebellions. In the Pure Land tradition, prayer, devotion, and acts of kindness are believed to be the path to rebirth in a higher form, and eventually, to Nirvana. Other less known traditions of Chinese Buddhism are T'ien-t'ai, Hua-yen, Tantric, Fa-Hsiang, Kosa, and the Sect of the Three Stages. The culture of China is deeply ingrained in each sect of Chinese Buddhism.

Early Chinese translations of Buddhist texts explained Buddhist concepts using Taoist terms. The Chinese religion of Taoism has greatly affected Buddhism. In fact, the Chinese Buddhist texts were so similar to Taoist texts that for a long time, Buddhism was thought to be a new form of Taoism. Also, Lao-tzu; the founder of Taoism and the Buddha were supposed by the Chinese to be the same deity. During the T'ang dynasty, Buddhism and Taoism competed for followers within the court and the general population.

One setback to Buddhism was the popularity of female deities in China. Buddhism was a very patriarchal religion, while Taoism included a goddess. Thus, as a result of the influences of traditional Chinese religions and the rivalry with Taoism, the Buddhist male deity, Kuan Yin, gradually came to be regarded as a female. During this period of religious rivalry, many aspects of Buddhism were "borrowed" by Taoism in its effort to gain followers. The many Buddhist sutras that came into China at that time were quickly but sloppily copied by Taoists. Most times all that was changed was the name "Buddha" to "Lao-tzu," and sometimes even this was overlooked. The remnants of the religious exchanges of the Tang dynasty still exist today.

In the interaction between Buddhism and China, the culture of China has also been greatly influenced. One of the main effects of Buddhism on Chinese culture was in art. Paintings and sculptures of the Buddha and Bodhisattvas (the Buddhist equivalent of a Catholic saint), in particular Guan Yin, or Kuan Yin, were very popular during the Chinese period of disunity. Carvings of the Buddha in rock caves were sometimes as tall as 45 feet.

Buddhism appealed to the Chinese as a way to be freed from suffering. The Four Noble Truths of Buddhism provided straightforward instructions as to how to escape from suffering. While the introspective nature of Buddhism seemed to conflict with the family-oriented ideals and beliefs of Confucianism, in actuality, the Mahayana form of Buddhism agreed with social aspects of Confucianism, as with mystical aspects of Taoism, and the Chinese culture of the time of its first appearance. Because of this, the influences of Buddhism can be seen in other Chinese religions, and the division of religions is more difficult to discern.

At present, Buddhism and China are very closely correlated, and each continues to influence the other. Even in the past half-century, there have been many developments in the relationship between China and Buddhism.

Records of Zhang Qian and Sima Qian: Zhang Qian was an imperial envoy to the outside world in the 2nd century BC, during the time of the Han Dynasty. He was the first official diplomat to bring back reliable information about Central Asia to the Chinese imperial court, then under Emperor Wu of Han, and played an important pioneering role in the Chinese colonization and conquest of the region now known as Xinjiang.

Zhang Quian's travels are linked with the major route of transcontinental trade, the Silk Road. In essence, his missions opened up to China the many kingdoms and products of Indai. Zhang Qian's accounts of his explorations of Central Asia are detailed in the Early Han historical chronicles.

Zhang Qian was born just east of Hanzhong in the north central province of Shaanxi, China. He entered the capital, Chang'an, today's Xi'an, between 140 BC and 134 BC as a Gentleman, serving Emperor Wu of Han of the Han Dynasty. At the time the nomadic Xiongnu tribes, the name given the Turkic peoples of Central Asia by the Chinese, controlled what is now Inner Mongolia and dominated the Western Regions, Xiyu, the areas surrounding the territory of the Han Dynasty. The Han emperor was interested in establishing commercial ties with distant lands but outside contact was prevented by the hostile Xiognu.

The Han court dispatched Zhang Qian to the Western Regions in 138 BC with a group of ninety-nine members to make contact and build an alliance with outside kingdoms.

The reports of Zhang Qian's travels are quoted extensively in the 1st century BC Chinese historic chronicles "Records of the Great Historian" by Sima Qian. Zhang Qian visited directly the kingdom of Dayuan in Ferghana, the territories of the Yuezhi in Transoxonia, the Bactrian country of Daxia with it remnants of Greco-Bactrian rule, and Kangju. He also made reports on neighbouring countries that he did not visit, such as Anxi (Parthia), Tiaozhi (Mesopotamia), Shendu (India) and the Wusun.

Zhang Qian also reports about the existence of India southeast of Bactria. The name Shendu comes from the Sanskrit word "Sindhu", used for the province of Sindh by its local people. Sindh was one of the most advanced regions of India at the time. Although it was part of India, it practiced separate authority over itself. Because of its coastal borders with Persia and the Arabian Sea, it invited great wealth from these regions. Parts of Northwestern India (modern Pakistan) were ruled by the Indo-Greek Kingdom at the time, which explains the reported cultural similarity between Bactria and India. His reports says:

"Southeast of Daxia is the kingdom of Shendu (India)... Shendu, they told me, lies several thousand *li* southeast of Daxia (Bactria). The people cultivate the land and live much like the people of Daxia. The region is said to be hot and damp. The inhabitants ride elephants when they go in battle. The kingdom is situated on a great river (Indus)."

Medieval Period

After the transmission of Buddhism from India to China from the first century onwards, many Indian scholars and monks travelled to China, such as Batuo (founder of the Shaolin Monastery) and Bodhidharma (founder of Chan/Zen Buddhism), while many Chinese scholars and monks travelled to India, such as Xuanzang and Yi Ching.

During the seventh Century, Tang Dynasty China gained control over large portions of the Silk Road and Central Asia. Wang Xuance had sent a diplomatic mission to northern India, which was embroiled by civil war just following the death of King Harsha. After the murder of thirty members of this mission by one usurpers claiments to the throne, Wang fled, and returned with allied Tibetan and central Asian troops to back the opposing claimant. With his forces, Wang besieged and captured the capital, while his deputy Jiang Shiren captured the usurper and sent him back to Emperor Tang Taizong in Chang'an as a prisoner.

Scholarly Travels: The Chinese were attracted to India for her fabulous wealth of learning since ancient times. Buddhabhadra, a Buddhist monk from India or Ba Tuo in Chinese, came to China during Emperor Xiaowen's reign during the Northern Wei Dynasty period in 495AD. The emperor liked Buddhabhadra and offered to support him in teaching Buddhism at court. Buddhabhadra declined and was given land to build a temple on Mt. Song. There he built Shaolin, which translates into small forest.

Thirty years after Shaolin was founded, another Buddhist monk called Bodhidharma from India came to China to teach Yogic concentration, known commonly today by the Japanese term "Zen" Buddhism. He travelled throughout China and finally came to Mt. Song where he found Shaolin Temple where he asked to be admitted.

The abbot, Fang Chang, refused and it is said Bodhidharma climbed high into the mountains to a cave where he meditated for nine years. It is believed that he sat, facing the cave wall for much of these nine years so that his shadow became permanently outlined on the cave wall. After nine years, Fang Chang finally granted Bodhidharma entrance to Shaolin where he became the First Patriarch of Zen Buddhism.

Xuanzang, a seventh century Buddhist pilgrim, made a historic pilgrimage to India along the Silk Road, one of the longest and oldest trade routes known to mankind. Along with silk and less glamorous articles of trade, the great trans-Asian roads carried ideas and religions which were to prove far more significant than silk. The gentle creed of Buddhism was to revolutionize art and thought not only in China but in Japan and Korea as well. The Lord Buddha was born in India in 656 BC. Centuries later, there were so many schools of Buddhism and so many conflicting texts, Xuanzang was clear that he had to go to the source. In 629 BC he set forth to seek "the sacred traces of the Buddha" and to find the true Buddhist scriptures in the land of its birth.

In 633, Xuanzang visited Kashmir and journeyed south to Chinabhukti (thought to be modern Firozpur), where he studied for a year with the monk-prince Vinitaprabha. In 634 he went east to Jalandhar in eastern Punjab, before climbing up to visit predominantly "Hinayana" monasteries in the Kulu valley and turning southward again to Bairat and then Mathura, on the Yamuna river. Mathura had 2,000 monks of both major Buddhist branches, despite being Hindu-dominated. Xuanzang travelled up the river to Srughna before crossing eastward to Matipura, where he arrived in 635, having crossed the river Ganges. From here, he headed south to Sankasya (Kapitha), said to be where Buddha descended from heaven, then onward to the northern Indian emperor Harsha's grand capital of Kanyakubja (Kanauji). Here, in 636, Xuanzang encountered 100 monasteries of 10,000 monks (both Mahayana and "Hinayana"), and was impressed by the king's patronage of both scholarship and Buddhism. Xuanzang spent time in the city studying Theravada scriptures, before setting off eastward again for Ayodhya (Saketa), homeland of the Yogacara school. Xuanzang now moved south to Kausambi (Kosam), where he had a copy made from an important local image of the Buddha.

Xuanzang now returned northward to Sravasti, travelled through Terai in the southern part of modern Nepal (here he found deserted Buddhist monasteries) and thence to Kapilavastu, his last stop before Lumbini, the birthplace of Buddha. Reaching Lumbini, he would have seen a pillar near the old Ashoka tree that Buddha is said to have been born under. This was from the reign of emperor Ashoka, and records that he worshipped at the spot. The pillar was rediscovered by A. Fuhrer in 1895.

In 637, Xuanzang set out from Lumbini to Kusinagara, the site of Buddha's death, before heading southwest to the deer park at Sarnath where Buddha gave his first sermon, and where Xuanzang found 1,500 resident monks. Travelling eastward, at first via Varanasi, Xuanzang reached Vaisali, Pataliputra (Patna) and Bodh Gaya. He was then accompanied by local monks to Nalanda, the great ancient university of India, where he spent at least the next two years. He was in the company of several thousand scholar-monks, whom he praised. Xuanzang studied logic, grammar, Sanskrit, and the Yogacara school of Buddhism during his time at Nalanda.

Hiuen-Tsiang (603-664 A.D.) was one of the outstanding Chinese scholars who visited India in search of knowledge. He traveled extensively in India. He passed through Kashmir valley, visited Takshashila, and reached Mathura, where he saw the sacred traces of Lord Buddha at Kashi. He went to Kapilavastu, Kushinagar, Pataliputra, Vaishali, Mahabodhi, and stayed at the famed Nalanda university. Tsinag then visited Rajgir and Nepal. He also toured South India and paid a visit to Sri Lanka.

Hiuen Tsiang's visit to Nalanda Mahavihara meant the fulfillment of his life-long wishes which brought him to India. There he found profound learning, devotion, warm and cordial hospitality. Under the able guidance of Shilabhadra and Buddhabhadra, he was able to extend his scholarship in a wider sense than he could have done elsewhere. He could study subjects like logic, grammar, linguistics, medicine, crafts and the Vedas in great detail.

He returned by the same route by which he had come to India. He collected very valuable information and manuscripts. Unfortunately while crossing the Indus river on the way back, his boat capsized and a number of documents were lost. However, some of these he was able to recover from the libraries at Kusha and Kashghar monasteries.

In the year 645 A.D. he was back in China. He had carried with him relics, golden and sandalwood statues of Lord Buddha, 224 books of the sutras, 192 Shastras, 15 works of the Sthavira schools, 67 books of the Sarvastivada school, and 17 works of the Kasyapiya school. The emperor, although was upset by Hieun Tsiang's actions earlier, gave a him a hero's welcome upon return. The emperor also built a pagoda at the southern gate of the Hogn-Fu temple in Si-gan-fu, in which Hiuen Tsinag's entire collection is protected and preserved. This noble act of the Chinese emperor enables the scholars of Buddhist studies could make use of this extremely valuable source material even today.

Voyages of Zheng He: Between 1405 and 1433, the Ming Dynasty China sponsored a series of seven naval expeditions. Emperor Yongle designed them to establish a Chinese presence, impose imperial control over trade, and impress foreign peoples in the Indian Ocean basin. He also might have wanted to extend the tributary system, by which Chinese dynasties traditionally recognized foreign peoples.

Admiral Zheng was dispatched to lead a series of huge naval expeditions to explore these regions. The largest of his voyages included over 317 and 28,000 men, and the largest of his treasure ships were over 126.73 m in length. During his voyages, he visited numerous Indian kingdoms and ports. On the first three voyages, Zheng He visited southeast Asia, India, and Ceylon. The fourth expedition went to the Persian Gulf and Arabia, and later expeditions ventured down the east African coast, as far as Malindi in what is now Kenya. Throughout his travels, Zheng He liberally dispensed Chinese gifts of silk, porcelain, and other goods. In return, he received rich and unusual presents from his hosts, including African zebras and giraffes that ended their days in the Ming imperial zoo. Zheng He and his company paid respects to local deities and customs, and in Ceylon they erected a monument honouring Buddha, Allah, and Vishnu.

Early Modern Period

Sino-Gurkha Wars: The late 1760s saw the creation of a strong state under the Gurkhas, a warrior people originally from northern India that expanded outwards to include an area which includes modern Nepal. In 1788 the Gurkha rulers decided to invade southern Tibet, for which they probably thought they would have British backing. During the campaign between 1788 and 1791, Nepal invaded Tibet and robbed Tashilhunpo Monastery of Shigatse. Alarmed, the Chinese emperor Qianlong dispatched a sizeable army to Tibet. The two Manchu resident agents in Lhasa (Ambans) made no attempt at defence or resistance. Instead they took the child Panchen Lama to safety when the Nepalese troops came through and plundered the rich monastery at Shigatse on their way to Lhasa. Upon hearing of the first Nepalese incursions, the Qianlong Emperor commanded troops from Sichuan to proceed to Lhasa and restore order. By the time they reached southern Tibet, the Gurkhas had already withdrawn.

In 1791 the Gurkhas returned in force. Qianlong urgently dispatched an army of 10,000. It was made up of around 6,000 Manchu and Mongol forces supplemented by tribal soldiers under the able general Fukang'an, with Hailancha as his deputy. They entered Tibet from Xining (Qinghai) in the north, shortening the march but making it in the dead of winter 1791-1792, crossing high mountain passes in deep snow and cold. They reached central Tibet in the summer of 1792 and within two or three months could report that they had won a decisive series of encounters that pushed the Gurkha armies across the crest of the Himalaya and back into the valley of Kathmandu. Fukang'an fought on into 1793, when he forced the battered Gurkhas to accept surrender on Manchu terms. The Nepalese were forced to retreat and pay heavy repatriations. The victory of 1793, however, did not prevent repeated Nepalese incursions thereafter.

Sino-Sikh War: In the 18th to 19th centuries, the Sikh Confederacy of the Punjab region in India was expanding into neighbouring lands. It had annexed Ladakh into the state of Jammu in 1834. In 1841, they invaded Tibet with an army and overran parts of western Tibet.

Chinese forces defeated the Sikh army in December 1841, forcing the Sikh army to withdraw from Tibet, and in turn entered Ladakh and besieged Leh, where they were in turn defeated by the Sikh Army. At this point, neither side wished to continue the conflict, as the Sikhs were embroiled in tensions with the British that would lead up to the First Anglo-Sikh War, while the Chinese was in the midst of the First Opium War with the British. The Chinese and the Sikhs signed a treaty in September 1842, which stipulated no transgressions or interference in the other country's frontiers.

Post Independence

India's first Prime Minister Jawaharlal Nehru based his vision of rising Asia on friendship between the two largest states of Asia. However, the initial focus of the leaders of both the nations was not the foreign policy, but the internal development of their respective states. When they did concentrate on the foreign policies, their concern wasn't one another, but rather the United States of America and the Union of Soviet Socialist Republics and the alliance systems which dominated by the two superpowers.

1950s: On October 1st, 1949 the People's Liberation Army defeated the Kuomintang (Nationalist Party) of China in a civil war and established the People's Republic of China. On 15 August, 1947, India became an independent dominion under British Commonwealth and became a federal, democratic republic after its constitution came into effect on 26

January, 1950. Mao Zedong, the Commander of the Liberation Army and the Chairman of the Communist Party of China viewed Tibet as an integral part of the Chinese State. Mao was determined to bring Tibet under direct administrative and military control of People's Republic of China and saw Indian concern over Tibet as a manifestation of the Indian Government in the internal affairs of the People's Republic of China.

The PRC sought to reassert control over Tibet and to end Lamaism (Tibetan Buddhism) and feudalism, which it did by force of arms in 1950. To avoid antagonizing the People's Republic of China, Nehru informed Chinese leaders that India had neither political nor territorial ambitions, nor did it seek special privileges in Tibet, but that traditional trading rights must continue. With Indian support, Tibetan delegates signed an agreement in May 1951 recognizing PRC sovereignty but guaranteeing that the existing political and social system of Tibet would continue. Direct negotiations between India and the PRC commenced in an atmosphere improved by India's mediation efforts in ending the Korean War (1950-1953).

Meanwhile, India was the 16th state to establish diplomatic relations with the People's Republic of China, and did so on 1 April, 1950. In April 1954, India and the PRC signed an eight-year agreement on Tibet that set forth the basis of their relationship in the form of the Five Principles of Peaceful Coexistence (Panchsheel). Although critics called the Panchsheel naive, Nehru calculated that in the absence of either the wherewithal or a policy for defence of the Himalayan region, India's best guarantee of security was to establish a psychological buffer zone in place of the lost physical buffer of Tibet. Thus the catch phrase of India's diplomacy with China in the 1950s was Hindi-Chini bhai-bhai, which means, in Hindi, Indians and Chinese are brothers. Up until 1959, despite border skirmishes and discrepancies between Indian and Chinese maps, Chinese leaders amicably had assured India that there was no territorial controversy on the border though there is some evidence that India avoided bringing up the border issue in high level meetings.

In 1954, India published new maps that included the Aksai Chin region within the boundaries of India. When an Indian reconnaissance party discovered a completed Chinese road running through the Aksai Chin region of the Ladakh District of Jammu and Kashmir, border clashes and Indian protests became more frequent and serious. In January 1959, PRC premier Zhou Enlai wrote to Nehru, rejecting Nehru's contention that the border was based on treaty and custom and pointing out that no government in China had accepted as legal the McMahon Line, which in the 1914 Shimla Convention defined the eastern section of the border between India and Tibet. The Dalai Lama, spiritual and temporal head of the Tibetan people, sought sanctuary in Dharmsala, Himachal Pradesh, in March 1959, and thousands of Tibetan refugees settled in north-western India, particularly in Himachal Pradesh. The People's Republic of China accused India of expansionism and imperialism in Tibet and throughout the Himalayan region. China claimed 104,000 square of territory over which India's maps showed clear sovereignty, and demanded rectification of the entire border.

Zhou proposed that China relinquish its claim to most of India's northeast in exchange for India's abandonment of its claim to Aksai Chin. The Indian government, constrained by domestic public opinion, rejected the idea of a settlement based on uncompensated loss of territory as being humiliating and unequal.

1960s: Border disputes resulted in a short border war between the People's Republic of China and India in 20 October, 1962. The PRC pushed the unprepared and inadequately led Indian forces to within forty-eight kilometres of the Assam plains in the northeast and occupied strategic points in Ladakh, the PRC declared a unilateral cease-fire on 21 November and withdrew twenty kilometers behind its contended line of control.

At the time of Sino-Indian border conflict, a severe political split was taking place in the Communist Party of India. One section was accused by the Indian government as being pro-PRC, and a large number of political leaders were jailed. Subsequently, CPI split with the leftist section forming the Communist Party of India (Marxist) in 1964. CPI(M) held some contacts with the Communist Party of China in the initial period after the split, but did not fully embrace the political line of Mao Zedong.

Relations between the PRC and India deteriorated during the rest of the 1960s and the early 1970s as Sino-Pakistani relations improved and Sino-Soviet relations worsened. The PRC backed Pakistan in its 1965 war with India. Between 1967 and 1971, an all-weather road was built across territory claimed by India, linking PRC's Xinjiang Uyghur Autonomous Region with Pakistan India could do no more than protest. The PRC continued an active propaganda campaign against India and supplied ideological, financial, and other assistance to dissident groups, especially to tribes in northeastern India. The PRC accused India of assisting the Khampa rebels in Tibet. Diplomatic contact between the two governments was minimal although not formally severed.

The flow of cultural and other exchanges that had marked the 1950s ceased entirely. The flourishing wool, fur and spice trade between Lhasa and India through the Nathula Pass, an offshoot of the ancient Silk Road in the then Indian protectorate of Sikkim was also severed. However, the biweekly postal network through this pass was kept alive, which exists till today.

In late 1967, there were two skirmishes between Indian and Chinese forces in Sikkim. The first one was dubbed the Nathu La incident, and the other the Chola incident. Prior to these incidents had been the Naxalbari uprising in India by the Communist Naxalites and Maoists.

In 1967 a peasant uprising broke out in Naxalbari, led by pro-Maoist elements. A pronunciation by Mao titled Spring Thunder over India gave full moral support for the uprising. The support for the revolt marked the end for the relations between CPC and CPI(M). Naxalbari-inspired communists organized armed revolts in several parts of India, and in 1969 they formed the Communist Party of India (Marxist-Leninist). However, as the Naxalite movement disintegrated in various splits, the PRC withdrew its political support and turned non-committal towards the various Indian groups.

On 11 September, 1967, troops of the Indian Army's eighteenth Rajput Regiment were protecting an Engineering Company that was fencing the North Shoulder of Nathula, when Chinese troops opened fire on them. This escalated over the next five days to an exchange of heavy artillery and mortar fire between the Indians and the Chinese. Sixty two Indian soldiers, from the eighteenth Rajput, the second Grenadiers and the Artillery regiments were killed.

In the second, on 1 October, 1967, a group of Indian Gurkha Rifles soldiers (from the 7th Battalion of the 11th Regiment) noticed Chinese troops surrounding a sentry post near a boulder at the Chola outpost in Sikkim. After a heated argument over the control of the boulder, a Chinese soldier bayoneted a Gurkha rifleman, triggering the start of a close-quarters knife and fire-fight, which then escalated to a mortar and HMG duel. The Chinese troops signalled a ceasefire after three hours of fighting, but later scaled Point 15450 to establish themselves there. The Gurkhas outflanked them the next day to regain Point 15450 and the Chinese retreated across the LAC

1970s: In August 1971, India signed its Treaty of Peace, Friendship, and Cooperation with the Soviet Union, and the United States and the PRC sided with Pakistan in its December 1971 war with India. By this time, the PRC had just replaced the Republic of China in the UN where its representatives denounced India as being a tool of Soviet expansionism.

India and the PRC renewed efforts to improve relations after the Soviet Union invaded Afghanistan in December 1979. The PRC modified its pro-Pakistan stand on Kashmir and appeared willing to remain silent on India's absorption of Sikkim and its special advisory relationship with Bhutan. The PRC's leaders agreed to discuss the boundary issue, India's priority, as the first step to a broadening of relations. The two countries hosted each others' news agencies, and Mount Kailash and Mansarowar Lake in Tibet, the mythological home of the Hindu pantheon, were opened to annual pilgrimages from India.

1980s: In 1981 PRC minister of foreign affairs Huang Hua was invited to India, where he made complimentary remarks about India's role in South Asia. PRC premier Zhao Ziyang concurrently toured Pakistan, Nepal, and Bangladesh. In 1980, Indian Prime Minister Indira Gandhi approved a plan to upgrade the deployment of forces around the Line of Actual Control to avoid unilateral redefinitions of the line. India also increased funds for infrastructural development in these areas.

In 1984, squads of Indian soldiers began actively patrolling the Sumdorong Chu Valley in Arunachal Pradesh (formerly NEFA), which is north of the McMahon Line as drawn on the Shimla Treaty map but south of the ridge which Indian claims is meant to delineate the McMahon Line. The Sumdorong Chu valley seemed to lie to the north of the McMahon line but is south of the highest ridge in the area, and the McMahon line is meant to follow the highest points according to the Indian claims, while the Chinese did not recognize the McMahon Line as legitimate and were not prepared to accept an Indian claim line even further north than that. The Indian team left the area before the winter. In the winter of 1986, the Chinese deployed their troops to the Sumdorong Chu before the Indian team could arrive in the summer and built a Helipad at Wandung. Surprised by the Chinese occupation, India's then Chief of Army Staff, General K. Sundarji, airlifted a brigade to the region.

Chinese troops could not move any further into the valley and were forced to move sideways along the Thag La ridge, away from the valley. By 1987, Beijing's reaction was similar to that in 1962 and this prompted many Western diplomats to predict war. However, Indian foreign minister N.D. Tiwari and Prime Minister Rajiv Gandhi travelled to Beijing over the following months to negotiate a mutual de-escalation.

After the Huang visit, India and the PRC held eight rounds of border negotiations between December 1981 and November 1987. These talks initially raised hopes that progress could be made on the border issue. However, in 1985 the PRC stiffened its position on the border and insisted on mutual concessions without defining the exact terms of its package proposal or where the actual line of control lay. In 1986 and 1987, the negotiations achieved nothing, given the charges exchanged between the two countries of military encroachment in the Sumdorung Chu Valley of the Tawang tract on the eastern sector of the border. China's construction of a military post and helicopter pad in the area in 1986 and India's grant of statehood to Arunachal Pradesh (formerly the North-East Frontier Agency) in February 1987 caused both sides to deploy new troops to the area, raising tensions and fears of a new border war. The PRC relayed warnings that it would teach India a lesson if it did not cease nibbling at Chinese territory. By the summer of 1987, however, both sides had backed away from conflict and denied that military clashes had taken place.

A warming trend in relations was facilitated by Rajiv Gandhi's visit to China in December 1988. The two sides issued a joint communiqué that stressed the need to restore friendly relations on the basis of the Panchsheel and noted the importance of the first visit by an Indian prime minister to China since Nehru's 1954 visit. India and the People's Republic of China agreed to broaden bilateral ties in various areas, working to achieve a fair and reasonable settlement while seeking a mutually acceptable solution to the border dispute.

The communiqué also expressed China's concern about agitation by Tibetan separatists in India and reiterated China's position that Tibet was an integral part of China and that anti-China political activities by expatriate Tibetans was not to be tolerated. Rajiv Gandhi signed bilateral agreements on science and technology cooperation, on civil aviation to establish direct air links, and on cultural exchanges. The two sides also agreed to hold annual diplomatic consultations between foreign ministers, and to set up a joint ministerial committee on economic and scientific cooperation and a joint working group on the boundary issue. The latter group was to be led by the Indian foreign secretary and the Chinese vice minister of foreign affairs.

1990s: As the mid-1990s approached, slow but steady improvement in relations with China was visible. Top-level dialogue continued with the December 1991 visit of PRC premier Li Peng to India and the May 1992 visit to China of Indian president R. Venkataraman. Six rounds of talks of the Indian-Chinese Joint Working Group on the Border Issue were held between December 1988 and June 1993. Progress was also made in reducing tensions on the border via confidence-building measures, including mutual troop reductions, regular meetings of local military commanders, and advance notification of military exercises. Border trade resumed in July 1992 after a hiatus of more than thirty years, consulates reopened in Bombay (Mumbai) and Shanghai in December 1992, and, in June 1993, the two sides agreed to open an additional border trading post. During Sharad Pawar's July 1992 visit to Beijing, the first ever by an Indian minister of defence, the two defence establishments agreed to develop academic, military, scientific, and technological exchanges and to schedule an Indian port call by a Chinese naval vessel.

Substantial movement in relations continued in 1993. The sixth-round joint working group talks were held in June in New Delhi but resulted in only minor developments. However, as the year progressed the long-standing border dispute was eased as a result of bilateral pledges to reduce troop levels and to respect the cease-fire line along the India-China border. Prime Minister Narasimha Rao and Premier Li Peng signed the border agreement and three other agreements (on cross-border trade, and on increased cooperation on the environment and in radio and television broadcasting) during the former's visit to Beijing in September. A senior-level Chinese military delegation made a six-day goodwill visit to India in December 1993 aimed at fostering confidence-building measures between the defence forces of the two countries. The visit, however, came at a time when press reports revealed that, as a result of improved relations between the PRC and Burma, China was exporting greater amounts of military materiel to Burma's army, navy, and air force and sending an increasing number of technicians to Burma. Of concern to Indian security officials was the presence of Chinese radar technicians in Burma's Coco Islands, which border India's Union Territory of the Andaman and Nicobar Islands. Nevertheless, movement continued in 1994 on troop reductions along the Himalayan frontier. Moreover, in January 1994 Beijing announced that it not only favoured a negotiated solution on Kashmir, but also opposed any form of independence for the region.

Talks were held in New Delhi in February 1994 aimed at confirming established confidence-building measures and discussing clarification of the line of actual control, reduction of armed forces along the line, and prior information about forthcoming military exercises. China's hope for settlement of the boundary issue was reiterated.

The 1993 Chinese military visit to India was reciprocated by Indian army chief of staff General B. C. Joshi. During talks in Beijing in July 1994, the two sides agreed that border problems should be resolved peacefully through mutual understanding and concessions. The border issue was raised in September 1994 when PRC minister of national defence Chi Haotian visited New Delhi for extensive talks with high-level Indian trade and defence officials. Further talks in New Delhi in March 1995 by the India-China Expert Group led to an agreement to set up two additional points of contact along the 4,000 km border to facilitate meetings between military personnel. The two sides also were reported as seriously engaged in defining the McMahon Line and the line of actual control vis-à-vis military exercises and prevention of air intrusion. Talks in Beijing in July 1995 aimed at better border security and combating cross-border crimes and in New Delhi in August 1995 on additional troop withdrawals from the border made further progress in reducing tensions.

Possibly indicative of the further relaxation of India-China relations, at least there was little notice taken in Beijing, was the April 1995 announcement, after a year of consultation, of the opening of the Taipei Economic and Cultural Centre in New Delhi. The centre serves as the representative office of the Republic of China (Taiwan) and is the counterpart of the India-Taipei Association in Taiwan both institutions have the goal of improving relations between the two sides, which have been strained since New Delhi's recognition of Beijing in 1950.

Sino-Indian relations hit a low point in 1998 following India's nuclear tests in May. Indian Defence Minister George Fernandes declared that China is India's number one threat, hinting that India developed nuclear weapons in defence against China's nuclear arsenal. In 1998, China was one of the strongest international critics of India's nuclear tests and entry into the nuclear club. Relations between India and China stayed strained until the end of the decade.

2000s: With Indian President K. R. Narayanan's visit to China, 2000 marked a gradual re-engagement of Indian and Chinese diplomacy. In a major embarrassment for China, the seventeenth Karmapa, Urgyen

Trinley Dorje, who was proclaimed by China, made a dramatic escape from Tibet to the Rumtek Monastery in Sikkim. Chinese officials were in a quandary on this issue as any protest to India on the issue would mean an explicit endorsement on India's governance of Sikkim, which the Chinese still hadn't recognized. In 2002, Chinese Premier Zhu Rongji reciprocated by visiting India, with a focus on economic issues. 2003 ushered in a marked improvement in Sino-Indian relations following Indian Prime Minister Atal Bihari Vajpayee's landmark June 2003 visit to China. China officially recognized Indian sovereignty over Sikkim as the two nations moved toward resolving their border disputes.

2004 also witnessed a gradual improvement in the international area when the two countries proposed opening up the Nathula and Jelepla Passes in Sikkim which would be mutually beneficial to both countries. 2004 was a milestone in Sino-Indian bilateral trade, surpassing the Ten billion dollar mark for the first time. In April 2005, Chinese Premier Wen Jiabao visited Bangalore to push for increased Sino-Indian cooperation in high-tech industries. In a speech, Wen stated that Cooperation is just like two pagodas (temples), one hardware and one software. Wen stated that the twenty-first century will be the Asian century of the IT industry. The high-level visit was also expected to produce several agreements to deepen political, cultural and economic ties between the two nations. Regarding the issue of India gaining a permanent seat on the UN Security Council, on his visit, Wen Jiabao initially seemed to support the idea, but had returned to a neutral position on the subject by the time he returned to China. In the South Asian Association for Regional Cooperation (SAARC) Summit (2005) China was granted an observer status. While other countries in the region are ready to consider China for permanent membership in the SAARC, India seems reluctant.

A very important dimension of the evolving Sino-Indian relationship is based on the energy requirements of their industrial expansion and their readiness to proactively secure them by investing in the oilfields abroad - in Africa, the Middle East and Central Asia. On the one hand, these ventures entail competition (which has been evident in oil biddings for various international projects recently). But on the other hand, a degree of cooperation too is visible, as they are increasingly confronting bigger players in the global oil market. This cooperation was sealed in Beijing on 12 January, 2006 during the visit of Petroleum and Natural Gas Minister Mani Shankar Aiyar, who signed an agreement which envisages ONGC Videsh Ltd (OVL) and the China National Petroleum Corporation

(CNPC) placing joint bids for promising projects elsewhere. This may have important consequences for their international relations.

On 6 July, 2006, China and India re-opened Nathula, an ancient trade route which was part of the Silk Road. Nathula is a pass through the Himalayas and it was closed forty four years prior to 2006 when the Sino-Indian War broke out in 1962. The initial agreement for the re-opening of the trade route was reached in 2003, and a final agreement was formalized on 18 June, 2006. Officials say that the re-opening of border trade will help ease the economic isolation of the region. In November 2006, China and India had a verbal spat over claim of the north-east Indian state of Arunachal Pradesh. India claimed that China was occupying 38,000 square kilometres of its territory in Kashmir, while China claimed the whole of Arunachal Pradesh as its own. In May 2007, China denied the application for visa from an Indian Administrative Service officer in Arunachal Pradesh, saying that since Arunachal Pradesh is a territory of China, he won't need a visa to visit his own country. Later in December 2007, China appeared to have reversed its policy by granting a visa to Marpe Sora, an Arunachal born professor in computer science.

Two of the world's fastest growing economies are beginning to outgrow decades of rivalry and mistrust and starting to think of themselves as partners. It is perhaps too short sighted to see India and China as competitors. Typically large neighbouring countries have huge bilateral trade. By that benchmark, India and China have a long way to go. It is not that two countries should not or will not complete in the future. If is only that the scope of cooperation – so far unexplored and unrealized is enormous. The scale of interaction among all large neighbours in the world, be it Mexico and the US or Germany and France or South Africa and its neighbours, is much larger than what exists between India and China. And this when the two are the world's most populous nations.

REFERENCES

Avedon, John F.: In Exile from the Land of Snows, New York, HarperCollins, 1997.

Barnett, Robert and Shirin Akiner: Resistance and Reform in Tibet, London, Hurst and Company, 1994.

Bell, Charles: Tibet: Past and Present, Delhi, Motilal Banarsidass, 1992.

Bell, David V. J.: Resistance and Revolution, Boston, Houghton Mifflin Company, 1973.

Chandra, Bipan: India's Struggle for Independence 1857-1947, New Delhi, Penguin, 1989.

Conner, Victoria and Robert Barnett: Leaders in Tibet: A Directory, London, Tibet Information Network, 1997.

Edin, Maria: Transition to Democracy in Exile - A Study of the Tibetan Government's Strategy for Self-Determination, University of Uppsala, Department of Government Minor Field Study, 1992.

Fischer, Louis: The Life of Mahatma Gandhi, London, Jonathan Cape, 1951.

Jones, Ken: The Social Face of Buddhism: An Approach to Social and Political Activism, London, Wisdom, 1989.

Kelly, Petra K., Gert Bastian, and Pat Aiello: The Anguish of Tibet, Berkeley, Parallax Press, 1991.

Khilnani, Sunil: The Idea of India, London, Hamish Hamilton, 1997.

Lazar, E.: Tibet: The Issue is Independence, Berkeley, Parallax Press, 1994.

McKay, Alex: Tibet and the British Raj: The Frontier Cadre, 1904-1947, Surrey, Curzon Press, 1997.

Merton, Thomas: Gandhi on Non-Violence, Boston, Shambhala, 1996.

Mukherjee, R.: The Penguin Gandhi Reader, New Delhi, Penguin, 1993.

Norbu, Jamyang: Warriors of Tibet: The Story of Aten and the Khampas' Fight for the Freedom of their Country, London, Wisdom, 1986.

Pandey, B.N.: The Indian Nationalist Movement: Select Documents, London, MacMillan, 1979.

Philips, C.H. and Wainwright, M.D.:The Partition of India: Policies and Perspectives 1935-1947, London, George Allen and Unwin Ltd., 1970.

Radhakrishnan, S.: The Principal Upanishads, London, Allen and Unwin, 1953.

Richards, Glyn: The Philosophy of Gandhi, Surrey, Curzon Press, 1991.

Richardson, H. E.: Tibet and its History, London, Oxford University Press, 1962.

Robbins, Christopher: The Invisible Air Force: The True Story of the CIA's Secret Airlines, London, Pan, 1981.

Shakabpa, Tsepon W.D.: Tibet: A Political History, New York, Potala Publications, 1984.

Shakya, Tsering: 'Tibet and the Occident: The Myth of Shangri-La' in Lungta, 1991.

Smith, Warren W.: Tibetan Nation: A History of Tibetan Nationalism and Sino-Tibetan Relations, Boulder, Westview Press, 1996.

Snellgrove, David and H. E. Richardson: A Cultural History of Tibet, Boston, Shambhala, 1986.

Strong, Anna-Louise: When Serfs Stood Up in Tibet, Peking, New World Press, 1960.

Su Wenming: Tibet: Today and Yesterday, Beijing, Beijing Review, 1983.

Subba, T.A.: Flight and Adaptation: Tibetan Refugees in the Darjeeling - Sikkim Himalaya, Dharamsala, Library of Tibetan Works and Archives, 1990.

Wylie, Turrell: 'A Standard System of Tibetan Transcription' in Harvard Journal of Asiatic Studies, 1959.

Zaehner, R.C.: The Bhagavad-Gita, Oxford: Clarendon Press, 1969

3

History of Sino-Tibetan Relations

Introduction

While China claims that Tibet has always been a part of China, Tibet has a history of at least thirteen hundred years of independence from China. In 821 A.D China and Tibet ended almost two hundred years of fighting with a treaty engraved on three stone pillars, one of which still stands in front of the Jokhang cathedral in Lhasa.

The treaty reads in part: Both Tibet and China shall keep the country and frontiers of which they are now possessed. The whole region to the East of that being the country of Great China and the whole region to the West being assuredly the country of Great Tibet, from either side there shall be no hostile invasion, and no seizure of territory and in order that this agreement establishing a great era when Tibetans shall be happy in Tibet and Chinese shall be happy in China shall never be changed, the Three Jewels, the body of Saints, the sun and the moon, planets and stars have been invoked as witness. The three stone pillars were erected, one outside the Chinese Emperor's palace, one on the border between the two countries, and one in Lhasa.

During the 13th and 14th centuries both China and Tibet came under the influence of the Mongol empire. China claims today that Tibet and China during that time became one country, by virtue of the Mongols domination of both nations. In validating this claim, it must first be remembered that virtually all of Asia was dominated by the Mongols under Kublai Khan and his successors, who ruled the largest empire in human history. Second, the respective relationships between the Mongols and the Tibetans and between the Mongols and Chinese must be examined. These two relationships were not only radically different in nature, but they also started and ended at different times. Tibet came under Mongol influence before Kublai Khan's conquest of China and regaining complete independence from the Mongols several decades before China regained its independence.

While China was militarily conquered by the Mongols, the Tibetans and the Mongols established the historically unique priest patron relationship, also known as CHO-YON. The Mongol aristocracy had converted to Buddhism and sought spiritual guidance and moral legitimacy for the rule of their vast empire from the Tibetan theocracy. As Tibet's patrons they pledged to protect it against foreign invasion. In return Tibetans promised loyalty to the Mongol empire.

The Mongol-Tibetan relationship was thus based on mutual respect and dual responsibility. In stark contrast, the Mongol-Chinese relationship was based on military conquest and domination. The Mongols ruled China, while the Tibetans ruled Tibet. The Mongol empire ended in the mid-14th century.

In 1639, the Dalai Lama established another CHO-YON relationship, this time with the Manchu Emperor, who in 1644 ruled China and established the Qing Dynasty. By the middle of the 19th century, the Munchu influence in Tibet had waned considerably as the Manchu empire began to disintegrate. In 1842 and 1856 the Manchus were incapable of responding to Tibetan calls for assistance against repeated Nepalese Gorkha invasion. The Tibetans drove back the Gorkhas with no assistance and concluded bilateral treaties.

In 1911 the CHO-YON relationship came to its final end with the fall of the Manchu Dynasty. Tibet formally declared its Independence in 1912 and continued to conduct itself as a fully sovereign nation until its invasion by Communist China an 1949.

Ancient Period

Origin: The first known interaction between the two states came in 640 A.D., when the Tibetan King Songtsan Gampo married the Princess Wencheng, a niece of the Tang Emperor Taizong. He also married a Nepalese princess. Both wives were Buddhists, and this may have been the origin of Tibetan Buddhism. The faith grew when an influx of Central Asian Buddhists flooded Tibet early in the eighth century, fleeing from advancing armies of Arab and Kazakh Muslims.

During his reign, Songtsan Gampo added parts of the Yarlung River Valley to the Kingdom of Tibet his descendants would also conquer the vast region that is now the Chinese provinces of Qinghai, Gansu, and

Xinjiang between 663 AD and 692 AD. Control of these border regions would change hands back and forth for centuries to come.

In 692 AD, the Chinese retook their western lands from the Tibetans after defeating them at Kashgar. The Tibetan king then allied himself with the enemies of China, the Arabs and eastern Turks. Chinese power waxed strong in the early decades of the eighth century. Imperial forces under General Gao Xianzhi conquered much of Central Asia, until their defeat by the Arabs and Karluks at the Battle of Talas River in 751 A.D. China's power quickly waned, and Tibet resumed control of much of Central Asia.

The ascendant Tibetans pressed their advantage, conquering much of northern India and even seizing the Tang Chinese capital city of Chang'an (now Xian) in 763 A.D. Tibet and China signed a peace treaty in 821 A.D or 822 A.D, which delineated the border between the two empires. The Tibetan Empire would concentrate on its Central Asian holdings for the next several decades, before splitting into several small, fractious kingdoms.

Relations with Tang Dynasty of China: Early in the seventh century, the powerful Tang Dynasty was founded in the Central Plains, ending the disintegration and chaotic situation that had prevailed in the region for more than 300 years. Tubo was an ethnic group which formed on the Tibetan plateau. Ever since the founding of Tubo regime, hereditary system was followed. After several generations' ruling, Tubo society gradually turned from a primitive society into a slavery society and the social productivity developed rapidly.

In 629, a young headman aged thirteen and named Songtsan Gambo began to rule his group. In his ruling, the whole of Tibet was unified and the Tubo Dynasty was founded. It was in his reign that contact between Tang and Tubo was initiated and reached an unprecedented level. He twice sent ministers to the Tang court requesting a member of the imperial family be given to him in marriage. In order to propose marriage towards Tang, Songtsan Gambo sent an envoy with copious gold and treasures to Chang'an in 640 AD. Willing to make friendly relationship with Tubo, Emperor Taizong agreed to marry Wencheng Princess with Songtsan Gambo. In 710 AD, Tang Princess Jin Cheng was married to Tubo Tsenpo and she brought with her many craftsmen and ancient books and records in Chinese. There were frequent exchanges between the Tang Dynasty and the Tubo Kingdom. In the 213 years, there were 191 exchanges between officials from both sides and eight peace pledges were signed. During the reign of Songtsan Gambo, political, economic and cultural relations between the two nations became increasingly friendly and extensive. This pattern of friendly relations was carried on during the next 200 years or more.

Following the marriage of Wencheng Princess and Songtsan Gambo, the economical and cultural exchange between Tang and Tubo had been greatly accelerated. When the princess went to Tubo, she carried many vegetable seeds, handicraft articles, brewing and textile techniques, which had helped to improve Tubo's agriculture and handicraft industry. Meanwhile, merchants from Tubo bought lots of silk, paper and military arrows from the Tang Dynasty.

In 821, then Tubo King Tri Ralpachen dispatched envoys to Chang'an, capital of the Tang Dynasty for three times, asking for alignment. Muzong, then Emperor of the Tang Dynasty, appointed his senior officials to hold a grand alignment ceremony in the western suburb of Chang'an. In the next year, the Tang Dynasty and the Tubo Kingdom formally concluded their alliance pact in the eastern suburb of Lhasa. The two sides of the alliance reiterated their close relations bound by marriage and decided to treat each other as a member of one family. The alignment was recorded on three Tang-Tubo Peace Pledgement Monuments, one of which still stands in front of the Jokhang Monastery in Lhasa. The monument, a treaty of friendship, is written in both Tibetan and Chinese and is somewhat difficult to interpret. The relations between the two countries appears to have been complex. On the one hand, the monument describes connections between China and Tibet as similar to those between uncle and nephew. The two dynasty of Tibet were indeed related by marriage, yet the terms uncle and nephew are not used in relation to other groups with whom the Chinese had connections by marriage. On the other hand, the monument seems to describe the two countries as equals.

An important thread that linked Tang cultural and Tubo culture was the faith of Buddhism. The formation of Tubo's Buddhism was based on Tianzhu (currently India) Buddhism, Nipoluo (currently Nepal) Buddhism and Buddhism from Tang. Among them, Buddhism from Tang was more suitable to Tubo's local culture. On this basis, Tubo developed its own Buddhist culture which was specifically the predecessor of Tibetan Buddhism. Historical records clarify that when Wencheng Princess entered Tubo, she also brought a figure of Sakyamuni and 360 Buddhist classical sutras with her. Additionally, Tubo used to send envoys to visit Tang's temples including Buddhist temples in Wutaishan Mountain and Da Ci'en Temple in Big Wild Goose Pagoda. Later, Tubo people built their own Buddhist temple - the Jokhang Temple in current Lhasa.

In 842, the Tubo Kingdom broke up, and rival groups of ministers, members of the royal family and various tribes plunged into internecine struggle that was to last in varying levels of intensity for the next 400 years. Reeling under the detrimental impact of such activities on their economic and cultural development, people on the Tibetan Plateau looked to the emergence of a formidable regime on the Central Plains to someday come to their rescue. Those who could no longer stand the bitterness fled to areas in present-day Gansu, Qinghai, Sichuan and Yunnan provinces.

Buddhist Revolution in Tibet and Song Dynasty: Tibetan Buddhism is the body of religious Buddhist doctrine and institutions characteristic of Tibet and the Himalayan regions, which include northern Nepal, Bhutan, India (Arunachal Pradesh, Ladakh and Sikkim), Mongolia, Russia (Kalmykia, Buryatia and Tuva) and northeastern China (Manchuria: Heilongjiang, Jilin). It includes the teachings of the three vehicles of Buddhism: the Foundational Vehicle, Mahayana, and Vajrayana.

Probably Buddhism was first introduced to Tibet in 173 AD during the reign of the 28th Yarlung king Lha Thothori Nyantsen, but had apparently no impact. The first official historic introduction of a Buddhist scripture into Tibet happened during reign of King Hlato Ri Nyentsen (28th king of Tibet - around 500 AD), however, the book was not translated at the time. The 33rd King of Tibet, Song Tsen Gampo (born 617) had the book translated and married two Buddhist princesses. With this, one can say that Buddhism was first really introduced to Tibet as a practice. The 37th King of Tibet, Trisong Detsen invited Indian Pandit Shantarakshita and Kamalasila, who suggested to invite Padmasambhava (or Guru-Rinpoche) to Tibet, who arrived in 817.

An ordained spiritual community was established in the first Buddhist monastery Samye, which was built by Padmasambhava. In this period, translation of scriptures genuinely began. As of this time, one can say that Buddhism was firmly established in Tibet, as the presence of Sangha is considered essential. In 792, after a great philosophical debate, King Trisong Detsen officially declared Indian Buddhism and not Chinese Buddhism to be the religion of Tibet. Before the propagation of Buddhist doctrines in Tibet the religion of the inhabitants of this country was most probably a kind of worship differing but little from that prevalent among all rude nations, viz. a mingled system of idolatry and sorcery administered by priests enjoying great reputation and power, in consequence of their supposed intercourse with the Gods, and presumed knowledge of the means whereby the divine favour and assistance can be obtained.

The first attempt of Buddhist followers to extend their creed to Tibet doubtless met with general opposition at the hands of both priesthood and people. The latter indeed must have found it far less troublesome to pay a clerical class to obtain a sensual prosperity for them, than by painful discipline, combined with profound meditation, to seek salvation and eternal welfare in a future re-birth and final emancipation from metempsychosis. In order to attain success and the more readily impose upon the tribes they were about to convert to a new religion, the first teachers of Buddhism in Tibet were most probably induced to ascribe to themselves supernatural qualities, and to yield, in minor points of discipline, to some of the ideas of their neophytes.

Many suggestions to this effect are to be found in the sacred Tibetan books, as in the Bodhimor, and in the history of Ssanang Ssetsen, which teems with the miraculous and wonderful works performed by early Buddhist priests. Again, it is related that Padma Sambhava's first labour was the subduing of the dreadful demon who rose up in opposition to prevent his entering Tibet. His scholars are said to have derived from the instructions he gave them on the proper employment of charms, the power of performing most extraordinary deeds. Thus, they caused good harvests, and similar prosperous events, taught the Tibetans some of the arts and sciences which were then practised in the, more advanced civilization of China and India (whence they came), but were discreet enough, after a while, to attribute all their successes to the worship of the images and relies of Sakyamuni.

With regard to the introduction of Buddhism into the Eastern part of Tibet are now in possession of many positive data, though here also the early history is involved in darkness and myth. The first attempts apparently led to very unsatisfactory results at least, the monastery which is reported to have been erected in the year 137 B.C. on the slopes of the Kailas range seems to have been soon abandoned and to have fallen into ruins. The legends attribute the conversion of the Tibetans to Buddhism to the Dhyani Bodhisattva Avolokitevara, the celestial son of Amitaha, whose Chosen land is Tibet many of the rulers and priests who took an active part in the consolidation of Buddhist faith in this country were regarded by its inhabitants as incarnations of these two sacred persons.

In the year 371 A.D. there, suddenly appeared five foreigners before the king Thothori Nyan tsan, who instructed him, how he might use for the general welfare of Tibet four objects, which, in the year 331 A.D., had fallen from heaven, enclosed in a precious chest, but of' the intrinsic value of which no one had hitherto entertained any adequate idea. These instructions being given, the five foreigners at once disappeared. The four precious objects were; Two hands folded in prayer, A small Chorten, A gem with an inscription of the prayer, The religious work Zamatog, constructed vessel, a work on moral subjects forming part of the Kanjur.

The king Thothori strictly obeyed the advice received from the five foreigners,. and paid great reverence to the said four objects by their blessing and powerful influence he contrived to live one hundred and nineteen years, during which time universal prosperity and welfare prevailed throughout the kingdom. Ssanang Ssetsen connects the introduction of Buddhism with the date of this event but according to Tibetan historians the earliest period of the propagation of Buddhism, which reached down till the end of the tenth century AD begins with King Srongtsan Gampo, who was born in the year 617 AD and died in 698 AD. This king is highly extolled by them on account of his successful efforts in propagating Buddhism.

He even went so far as to send to India, in the year 632 AD his prime-minister, Thumi Sambhota, with sixteen companions, who had orders to study carefully the sacred Buddhist books and the Indian language the members of this mission were also instructed to bring back to Tibet a complete system of the alphabet as used in India, with a view to its being hereafter adapted to the Tibetan language. After the safe return of the party from a journey which is described as fraught with incredible difficulties, Thumi Sambhota constructed the Tibetan letters from the Devanagari alphabet whereupon King Srongtsan Gampo ordered the sacred Indian books treating on Buddhists doctrines to the translated into Tibetan.

King Srongtsan Gampo was most energetically supported by his two wives, one of whom was a Nepalese the other a Chinese princess. Who throughout their life-time proved most faithful votaries to the faith of

Buddha, are worshipped either under the general name of Dolma (in Sanskrit Tara), or under the respective names of Dolkar and Doljang. These princesses are said to have brought with them to Tibet.a variety of valuable religious books, with wonderful miracle-working images, and relies of Sakyamuni, besides building numerous temples and colleges.

Under the successors of King Srongtsan Gampo the religion did not greatly flourish, but under one of them, Thisrong de tsan, who lived in the years 728-786 AD. Buddhism began to revive, owing to the useful regulations proclaimed by this king. He it was who successfully crushed an attempt made by the chiefs during his minority to suppress the new creed, and it is principally due to him that the Buddhist faith became henceforth permanently established. He induced the learned Pandit Santa Rakshita (Zhiva tso), commonly called Bôdhisattva, to leave Bengal and settle in Tibet and at his recommendation the great Guru Padma Sambhava (in Tibetan Padma jungue, or Urgyen) from Kafiristan (Udyana), who was famed far and wide for his extraordinary knowledge of Dharanis and their application and rites, also changed his residence to become a Tibetan subject. The Indian sages were now induced to settle in Tibet. The latter had been the first Buddhist missionaries in Tibet and seem to have taught the principles of Nagarjuna with the modifications established by the Yogacharya school from the history of Buddhism of the Tibetan Puton or Buston who wrote in the fourteenth century that in their system man is not allowed to make any notion the object of his meditation.

Padma Sambhava and subsequent Indian priests, however, explained the law in the sense of the Madhyamika school, which in India at this period had just gained influence over the Yogacharya system they insisted upon assiduity in undisturbed meditation. But King Thisrong de tsan, who did not wish two opposing doctrines to be taught, ordered a disputation to take place between the Chinese Mahayana (a name evidently symbolical of the system he defended) and the Hindu Kamalasila. Mahayana was defeated and obliged to leave Tibet, and since this period Indian priests only were called and Madhyamika doctrines taught. King Thisrong built the large monastery and temple of Bima at Samyé, and ordered the translation of the sacred books into the Tibetan language to be carried on energetically.

A later ruler of the name of Langdar, or Langdharma, again tried to abolish Buddhist doctrines. He commanded all temples and monasteries to be demolished, the images to be destroyed, and the sacred books to be burnt but so intense was the indignation excited by these acts of sacrilege that he was murdered, in the year 900 A.D. Langdar's son and successor is also said to have died in his 64th year without religion. Bilamgur Tsan, Langhdarma's grandson, proved, on the other hand, favourably inclined to Buddhism he re-built eight temples, and died after a glorious reign of eighteen years.

With this period it is connect to the second propagation of Buddhism it received, especially from the year 971, a powerful impetus from the joint endeavours of the returned Tibetan priests (who had fled the country under the preceding kings), and of the learned Indian priest Pandita Atisha and his pupil Bromston. Shortly before Atisha came to Tibet, 1041 A.D., the Kalchakra doctrine, or Tantrika mysticism, was introduced into Tibet, and in the twelth and thirteenth centuries, many Indian refugees settled in the country, who greatly assisted the Tibetans in the translation of Sanskrit books.

Three hundred years from the time of Atisha's death bring us to the period of Tsonkhapa, the extraordinary reformer, who was born in the year 1355 A.D., in the district of Amdo, where is now the famous monastery of Kunbum. Tsonkhapa had imposed upon himself the difficult task of uniting and reconciling the dialectical and mystical schools which Tibetan Buddhism had brought forth, and also of eradicating the abuses gradually introduced by the priests, who had returned to the ordinary tricks and pretended miracles of charlatanism, in order to prove to the crowd their extraordinary mission. Tsonkhapa strictly prohibited such proceedings, and enforced a rigid observance of the laws binding upon the priests he also distinguished himself by publishing most comprehensive works, in which the principles of the faith of the Buddha are explained from his particular point of view.

Though all the innovations introduced by Tsonkhapa, were never universally acknowledged, yet he obtained numerous followers, whose numbers rapidly increased during the next two centuries, until they predominated in Tibet and High Asia. The rigour of his ordinances against the priests has been, however, considerably relaxed, and how widely the practice now differs from theory, it may infer from the fact, that the entrance into the clerical profession is an object of general ambition, and that a considerable part of the priestly revenues is derived from rites of an emphatically shaman character, performed at the request of the lay population to drive off the evil spirits.

There were many reasons for the decline of Buddhism after the Tang period. The most apparent factor destroying the eminent position of Buddhism in Chinese society, economy and politics were the several persecutions of Buddhism and other religions during the 8th and 9th centuries. It was in first place economical reasons for these persecutions - monasteries were tax-free units, and monks were not obliged to pay taxes. The more people were hiding inside the ranks of the clergy, the less people were tax-liable and could be mobilized for official works or military service. The Song Dynasty government developed a regular tool to increase state revenues by selling certificates to ordained monks by which they could prove that they were exempted from tax and labour services. But as soon as buying such a certificate was enough for being tax-exempted there was no further duty for a monk to exert the life of a monk as he was expected to do. People wealthy enough to buy a monk certificate could enter any monastery. This practice lowered the quality of the monasterial community and discredited moral integrity and the reputation of Buddhist sanghas, even the highest dignitaries by selling their titles and their privilege to wear the purple robe of a patriarch During the Southern Song, the sales of monk certificates were abolished, and a poll tax imposed upon clergymen was introduced.

The rise of Neo-Confucianism with its interest in metaphysical discussions became a far more attractive ideology for the scholar-officials of the Song period than the purely religious Buddhism. Neo-Confucian theoreticians incorporated Buddhist problems into the framework of traditional Chinese, especially Confucian, thinking, and made it obsolete for the scholars to be a true Buddhist believe - the study of Buddhism and the adaption of some of its ideas was sufficient, and Neo-Confucians produced their counter-theories against Buddhist doctrines, like the emptiness of the phenomenal world as opposed to the Neo-Confucian ether-essence qi that is incorporated in every substantial and non-substantial phenomenon through an immmanent principle of order li. The emergence of Neo-Confucian ideas experienced an intensive support by government with the introduction of the state examinations that required the studies of the Confucian Classics) and totally neglected Buddhis sutras.

While some Tang period monks undertook long journeys to go to India and to bring back sutras and other Buddhist writings in the Sanskrit original to translate them into Chinese when back, the occupation of the gateway to the west by the Uighurs and the Tangut empire of Western

Xia as well as the decline of Buddhism in its home country in India also contributed to the stagnation of Buddhism in China. Here, the old traditional schools or sects were gradually replaced by new sects that became much more popular and are often equalized with Buddhism itself: The Chan Sect and the Pure Land Sect. Both sects disregarded the study of sutras and the observation of monastic rules and emphasized instead intuition, simple faith and the mechanical recitation of formulas. Such simple types of beliefs were very attractive for the broad masses but they did not lead to a productive development of religious scholarship. Nonetheless these two sects were a very handsome tools for the Song period emperors who wanted to control the Buddhist communities and who founded many Chan monasteries throughout the country and bestowed the highest titles of Buddhist clergy through imperial order It was easier to cope with one single sect and its representants than with many different concurring streamings.

Taxation of monasteries became more and more the regular case during the Song period. Persecutions of Buddhism did never occur after the Tang period, and the only attempt to attack Buddhism by Emperor Huizong was rather an experiment to dao-ise Buddhism by changing terms and titles.

State sponsoring of Buddhism began early in Song, when Emperor Taizu dispatched an envoy of monks to India had printed the Buddhist canon in Chengdu /Sichuan, contemporary center of printing technology and had insiced Buddhist writings - including imperial prefaces - into stone slabs. Emperor Taizong had erected several large pagodas in the largest cities of the empire. The most important editions of the Buddhist Tripitaka during Song were the Kaibao Tripitaka from 983, Chongning Tripitaka from 1103 and the Pilu Tripitaka from 1151, the first printed in Chengdu, the others in Fuzhou /Fujian.

Medieval Period

Sakya Lamas and Mongol Empire: Mongols were highly tolerant of most religions, and typically sponsored several at the same time. At the time of Genghis Khan, virtually every religion had found converts, from Buddhism to Christianity and Manichaeanism to Islam. To avoid strife, Genghis Khan set up an institution that ensured complete religious freedom, though he himself was a shamanist. Under his administration, all religious leaders were exempt from taxation, and from public service.Initially there were few formal places of worship, because of the nomadic lifestyle. However, under Ogedei, several building projects were undertaken in Karakorum. Ogedei's son and Guyuk's younger brother, Khoten, became the governor of Ningxia and Gansu. He launched a military campaign into Tibet under the command of Generals Lichi and Dhordha. The marauding Mongols burned down Tibetan monuments such as the Reting monastery and the Gyal temple in 1240. Prince Koton was convinced that no power in the world exceeded the might of the Mongols. However, he believed that religion was necessary in the interests of the next life. Thus he invited Sakya Pandita to Mongolia. Prince Koton was impressed by Sakya Pandita's teachings. Then he became the first known buddhist prince of Mongol empire.

In 1244 Sakya Pandita left for Prince Godan's royal camp with two of his young nephews, the ten year-old Phagpa and six year-old Chhana, who later published a collection of Sakya Pandita's writings. On the way, they stopped in Lhasa, where Phagpa pronounced its vows of young buddhist monk at the Jokhang monastery in front of the statue of the Jowo offered by the Princess Wencheng, the Chinese wife of Songsten Gampo. Sakya Pandita preached sermons along his way and arrived at Prince Godan's camp in 1247 in Lanzhou in the current province of Gansu, where the mongol troops were exterminating Han Chinese by throwing them in a river. Sakya Pandita, horrified, gave religious instructions, and in particular that killing a sentient being is one of the worse acts according to Buddha Dharma. He gave religious instruction to the prince and greatly impressed the court with his personality and powerful teachings. He is also said to have cured Prince Godan of a serious illness and, with the help of his nephew, Phagpa, he adapted the Uighur script so that the Buddhist Scriptures could be translated into Mongolian, which was a previously unwritten language. In return, was given temporal authority over the 13 myriarchies of Central Tibet.

After the death of Sakya Pandita, Phagpa remained at the camp of Prince Godan and learned Mongolian language. Five years later, Kublai Khan asked Godan to give him Chogyal Phagpa, who was then 23, and converted him to Buddhism. Shortly after, Kublai Khan in a succession fight, took over his brother, Mongke, and became the khan, the ruler of the Mongols and even later on became emperor of China. Kublai Khan in turn appointed Chogyal Phagpa as his Imperial Preceptor in 1260 the year when he became emperor of Mongolia. According to nowadays Mongols, Phagpa was the first one to inaugurate theology politics of the relation between the State and the religion in the tibet-mongol buddhist world. With the support of Kublai Khan, Chogyal Phagpa established himself and his sect as the preeminent political power in Tibet.

Kublai Khan commissioned Chogyal Phagpa to design a new writing system to unify the writing of the multilingual Mongolian Empire. Chogyal Phagpa in turn modified the traditional Tibetan script and gave birth to a new set of characters called Phagspa script which was completed in 1268. Kublai Khan decided to use the Phagspa script as the official writing system of the empire, including when he became emperor of China in 1271, instead of the Chinese ideogrammes. The script was used for 110 years and is thought to have influenced the development of modern Korean script. However, it fell into disuse after the collapse of the Mongol Empire and the associated Yuan Dynasty in 1368.

Pagspa's diaries for 1271 mention a foreign friend of Kublai Khan, who was quite possibly one of the elder Polos or even Marco Polo, although, unfortunately, no name is given

Thus began a strong alliance and the capital of Sakya became the capital of Tibet. This lasted until about the middle of the 14th century. During the reign of the 14th Sakya Trizin, Sonam Gylatsen, the Central Tibetan province of U was taken by the Myriarch, marking the beginning of the end of the period of Sakya power in Central Tibet

Khatun Chabi influenced Kublai to be converted to Buddhism. She received the Hévajra tantra initiations from Phagspa and was very impressed. Khubilai offered Phagpa rule over the thirteen trikhors of Tibet. On the completion of the second stage, Khubilai offered Phagpa a white dharma conch shell and rule over all the three provinces of Tibet. The influence of the *Sakya* school in Tibet waned after the end of Mongol power in the mid-fourteenth century

Tibet and the Ming Dynasty: The exact nature of Sino-Tibetan relations during the Ming Dynasty (1368–1644 AD) of China is unclear. Some modern scholars living and working in the People's Republic of China assert that the Ming Dynasty had unquestioned sovereignty over Tibet, pointing to the Ming court's issuing of various titles to Tibetan leaders, Tibetans' full acceptance of these titles, and a renewal process for successors of these titles that involved travelling to the Ming capital. Scholars also argue that Tibet has been an integral part of China since the 13th century, thus a part of the Ming Empire. But most scholars outside the PRC say that the relationship was one of suzerainty, that Ming titles were only nominal, that Tibet remained an independent region outside

Ming control, and that it simply paid tribute until the reign of Jiajing (1521–1566), who ceased relations with Tibet.

Some scholars note that Tibetan leaders during the Ming frequently engaged in civil war and conducted their own foreign diplomacy with neighbouring states such as Nepal. Some scholars underscore the commercial aspect of the Ming-Tibetan relationship, noting the Ming Dynasty's shortage of horses for warfare and thus the importance of the horse trade with Tibet. Others argue that the significant religious nature of the relationship of the Ming court with Tibetan lamas is underrepresented in modern scholarship. In hopes of reviving the unique relationship of the earlier Mongol leader Kublai Khan and his spiritual superior Drogon Chogyal Phagpa of the Tibetan Sakya sect, the Ming Chinese Yongle Emperor made a concerted effort to build a secular and religious alliance with Deshin Shekpa, the Karmapa of the Tibetan Black Hat sect. However, Yongle's attempts were unsuccessful.

The Ming initiated sporadic armed intervention in Tibet during the 14th century, but did not garrison permanent troops there. At times the Tibetans also used armed resistance against Ming forays. The Wanli Emperor made attempts to re-establish Sino-Tibetan relations after the Mongol-Tibetan alliance initiated in 1578 AD, which affected the foreign policy of the subsequent Qing Dynasty of China in their support for the Dalai Lama of the Yellow Hat sect. By the late 16th century, the Mongols were successful armed protectors of the Yellow Hat Dalai Lama, after increasing their presence in the Amdo region. This culminated in Gushi Khan's conquest of Tibet.

According to the official historical work on the Ming Dynasty, the History of Ming compiled in 1739 by the subsequent Qing Dynasty, the Ming Dynasty established the Army-Civilian Marshal Office in western Tibet and installed the Dbus-Gtsang Itinerant High Commandery and Mdo-khams Itinerant High Commandery to administer eastern Tibet. The Mingshi states that administrative offices were set up under these high commanderies, including one Itinerant Commandery, three Pacification Commissioner's Offices, six Expedition Commissioner's Offices, four Wanhu offices, and seventeen Qianhu offices.

The Ming court appointed three Princes of Dharma and five Princes, and granted many other titles, such as Grand State Tutors and State Tutors, to the important schools of Tibetan Buddhism, including the Karma Kagyu sect, Sakya sect, and Gelug sect. Leading officials of these organs were all appointed by the central government and were subject to the rule of law. Yet Van Praag describes the distinct and long-lasting Tibetan law code established by the Phagmodru ruler Janchub Gyaltsän as one of many reforms to revive old Imperial Tibetan traditions.

Other historians also assert that these Ming titles were nominal and did not actually confer the authority that the earlier Yuan titles had. Van Praag writes that the numerous economically motivated Tibetan missions to the Ming Court are referred to as 'tributary missions' in the Ming Shih. Van Praag writes that these tributary missions were simply prompted by China's need for horses from Tibet, since a viable horse market in Mongol lands was closed due to incessant conflict.

According to the Ministry of Foreign Affairs of the People's Republic of China, the Ming implemented a policy of managing Tibet according to conventions and customs, granting titles and setting up administrative organs over Tibet. The Information Office of the State Council of the People's Republic of China states that the Ming Dynasty's U-Tsang Commanding Office governed most areas of Tibet. It also states that while the Ming abolished the policy council set up by the Mongol Yuan to manage local affairs in Tibet and the Mongol system of Imperial Tutors to govern religious affairs, the Ming adopted a policy of bestowing titles upon religious leaders who had submitted to the Ming Dynasty.

Ming court conferred new official positions on ex-Yuan Tibetan leaders of the Phachu Kargyu and granted them lower-ranking positions. Of the county leaders of Neiwo Zong and Renbam Zong, Chen states that when the Emperor learned the actual situation of the Phachu Kargyu, the Ming court then appointed the main Zong leaders to be senior officers of the Senior Command of Dbus and Gtsang. The official posts that the Ming court established in Tibet, such as senior and junior commanders, offices of Qianhu (in charge of 1,000 households), and offices of Wanhu (in charge of 10,000 households), were all hereditary positions according to Chen, but he asserts that the succession of some important posts still had to be approved by the emperor, while old imperial mandates had to be returned to the Ming court for renewal.

In his usurpation of the throne from the Jianwen Emperor, the Yongle Emperor was aided by the Buddhist monk Yao Guangxiao, and like his father Hongwu, Yongle was well-disposed towards Buddhism, claims Rossabi. On 10 March, 1403, the Yongle Emperor invited Deshin Shekpa, the fifth Karmapa, to his court, even though the fourth Karmapa had rejected the invitation of the Hongwu Emperor of China. A Tibetan translation in the 16th century preserves the letter of Yongle, which the Association for Asian Studies notes is polite and complimentary towards the Karmapa. The letter of invitation read, My father and both parents of the queen are now dead. You are my only hope, essence of buddhahood. Please come quickly. In order to seek out the Karmapa, Yongle dispatched his eunuch Hou Xian and the Buddhist monk Zhi Guang to Tibet. Travelling to Lhasa either through Qinghai or via the Silk Road to Khotan, Hou Xian and Zhi Guang did not return to Nanjing until 1407.

During his travels beginning in 1403, Deshin Shekpa was induced by further exhortations by the Ming court to visit Nanjing by 10 April, 1407. Norbu writes that Yongle, following the tradition of Mongol emperors and their reverence for Tibetan Sakya lamas, showed an enormous amount of deference towards Deshin Shekpa. Yongle came out of the palace in Nanjing to greet the Karmapa and did not require him to kowtow like a tributary vassal. The emperor gave the Karmapa the place of honour at his left, and on a higher throne than his own. Rossabi describes a similar arrangement made by Kublai Khan and the Sakya Phagpa lama, writing that Kublai would sit on a lower platform than the Tibetan cleric when receiving religious instructions from him. Throughout the following month, the Yongle Emperor and his court showered Deshin Shekpa with presents. At Linggu Temple in Nanjing, he presided over the religious ceremonies for Yongle's deceased parents, while twenty-two days of his stay were marked by religious miracles that were recorded in five languages on a gigantic scroll that bore the Emperor's seal. During his stay in Nanjing, Deshin Shekpa was bestowed the title Great Treasure Prince of Dharma by Yongle. Elliot Sperling asserts that Yongle, in bestowing Deshin Shekpa with the title of King and praising his mystical abilities and miracles, was trying to build an alliance with the Karmapa as the Mongols had with the Sakya lamas, but Deshin Shekpa rejected Yongle's offer. In fact, this was the same title that Kublai Khan had offered the Sakya Phagpa lama, but Deshin Shekpa persuaded Yongle to grant the title to religious leaders of other Tibetan Buddhist sects.

Tibetan sources say Deshin Shekpa also persuaded Yongle not to impose his military might on Tibet as the Mongols had previously done. Thinley writes, before Deshin Shekpa returned to Tibet, the emperor began planning to send a military force into Tibet to forcibly give the Karmapa authority over all the Tibetan Buddhist sects, but Deshin Shekpa dissuaded him.

Deshin Shekpa's miracles testified to the power of both the emperor and his guru and served as a legitimizing tool for the emperor's problematic succession to the throne. Deshin Shekpa aided the legitimacy of Yongle's rule by providing him with portents and omens which demonstrated Heaven's favour of Yongle on the Ming throne.

Meetings of lamas with the emperor were exchanges of tribute between the patron and the priest and were not merely instances of a political subordinate paying tribute to a superior. Items of tribute were Buddhist artefacts which symbolized the religious nature of the relationship. Ming Dynasty did not exercise any direct political control over Tibet, content with their tribute relations that were almost entirely of a religious character. Yongle's courting and granting of titles to lamas was his attempt to resurrect the relationship between China and Tibet established earlier by the Yuan dynastic founder Khubilai Khan and his guru Phagpa. Later Qing emperors and their Mongol associates viewed Yongle's relationship with Tibet as part of a chain of reincarnation that saw this Han Chinese emperor as yet another emanation of Manjusri.

In year 1446 the Ming court cut off all relations with the Karmapa hierarchs. Until that year, the Ming court was unaware that Deshin Shekpa had died in 1415. Before discovering this, the Ming court believed that the representatives of his sect who continued to visit the Ming capital were sent by him.

Shortly after the visit by Deshin Shekpa, Yongle ordered the construction of a road and trading posts at the upper reaches of the Yangzi River and Mekong River in order to facilitate trade with Tibet in tea, horses, and salt. The trade route passed through Sichuan and crossed Shangri-La County in Yunnan. Rossabi and Sperling note that this trade in Tibetan horses for Chinese tea existed long before the Ming was established. Obtaining horses from Inner Asia in exchange for Chinese tea was also the goal of the earlier Wang Anshi, who realized that China could not produce enough militarily capable steeds. Horses were needed not only for cavalry but also as draft animals for the army's supply wagons. The Tibetans required Chinese tea not only as a common beverage but also as a religious ceremonial supplement. The Ming government imposed a monopoly on tea production and attempted to regulate this trade with state-supervised markets, but these collapsed in 1449 due to military failures and internal ecological and commercial pressures on the tea producing regions.

Ming's establishment of diplomatic delegations with Tibet was merely an effort by the Ming court to secure urgently needed horses. Tibetan areas were ruled by the Ming since Tibetan leaders were granted positions as Ming officials, that horses were collected from Tibet as a mandatory corvée tax, and therefore Tibetans were undertaking domestic affairs, not foreign diplomacy.

Ming simultaneously bought horses in the Kham region while fighting Tibetan tribes in Amdo and receiving Tibetan embassies in Nanjing. Embassies of Tibetan lamas visiting the Ming court were for the most part efforts to promote commercial transactions between the lamas' large, wealthy entourage and Ming Chinese merchants and officials. While the Ming maintained a laissez-faire policy towards Tibet and limited the numbers of the Tibetan retinues, the Tibetans sought to maintain a tributary relationship with the Ming because imperial patronage provided them with wealth and power. Tibetans eagerly sought Ming court invitations since the gifts the Tibetans received for bringing tribute were much greater in value than the latter.

As for Yongle's gifts to his Tibetan and Nepalese vassals such as silver wares, Buddha relics, utensils for Buddhist temples and religious ceremonies, and gowns and robes for monks, it was his effort to draw neighbouring states to the Ming orbit so that he could bask in glory, Yongle was quite willing to pay a small price. Silk workshops during the Ming also catered specifically to the Tibetan market with silk clothes and furnishings featuring Tibetan Buddhist iconography.

While the Ming Dynasty traded horses with Tibet, it upheld a policy of outlawing border markets in the north, which Laird says was an effort to punish the Mongols for their raids and to drive them from the frontiers of China. However, when Altan Khan, leader of the Tümed Mongols who overthrew the Oirat Mongol confederation's hegemony over the steppes, made peace with the Ming Dynasty in 1571, he persuaded the Ming to reopen their border markets in 1573. This provided the Chinese with a new supply of horses that the Mongols had in excess it was also a relief to the Ming, since they were unable to stop the Mongols from periodic raiding. Despite the fact that later Mongols believed Altan forced the Ming to view him as an equal, Chinese historians argue that he was simply a loyal Chinese citizen. By 1578, Altan Khan formed a formidable Mongol-Tibetan alliance with the Yellow Hat sect that the Ming viewed from afar without intervention.

Early Modern Period

Soon afterwards the Manchurian Qing Dynasty (1644-1911 AD) came to power in China. In 1652, the Fifth Dalai Lama was summoned to Beijing, he was re-conferred with the title Dalai Lama and made religious leader of Tibetan Buddhism by Emperor Shunzhi. The Potala Palace in Lhasa was constructed as a symbol of this new synthesis of power. The Dalai Lama made a state visit to the Qing Dynasty's second Emperor, Shunzhi, in 1653. The two leaders greeted one another as equals. Each man bestowed honours and titles upon the other, and the Dalai Lama was recognized as the spiritual authority of the Qing Empire. In 1654, the Fifth Dalai Lama had the Potala Palace renovated making it the base for Dalai Lamas to live, work and practice Buddhism. In 1682, the Fifth Dalai Lama passed away and dispute arose around the identification of the Sixth Dalai Lama. In 1709, Emperor Kangxi of Qing Dynasty sent his imperial envoy to assist the local magistrate Lhabzang Khan, grandson of Gushri Khan to confirm the Sixth Dalai Lama.

Qing Dynasty Control: According to Tibet, the priest/patron relationship established at this time between the Dalai Lama and Qing China continued throughout the Qing Era, but it had no bearing on Tibet's status as an independent nation. China, naturally, disagrees. Lobsang Gyatso died in 1682, but his Prime Minister concealed the Dalai Lama's passing until 1696 so that the Potala Palace could be finished and the power of the Dalai Lama's office consolidated.

The Panchen Lama was conferred with the title Panchen Erdeni in 1713 by Qing Dynasty. King Lobsang would rule for 12 years, until the Dzungar Mongols invaded and took power. Dzungar Mongols attacked Tibet in 1717. They killed the pretender to the Dalai Lama's throne, to the joy of the Tibetan people, but then began to loot monasteries around Lhasa. This vandalism brought a quick response from the Qing Emperor Kangxi, who sent troops to Tibet. The Dzungars destroyed the Imperial Chinese battalion near Lhasa in 1718.

In 1720, the angry Kangxi sent another, larger force to Tibet, which crushed the Dzungars. The Qing army also brought the proper Seventh Dalai Lama, Kelzang Gyatso (1708-1757) to Lhasa. China took advantage of this period of instability in Tibet to seize the regions of Amdo and Kham, making them into the Chinese province of Qinghai in 1724. Three years later, the Chinese and Tibetans signed a treaty that laid out the boundary line between the two nations. It would remain in force until 1910.

Qing China had its hands full trying to control Tibet. The Emperor sent a commissioner to Lhasa, but he was killed in 1750. The Imperial Army then defeated the rebels, but the Emperor recognized that he would have to rule through the Dalai Lama rather than directly. Day-to-day decisions would be made on the local level.

Despite much assistance from the Chinese Empire, the people of Tibet chafed under increasingly meddlesome Qing rule. Between 1804, when the Eighth Dalai Lama died, and 1895, when the Thirteenth Dalai Lama assumed the throne, none of the incumbent incarnations of the Dalai Lama lived to see their nineteenth birthdays. If the Chinese found a certain incarnation too hard to control, they would poison him. If the Tibetans thought an incarnation was controlled by the Chinese, then they would poison him themselves.

A Lot Drawing Process was introduced to avoid dispute over the identification of high lamas and their installation has been approved by the central government since 1793. In 1904, a British force invaded Lhasa and remained for 50 days. The 13th Dalai Lama, Thubten Gyatso, fled the country in 1904 at the urging of his Russian disciple, Agvan Dorzhiev. He went first to Mongolia, then made his way to Beijing. The Chinese declared that the Dalai Lama had been deposed as soon as he left Tibet, and claimed full sovereignty over not only Tibet but also Nepal and Bhutan. The Dalai Lama went to Beijing to discuss the situation with the Emperor Guangxu. Thubten Gyatso stayed in the Chinese capital from 1906 to 1908. He returned to Lhasa in 1909, disappointed by Chinese policies towards Tibet. China sent a force of 6,000 troops into Tibet, and the Dalai Lama fled to Darjeeling, India later that same year.

The Chinese Revolution swept away the Qing Dynasty. In 1911, the Qing Dynasty collapsed and the Republic of China was founded. The Thirteenth Dalai Lama's title, which was withdrawn by the Qing Dynasty in 1910, was restored by the Republic of China in 1912. Later, the Thirteenth Dalai Lama returned to Lhasa. In 1923, a dispute occurred between the Thirteenth Dalai Lama and the Ninth Panchen Lama.

China's new revolutionary government issued a formal apology to the Dalai Lama for the Qing Dynasty's insults, and offered to reinstate him. Thubten Gyatso refused, stating that he had no interest in the Chinese offer. He then issued a proclamation that was distributed across Tibet, rejecting Chinese control and stating that Tibet is a small, religious, and independent nation.

The Dalai Lama took control of Tibet's internal and external governance in 1913, negotiating directly with foreign powers, and reforming Tibet's judicial, penal, and educational systems. The Panchen Lama fled to Qinghai and died there in 1937. The Chinese government approved the identification of the reincarnations of the Fourteenth Dalai Lama and the Tenth Panchen Lama in 1940 and 1949 respectively.

Gelugpa Domination and Manchu Empire: In the 15th century, the rise to power of the Gelugpa order of monks, whose lamas were believed to be reincarnations of their predecessors, once more attracted Mongol approval. The third such lama received the title of 'Dalai', meaning 'Ocean', and implying 'Ocean of Wisdom'. It marked the Gelugpa's entry into the turbulent waters of worldly affairs. Not surprisingly, the local monastic elite saw the alliance as a threat, and conflict ensued. In 1611 the Tsang king attacked Drepung and Sera monasteries. The fourth Dalai Lama fled Tibet and died at the age of 25 (he was probably poisoned) in 1616. His death marked the start of a period of persecution of the Gelugpa by the Kagyupa (Red Hat) order, which was powerful in western and eastern Tibet. In 1640 Mongol forces intervened. The Tibetan king was taken captive and later executed. The great fifth Dalai Lama assumed power within Tibet, which was pacified with Mongol backing by 1656.

When he died in 1682, the Tibetan government encountered succession problems: the hastily enthroned sixth Dalai Lama was noted for his 'unbridled licentiousness'. At the same time, relations with the new Chinese Manchu Qing Dynasty quickly soured and in 1705 Mongol forces descended on Lhasa, capturing the Dalai Lama. The choice of his successor was just as controversial. He was deposed during the invasion of a rival group of Mongols in 1717, who were ousted in turn by the Chinese, who brought the seventh Dalai Lama with them. The Chinese were received as liberators by the Tibetans, and Emperor Kang Xi declared Tibet a protectorate of China - a historical precedent for the Communist takeover nearly 250 years later.

The Manchu overlordship appointed a king at one stage, but temporal rule reverted in 1750 to the seventh Dalai Lama, who ruled successfully until his death in 1757. The last Chinese military intervention took place in reaction to a Gurkha invasion from Nepal in 1788. From this time Manchu influence in Tibet receded. One significant outcome of that intervention was a ban on foreign contact, imposed because of fears of British collusion with the Gurkhas.

British Invasion of Tibet: The British expedition to Tibet in 1903 and 1904 was an invasion of Tibet by British Indian forces, seeking to prevent the Russian Empire from interfering in Tibetan affairs and thus gaining a foothold in one of the buffer states surrounding British India, under similar reasoning which had led British forces into Afghanistan twenty years before. Whilst British forces were remarkably successful in achieving their aims militarily, politically the invasion was very unpopular back in Britain, where it was virtually disowned post-war. The effects on Tibet, despite higher casualties and some economic disruption were also not significant, and any changes were not long retained.

The causes of the war are obscure, and it seems to have been primarily provoked by rumours circulating amongst the Calcutta-based British administration (Delhi was made imperial capital of India in 1911) that the Chinese government, (who nominally controlled Tibet), were planning to turn it over to the Russians, thus providing Russia with a direct route to British India and breaking the chain of semi-independent, mountainous buffer-states which separated India from the empires to the north. These rumours reached the current Viceroy, Lord Curzon, who decided to counter such a move by sending a diplomatic mission of 500 troops lead by a young officer named Major Francis Younghusband to Khamber Jong, a tiny Tibetan village north of Sikkim to meet Chinese and Tibetan representatives and discuss mutual non-aggression and trade agreements. The expedition arrived in June 1903 but by November no Chinese or Tibetan delegates had arrived and the force was recalled. Curzon decided at this stage to reinforce his message that foreign interference in the region would not be tolerated by dispatching a much larger armed force to the Tibetan capital Lhasa to dictate a treaty to the state's rulers.

Tibet's government, guided by the Dalai Lama was understandably unhappy about the presence of a large acquisitive foreign power dispatching a military mission to its capital, and began marshalling its armed forces. The government was fully aware that no help could be expected from the Chinese government, and so intended to use their arduous terrain and mountain-trained army to block the British path. The British authorities had anticipated this, and so dispatched a force heavy with Gurkha and Pathan troops, who came from mountainous regions of British India. The entire British force numbered just over 3,000 fighting men and was accompanied by 7,000 sherpas, porters and camp followers. Permission for the operation was received from London, but it is not clear that the Balfour government was fully aware of the scale of the operation, or of the Tibetan intention to resist it.

The British army which departed Gnatong in Sikkim on the 11 December 1903 was well prepared for the coming conflict due to its lengthy experience of service in Indian border wars. Its commander, Brigadier J. R. Macdonald wintered in the border country, using the time to train his troops near regular supplies of food and shelter before advancing properly in March, and making over 50 miles before his first major obstacle was presented on the 31 March at the pass of Guru, near Lake Bhan Tso.

Facing the vanguard of Macdonald's army and blocking the road was a 3,000 strong Tibetan force armed with primitive matchlock muskets and crouching behind rock sangers ready to fire on encroaching British forces. Their general rode to meet with Younghusband and Macdonald, but displayed his inexperience by not fortifying the western side of the pass, leaving his soldiers there exposed in plain view of his opponents. He hoped to prevent bloodshed, as the conflict was not yet a shooting war, and perhaps as a gesture of goodwill appears to have ordered his men to extinguish the fuses on their muskets, the relighting of which is a lengthy and difficult operation. Macdonald refused to accept the warnings of the Tibetan general and dispatched Sikh and Gurkha soldiers to disarm the Tibetan forces, who were unable to resist the advance due to their extinguished fuses, but still refused to give up their arms, resulting in a brawl amidst the sangers which while violent, was not yet deadly.

It was at this stage that war was irreparably declared, although the cause of it has never been established and probably never will be. British accounts insist that the Tibetan general became angry at the sight of the brawl developing and shot a Sikh soldier in the face rather than give up his modern pistol, prompting a violent response from the soldier's comrades which rapidly escalated the situation. The Tibetan accounts differ by claiming that the British tricked the general into extinguishing his troop's fuses and that once this was done the British opened fire first anyway, the fatal shot from the general's pistol only occurring once battle had been joined.

Whatever the truth of the opening round of the battle, the actual fighting did not last long. Once disarmed, the Tibetan forces attempted to retreat, but became entangled with each other and the steep landscape, opening them to disciplined rifle volleys from the Sikh and Gurkha regiments as well as the deadly fire of British Maxim Guns. Despite this withering attack, the Tibetan forces fell back in good order, refusing to turn their backs or run, and holding off cavalry pursuit at bayonet point. Half a mile from the battlefield the Tibetan forces reached shelter and were allowed to withdraw by Brigadier Macdonald. Behind them they left between 600 and 700 fatalities and 168 wounded, 148 of who survived in British field hospitals as prisoners. Amongst the dead was the general whose impetuous and inexperienced decision to extinguish his men's muskets had led to disaster. British losses were just a handful of wounded, including the unfortunate Sikh who had been shot in the face.

Past the first barrier and with increasing momentum, Macdonald's force crossed abandoned defences at Kangma a week later, and on the 9 April attempted to pass through Red Idol Gorge, which had been fortified to prevent passage. Macdonald ordered his Gurkha troops to scale the steep hillsides of the gorge and drive out the Tibetan forces ensconced high on their cliffs. This they began, but soon were lost in a furious blizzard, which cut all communications with the Gurkha force. Some hours later, exploratory probes down the pass encountered fire and a desultory exchange continued till the storm lifted around noon, which showed that the Gurkhas had by chance found their way to a position above the Tibetan troops. Thus faced with fire from both sides as Sikh soldiers pushed up the hill, the Tibetans moved back, again coming under severe fire from British artillery and retreated in good order, leaving behind 200 dead. British losses were again negligible.

It was clear that the mission was going to have to contest almost every pass and village it crossed, a problem Macdonald attempted to solve by splitting his forces, packets of several hundred being dispatched to various points on his route to drive in smaller Tibetan defences to speed the passage of the main force. Two minor actions occurred around this time, one on the 5 May at a fortified farm named Chang Lo involved an assault by an estimated 800 Tibetans on the British garrison of the fort, who were alerted by the cries of the Tibetan war whoops in time to form ranks and drive back the assailants with 160 dead. The other skirmish on the 9 May was possibly the highest action ever fought, when a Tibetan position at the Garo Pass (19,000 feet above sea level) was assaulted by Gurkha troops who climbed a vertical cliff under fire to outflank the Tibetans who were driven back by a charge of Gurkha, Sikh and British soldiers. For once, casualties were more evenly distributed, although the Tibetans still suffered heavily.

In the following two months, Macdonald collected his forces near Chang Lo and cleared minor obstacles with the intention of assaulting the main Tibetan stronghold at Gyantse Jong. Once this obstacle was cleared, the road to Lhasa would be opened, due to the removal of the small Tibetan forces occupying it by the dispersal of the British force. Gyantse Jong was however too tough for a small raiding force to take and it overlooked British supply routes, making it the primary target of Macdonald's army. On 28 June the final obstacle to the assault was cleared when a fortified monastery which covered the approach was taken in house to house fighting by Pathan soldiers.

Tibetan responses to the invasion so far had relied totally on static defences and sniping from the mountains at the passing column neither of which had proved effective, and apart from the failed assault on Chang Lo two months previously that had made no sallies against British positions or any aggressive movements against the besieging army. This attitude was a mix of justifiable fear of the Maxim Guns, and partly faith in the solid rock of their defences, but in every battle they were primarily let down by their poor weaponry and inexperienced leadership.

The Gyantse Jong was a massively well protected fortress, which possessed the best Tibetan troops and the country's only artillery as well as forbidding position high over the valley below. The British had no time for a lengthy formal siege and so Macdonald proposed that feints would draw Tibetan soldiers away from the walls over several days before an artillery bombardment with mountain guns would create a breach which would immediately be stormed by his main force. This plan was put into action, when Gurkha troops took several batteries in the vicinity of the fortress by climbing vertical cliffs under fire, a feat they achieved with impressive regularity.

The eventual assault on the 6 July did not go as planned, as the Tibetan walls were stronger than previously believed, and took eleven hours to break through. As Gurkhas and Royal Fusiliers charged the broken wall, they came under heavy fire and suffered some casualties. After several failed attempts to gain the walls, two soldiers broke through a bottleneck under fire and stormed the walls despite both being wounded. They gained a foothold which following troops exploited, enabling the walls to be taken. Knowing by now the power of British weaponry upon a defeated force, the Tibetans retreated in good order from the fort, allowing the British control of the road to Lhasa, but denying Macdonald a rout and thus remaining a constant threat (although never a serious problem) in the British rear for the remainder of the war.

Younghusband now assumed command of the mission, as the road had been successfully cleared. He took on his procession to Lhasa nearly 2,000 soldiers, all those not required to protect the road back to Sikkim. Crossing several obviously fortified ambush points without incident and recrossing the Garo Pass, the force arrived in Lhasa on August 3, 1904 to discover that the Dalai Lama and all the Tibetan officials had fled. Meeting with the Chinese resident official, who escorted the British into the city with his personal guard, a triumphal procession to the Potala Palace was followed by a dictation of treaty terms, which now included a demanded Tibetan apology for starting the war. The Tri Rimpoche who governed the city in the Dalai Lama's absence agreed to all articles of the treaty, reportedly cryptically commenting that When one has known the scorpion (meaning China) the frog (meaning Britain) is divine.

The British mission departed in late September 1904, after a ceremonial presentation of gifts. In the event, neither side could be too unhappy with the outcome of the war. Britain had won and had received the agreements it desired, but without actually receiving any tangible results. The Tibetans had lost the war but had seen China humbled in its failure to defend their client state from foreign incursion, and had pacified the invader by signing an unenforceable and largely irrelevant treaty. Damage to civilian life and property was virtually nil, and there are no contemporary reports of looting or wanton destruction by the soldiers of either side. Captured Tibetan troops were all released without condition upon the war's conclusion, many after receiving medical treatment. Some Chinese historians of a much later date have attempted to portray this as a series of savage massacres of unarmed men during a vicious war of expansion, but apart from the controversial opening battle at Guru, such tragedies did not occur, the war instead being conducted with the minimum possible bloodshed, all British commanders keeping a keen eye towards London, where their actions were thoroughly scrutinized at the distance of some weeks.

It was in fact the reaction in London which was fiercest in condemnation of the war. By the Edwardian period, colonial wars had become increasingly unpopular, and public and political opinion were unhappy with the waging of a war for such slight reasons as those provided by Curzon, and with the opening battle, which was portrayed in Britain as something of a deliberate massacre of unarmed men. It was only the support given to them by King Edward VII that provided Younghusband, Macdonald, Grant and others with the recognition they did eventually receive for what was quite a remarkable feat of arms in taking an army across the rooftop of the world, driving through courageous defenders through freezing weather in impassable positions and achieving all their objectives in just six months, losing just 202 men to enemy action and 411 to other causes. Tibetan casualties have never been calculated, but must have reached the several thousands over the course of 16 major and minor actions, including two battles.

Early 20th Century Events

The area of contention between China and Tibet is so remote that it is not easy even to describe exactly where we are talking about. It comprises roughly the north-eastern quarter of what is now the Chinese province of Chinghai, south of the Koko Nor or "Blue Lake" - a bleak, rolling steppe averaging about 12,000 feet above sea level, bisected by the gorges of the Yellow River and overshadowed by the inaccessible Amne Machin mountain massif. Until the 1950s, even the political status of this area was uncertain. It was claimed by the Tibetans, who regarded it as part of their province of Amdo, but until 1912 it had been nominally subject to the Manchu dynasty of China, which had maintained a handful of ineffectual garrisons there. Then the Chinese were withdrawn, but the Tibetan government in Lhasa was no more successful than the Manchus at establishing effective authority on this remote frontier.

For generations, the Turkish and Tungan (Chinese Muslim) clans on the Chinese side of the frontier had maintained a brutal feud with the Tibetan Ngolok tribesmen living further west. And yet, in 19th century the nomadic Ngoloks already had a reputation as rapacious horse rustlers and caravan raiders, who escaped retaliation by retiring into inaccessible mountain gorges. Several 19th century travellers mention these people, but for numerous reasons - the reluctance of the Chinese and Tibetan governments to allow outsiders into the region, the density and hostility of the population, and the sheer remoteness of the place from anywhere that seemed worth going to. One of the very few outsiders to encounter them was the Russian explorer Roborovski, who in 1895 had been attacked and driven back on the approaches to Amne Machin. Like most Tibetan Buddhists the Ngoloks regarded the mountain as sacred, and they were always unhappy about foreigners going anywhere near it.

The past history of the Tungans was just as turbulent. In 1895 the Muslims of Sining, the provincial capital of Chinghai, rebelled against the Manchus and inflicted several defeats on Chinese armies. Eventually they were suppressed, after a massacre which reportedly left no able-bodied Tungan males alive, except for 10,000 or so who fled west into the Koko Nor region. But by the 1920s the Muslims of eastern Chinghai were again on fairly good terms with their Chinese neighbours, and under the leadership of General Ma Chi one of many independent warlords who claimed to rule their own parts of China in the name of the defunct Republic they found themselves holding the frontier against the Mongolian and Tibetan nomads.

In fact, despite the warlike reputation of the latter, they seem more often than not to have been the victims of aggression by their settled neighbours. In about 1928, as the Nationalist Northern Expedition was bringing the warlord era in the rest of China to a close, Ma Chi launched what was declared at the time to be a war of extermination against the Ngoloks. After many setbacks, he defeated them and captured the great Buddhist monastery complex at Labrang, situated across the Yellow River south of Sining.

But twenty years later, the next outsider to try to get through to Amne Machin - the American Leonard Clark - found the Ngoloks far from exterminated, and still as belligerent as ever.At that time the Nationalist General Ma Pu-fang was based in Sining, with a predominantly Muslim army which was said to be over a million strong. (Confusingly, just about every Tungan was called Ma.) General Ma was regarded by many foreign powers as one of the anti-Communist forces' best hopes, and it appears that one of the factors which encouraged the Tibetan government to resist the Communists was the belief that he was a reliable buffer against invasion from the north-east. In 1949 Ma sent a mounted expeditionary force west into the Ngolok country to reconnoitre a route by which he could retire into Tibet if forced out of Sining by Mao's armies. This party was commanded by Colonel Ma Sheng-lung. In the event Ma failed to put up much resistance to the Communists, instead escaping to Hong Kong by plane with his gold and his concubines, and the planned fighting withdrawal into Tibet never materialised. During the 1950s the People's Liberation Army finally succeeded in pacifying the Ngoloks subdued and impoverished but still not assimilated into mainstream Chinese culture. (Amne Machin, incidentally, was first climbed in 1981, when it was found to be nearly 5,000 feet lower than Mount Everest.).

China's Contention of Sovereignty: The government of the People's Republic of China and the Government of Tibet in Exile, however, disagree over the issue of Tibet, when Tibet became a part of China, and whether this incorporation into China is legitimate according to international law. The government of the PRC contends that China has had control over Tibet since the Yuan Dynasty.

The government of Republic of China (ROC), which ruled mainland China from 1912 until 1949 and now controls Taiwan, has had cabinet level Mongolian and Tibetan Affairs Commission in charge of administration of Tibet and Mongolia regions since 1912. The Commission retained its cabinet level status after 1949, but no longer executes that function. On 10 May 1943, Chiang Kai-shek asserted that Tibet is part of Chinese territory. He again declared in 1946 that the Tibetans were Chinese. ROC still claims sovereignty over Tibet and Mongolia in its constitution.

In the late 19th century, China adopted the Western model of nation-state diplomacy and concluded a series of treaties regarding Tibet's boundaries and status. Chinese government sources consider this a sign of sovereignty rather than suzerainty.

According to historian Zahiruddin Ahmad, since at least the 18th century, when the Qing Government was setting up its local government structure and promulgated laws for the governing, Beijing has, in the words of a foreign missionary who witnessed, had absolute dominion over Tibet

The Chinese Resident Ministers in Tibet, namely Ambans, were bestowed power which, according to the Imperial Ordinance promulgated in 1793, was on a par with the local spiritual leaders of Dalai Lamas and Panchen Lamas. According to the Ordinance, the Ambans were in absolute charge of financial, diplomatic, and trade matters.

The Patron-Priest relationship held between the Chinese central authorities and the Tibetan local governments was one of superior to inferior. The 13th Dalai Lama, for example, knelt before the Empress Dowager and the young Emperor while he delivered his petition in Beijing. He was awarded the humiliating title of Loyally Submissive Vice-Regent, and ordered to follow China's commands and communicate with the Emperor only through the Chinese Amban in Lhasa. The kneeling before the Emperor followed the 17th-century precedent in the case of the 6th Dalai Lama.

The position of the PRC, which has ruled mainland China since 1949, as well as the official position of the Republic of China, which ruled mainland China before 1949 and currently controls Taiwan, is that Tibet has been an indivisible part of China de jure since the Yuan Dynasty of Mongol-ruled China in the 13th century. Comparable to other states such as the Kingdom of Dali and the Tangut Empire that were also incorporated into the Middle Kingdom at the time. The PRC contends that according to the Succession of states theory in international law all subsequent Chinese governments (Ming Dynasty, Qing Dynasty, ROC and PRC) have succeeded the Yuan Dynasty in exercising de jure sovereignty and de facto power over Tibet.

According to the current government, successive Chinese governments have recognized Tibet as having its own unique culture and language however, they believe that this situation, does not necessarily argue in favour of independence, because China has over 56 unique ethnic groups and is one of many multi-national states in the world.

The ROC government had no effective control over Tibet from 1912 to 1951 however, in the opinion of the Chinese government, this condition does not represent Tibet's complete independence as many other parts of China also enjoyed de facto independence when the Chinese nation was torn by warlords, Japanese invasion, and civil war. Goldstein explains what is meant by de facto independence in the following statement:

While at times the Tibetans were fiercely independent-minded, at other times, Tibet indicated its willingness to accept subordinate status as part of China provided that Tibetan internal systems were left untouched and China relinquished control over a number of important ethnic Tibetan groups in Kham and Amdo. China insists that during this period the ROC government continued to maintain sovereignty over Tibet. The Provisional Constitution of the Republic of China (1912) stipulated that Tibet was a province of the Republic of China. Provisions concerning Tibet in the Constitution of the Republic of China promulgated later all stress the inseparability of Tibet from Chinese territory, and the Central Government of China exercise of sovereignty in Tibet. In 1927, the Commission in Charge of Mongolian and Tibetan Affairs of the the Chinese Government contained members of great influence in the Mongolian and Tibetan areas, such as the 9th Panchen Lama, the 13th Dalai Lama and other Tibetan government representatives. In 1934, on his condolence mission for the demise of the Dalai Lama, the Chinese General Huang Musong posted notices in Chinese and Tibetan throughout Lhasa that alluded to Tibet as an integral part of China while expressing the utmost reverence for the Dalai Lama and religion.

The 13th Dalai Lama's attitude towards the Central Government vacillated but had been gradually improving. He began to see the possibility of unceasing wars between Tibet and contiguous provinces under the control of various warlords, and Tibet would benefit if there was effective intervention by the Central Government. These territorial disputes became for him local disputes instead of China-Tibet disputes. When wars of warlords were about to come to end, a unified Central Government would also be detrimental to the Dalai Lama - if the Panchen Lama were to oppose him with Chinese support. So in 1931, he sent delegates to attend the National Assembly. After his death, the Tibetan Kashag Government continued the policy of sending delegates to the National Assembly of 1936. Also, delegates from Tibetan areas attended the Drafting Committee for a new constitution of the Republic of China in 1925, the fourth National Congress of the Kuomintang in 1931, and a National Assembly for drafting a new Chinese constitution in 1946. A Trade Mission sent by the Tibetan government attended another National Assembly for drafting a new Chinese constitution in 1948.

The 9th Panchen Lama traditionally ruled over one-third of Tibet. On 1 February 1925, the Panchen Lama attended the preparatory session of the National Reconstruction Meeting meant to identify ways and means of unifying the Chinese nation, and gave a speech about achieving the unification of five nationalities, including Tibetans, Mongolians and Han Chinese. In 1933, he called upon the Mongols to national unity and to obey the Chinese Government to resist Japanese invasion. In February 1935 the Chinese government appointed Panchen Lama Special Cultural Commissioner for the Western Regions and assigned him 500 Chinese troops. He spent much of his time teaching and preaching Buddhist doctrines - including the principles of unity and pacification for the border regions - extensively in inland China, outside of Tibet, from 1924 until 1 December 1937, when he died on his way back to Tibet under the protection of Chinese troops.

The approval of the Kuomintang government was needed to validate the choice of the Dalai Lama and Panchen Lama. When the current 14th Dalai Lama was first installed in Lhasa, it was with an armed escort of Chinese troops and an attending Chinese minister, in accordance with centuries-old tradition.

During China's resistance war against Japanese invasion, Chiang Kai-shek ordered Ma Bufang, Governor of Qinghai (1937–1949), to repair the Yushu airport at Qinghai Province to deter Tibetan independence. In

May 1943, Chiang warned that Tibet must accept and follow the instructions and orders of the Central Government, that they must agree and help to build the Chinese-India road, and that they must maintain direct communications with the Office of the Mongolian and Tibetan Affairs Commission in Lhasa and not through the newly established Foreign Office of Tibet. He sternly warned that he would send an air force to bomb Tibet immediately should Tibet be found to be collaborating with Japan. Throughout the Kuomintang years, no country gave Tibet diplomatic recognition.

REFERENCES

Kelly, Petra K., Gert Bastian, and Pat Aiello: The Anguish of Tibet, Berkeley, Parallax Press, 1991.

Khilnani, Sunil: The Idea of India, London, Hamish Hamilton, 1997.

Klieger, P. Christiaan: Tibetan Nationalism: The Role of Patronage in the Accomplishment of a National Identity, Meerut, Archana Publications, 1992.

Lazar, E.: Tibet: The Issue is Independence, Berkeley, Parallax Press, 1994.

Lopez, Donald S.: Prisoners of Shangri-La: Tibetan Buddhism and the West, Chicago, University of Chicago Press, 1998.

Marshall, Steven D.: Hostile Elements: A Study of Political Imprisonment in Tibet, 1987-1998, London, Tibet Information Network, 1999.

Mukherjee, R.: The Penguin Gandhi Reader, New Delhi, Penguin, 1993.

Mullin, Chris: 'Tibetan Conspiracy' in Far Eastern Economic Review, 1975.

Nehru, Jawaharlal: The Discovery of India, London, Meridian Books, 1956.

Nhat Hanh: Vietnam: The Lotus in the Sea of Fire, New York, The Fellowship of Reconciliation, 1967.

Norbu, Dawa: 'The 1959 Tibetan Rebellion: An Interpretation' in China Quarterly, 1979.

Parekh, Bhikhu: Gandhi's Political Philosophy: A Critical Examination, London, Macmillan, 1989.

Parrinder, Geoffrey: The Bhagavad Gita, Oxford, Oneworld, 1996.

Patterson, George N.: Tibet in Revolt, London, Faber and Faber, 1960.

Peissel, Michel: Cavaliers of Kham: The Secret War in Tibet, London, Heinemann, 1972.

Powers, John: Introduction to Tibetan Buddhism, Ithaca, Snow Lion Publications, 1995.

Queen, C.S. and King, S.B.: Engaged Buddhism: Buddhist Liberation Movements in Asia, Albany: State University of New York Press, 1996.

Ray, S.: Gandhi, India and the World: An International Symposium, Melbourne, Hawthorn Press, 1970.

Sartori, Giovanni: The Theory of Democracy Revisited, Chatham, N.J., Chatham House, 1987.

Schwartz, Ronald D.: Circle of Protest: Political Ritual in the Tibetan Uprising, London, Hurst and Company, 1994.

Seymour, J. P. and Cao, C.: Tibet Through Dissident Chinese Eyes: Essays on Self-Determination, Armonk, M. E. Sharpe, 1992.

Smith, Warren W.: Tibetan Nation: A History of Tibetan Nationalism and Sino-Tibetan Relations, Boulder, Westview Press, 1996.

Snellgrove, David and H. E. Richardson: A Cultural History of Tibet, Boston, Shambhala, 1986.

Snow, Edgar: Red China Today: The Other Side of the River, Harmondsworth, Penguin, 1962.

Su Wenming: Tibet: Today and Yesterday, Beijing, Beijing Review, 1983.

Subba, T.A.: Flight and Adaptation: Tibetan Refugees in the Darjeeling - Sikkim Himalaya, Dharamsala, Library of Tibetan Works and Archives, 1990.

Text of speeches given by Professor Samdhong Rinpoche on his visit to Britain, October 1997.

Westerlund, David: Questioning the Secular State: The Worldwide Resurgence of Religion in Politics, London, Hurst and Co., 1996.

Williams, Paul: Mahayana Buddhism: The Doctrinal Foundations, London, Routledge, 1989.

4

Indo-China Foreign Policy

Introduction

After India gained independence from the United Kingdom, New Delhi tried to establish friendly diplomatic relationship with several countries. The communal riots following the Partition of India and dispute over Junagadh and Kashmir created tense relations between India and Islamic Republic of Pakistan. Within a year after attaining independence, Pakistan-backed guerrillas invaded the Dogra Kingdom of Kashmir, which subsequently acceded to India, resulting in a full-scale war. The region continues to be a bone of contention between the neighbours. The military operation in Kashmir was followed by Operation Polo and various other military operations, such as Operation Vijay resulting in the political integration of India.

India's Foreign Policy

India played a key role in establishing the Non-Aligned Movement in 1961. Though India pursued close relations with both US and USSR, it decided not to join any major power bloc and refrained from joining military alliances. India, however began establishing close military relationship with the Soviet Union.

In the 1950s, India showed keen interest in establishing close relationship with the People's Republic of China. The Panchsheel was seen as a landmark agreement between the two. However, several border disputes and the Chinese invasion of Tibet continued to plague Sino-Indian relations. In 1962, India detected Chinese infiltration into Indian territory, which resulted in a brief war between the two. India has remained suspicious towards China since then. China also became a close ally of Pakistan, India's neighbour, adding to the rift between the two. Even though there has been a significant improvement in trade and diplomatic relations, India remains wary of China.

After the Sino-Indian War and the Indo-Pakistani War of 1965, India made considerable changes to its foreign policy. It developed a close relationship with the Soviet Union and started receiving massive military equipment and financial assistance from the USSR. This had an adverse effect on the Indo-American relationship. The United States saw Pakistan as a counter-weight to pro-Soviet India and started giving the former military assistance. This created an atmosphere of suspicion between India and US. The US-India relationship suffered a considerable setback during the Soviet invasion of Afghanistan when India openly supported the Soviet invasion.

After the collapse of the Soviet Union, India improved its relations with the United States, Canada, France, Japan and Germany. In 1992, India established formal diplomatic relations with Israel.

In the mid-1990s, India tried to attract the world attention towards the alleged Pakistan backed terrorism in Kashmir. The Kargil War resulted in a major diplomatic victory for India. The United States and European Union recognized the fact that Pakistani military had illegally infiltrated into Indian territory and pressurized Pakistan to withdraw from Kargil. Several anti-India militant groups based in Pakistan were labelled as terrorist groups by the United States and European Union.

In 1998, India tested nuclear weapons (see Pokhran-II) which resulted in several U.S., Japanese and European sanctions on India. India's then defence minister, George Fernandes, said that India's nuclear program was necessary as it provided a deterrence to potential Chinese nuclear threat. Most of the sanctions imposed on India were removed by 2001.

After the September 11, 2001 attacks, Indian intelligence agencies provided the U.S. with significant information on Al-Qaeda and related groups' activities in Pakistan and Afghanistan. India's extensive contribution to the War on Terrorism, coupled with a surge in its economy, has helped India's diplomatic relations with several countries. Over the past three years, India has held numerous joint military exercises with U.S. and European nations that have resulted in a strengthened U.S.-India and E.U.-India bilateral relationship. India's bilateral trade with Europe and U.S. has more than doubled in the last five years.

India has been pushing for reforms in the UN and WTO with mixed results. India's candidature for a permanent seat at the UN Security Council is currently backed by several countries including the Russian Federation,

United Kingdom, France, Germany, Japan, Brazil and African Union nations. In 2004, the United States signed a nuclear co-operation agreement with India even though the latter is not a part of the Nuclear Non-Proliferation Treaty. The US argued that India's strong nuclear non-proliferation record made it an exception and persuaded other Nuclear Suppliers Group members to sign similar deals with India.

Although India and China had relatively little political contact before the 1950s, both countries have had extensive cultural contact since the first century A.D., especially with the transmission of Buddhism from India to China (see Buddhism, ch. 3). Although Nehru based his vision of resurgent Asia on friendship between the two largest states of Asia, the two countries had a conflict of interest in Tibet (which later became China's Xizang Autonomous Region), a geographical and political buffer zone where India had inherited special privileges from the British colonial government. At the end of its civil war in 1949, China wanted to reassert control over Tibet and to liberate the Tibetan people from Lamaism (Tibetan Buddhism) and feudalism, which it did by force of arms in 1950. To avoid antagonizing China, Nehru informed Chinese leaders that India had neither political nor territorial ambitions, nor did it seek special privileges in Tibet, but that traditional trading rights must continue. With Indian support, Tibetan delegates signed an agreement in May 1951 recognizing Chinese sovereignty and control but guaranteeing that the existing political and social system in Tibet would continue. Direct negotiations between India and China commenced in an atmosphere improved by India's mediatory efforts in ending the Korean War (1950-53).

In April 1954, India and China signed an eight-year agreement on Tibet that set forth the basis of their relationship in the form of the Panchsheel. Although critics called the Panchsheel naive, Nehru calculated that in the absence of either the wherewithal or a policy for defence of the Himalayan region, India's best guarantee of security was to establish a psychological buffer zone in place of the lost physical buffer of Tibet. Thus the catch phrase of India's diplomacy with China in the 1950s was *Hindi-Chini bhai-bhai* (Hindi for India and China are brothers). Up to 1959, despite border skirmishes and discrepancies between Indian and Chinese maps, Chinese leaders amicably had assured India that there was no territorial contro-versy on the border.

When an Indian reconnaissance party discovered a completed Chinese road running through the Aksai Chin region of the Ladakh District of Jammu and Kashmir, border clashes and Indian protests became more frequent and serious.

In January 1959, Chinese premier Zhou Enlai wrote to Nehru, rejecting Nehru's contention that the border was based on treaty and custom and pointing out that no government in China had accepted as legal the McMahon Line, which in the 1914 Simla Convention defined the eastern section of the border between India and Tibet. The Dalai Lamaspiritual and temporal head of the Tibetan peoplesought sanctuary in Dharmsala, Himachal Pradesh, in March 1959, and thousands of Tibetan refugees settled in northwestern India, particularly in Himachal Pradesh. China accused India of expansionism and imperialism in Tibet and throughout the Himalayan region. China claimed 104,000 square kilometers of territory over which India's maps showed clear sovereignty, and demanded rectification of the entire border.

Zhou proposed that China relinquish its claim to most of India's northeast in exchange for India's abandonment of its claim to Aksai Chin. The Indian government, constrained by domestic public opinion, rejected the idea of a settlement based on uncompensated loss of territory as being humiliating and unequal.

Chinese forces attacked India on October 20, 1962. Having pushed the unprepared, ill-equipped, and inadequately led Indian forces to within forty-eight kilometers of the Assam plains in the northeast and having occupied strategic points in Ladakh, China declared a unilateral cease-fire on November 21 and withdrew twenty kilometers behind its new line of control (see The Experience of Wars, ch. 10).

Relations with China worsened during the rest of the 1960s and the early 1970s as Chinese-Pakistani relations improved and Chinese-Soviet relations worsened. China backed Pakistan in its 1965 war with India. Between 1967 and 1971, an all-weather road was built across territory claimed by India, linking China's Xinjiang Uygur Autonomous Region with Pakistan India could do no more than protest. China continued an active propaganda campaign against India and supplied ideological, financial, and other assistance to dissident groups, especially to tribes in northeastern India. China accused India of assisting the Khampa rebels in Tibet. Diplomatic contact between the two governments was minimal although not formally severed. The flow of cultural and other exchanges that had marked the 1950s ceased entirely. In August 1971, India signed its Treaty of Peace, Friendship, and Cooperation with the Soviet Union, and the United States and China sided with Pakistan in its December 1971 war with India. By this time, Beijing was seated at the UN, where its representatives denounced India as being a tool of Soviet expansionism.

India and China renewed efforts to improve relations after the Soviet Union invaded Afghanistan in December 1979. China modified its pro-Pakistan stand on Kashmir and appeared willing to remain silent on India's absorption of Sikkim and its special advisory relationship with Bhutan. China's leaders agreed to discuss the boundary issue India's priority as the first step to a broadening of relations. The two countries hosted each others' news agencies, and Kailash (Kangrinbogê Feng) and Mansarowar Lake (Mapam Yumco Lake) in Tibetthe mythological home of the Hindu pantheonwere opened to annual pilgrimages from India. In 1981 Chinese minister of foreign affairs Huang Hua was invited to India, where he made complimentary remarks about India's role in South Asia. Chinese premier Zhao Ziyang concurrently toured Pakistan, Nepal, and Bangladesh.

After the Huang visit, India and China held eight rounds of border negotiations between December 1981 and November 1987. These talks initially raised hopes that progress could be made on thc border issue. However, in 1985 China stiffened its position on the border and insisted on mutual concessions without defining the exact terms of its package proposal or where the actual line of control lay. In 1986 and 1987, the negotiations achieved nothing, given the charges exchanged between the two countries of military encroachment in the Sumdorung Chu valley of the Tawang tract on the eastern sector of the border. China's construction of a military post and helicopter pad in the area in 1986 and India's grant of statehood to Arunachal Pradesh (formerly the North-East Frontier Agency) in February 1987 caused both sides to deploy new troops to the area, raising tensions and fears of a new border war. China relayed warnings that it would teach India a lesson if it did not cease nibbling at Chinese territory. By the summer of 1987, however, both sides had backed away from conflict and denied that military clashes had taken place.

A warming trend in relations was facilitated by Rajiv Gandhi's visit to China in December 1988. The two sides issued a joint communiqué that stressed the need to restore friendly relations on the basis of the Panchsheel and noted the importance of the first visit by an Indian prime minister to China since Nehru's 1954 visit. India and China agreed to broaden bilateral ties in various areas, working to achieve a fair and reasonable settlement while seeking a mutually acceptable solution to the border dispute. The communiqué also expressed China's concern about agitation by Tibetan separatists in India and reiterated China's position that Tibet was an integral part of China and that anti-China political activities by expatriate Tibetans was not to be tolerated. Rajiv Gandhi signed bilateral agreements on science and technology cooperation, on civil aviation to establish direct air links, and on cultural exchanges. The two sides also agreed to hold annual diplomatic consultations between foreign ministers, and to set up a joint ministerial committee on economic and scientific cooperation and a joint working group on the boundary issue. The latter group was to be led by the Indian foreign secretary and the Chinese vice minister of foreign affairs.

As the mid-1990s approached, slow but steady improvement in relations with China was visible. Top-level dialogue continued with the December 1991 visit of Chinese premier Li Peng to India and the May 1992 visit to China of Indian president Ramaswami Venkataraman. Six rounds of talks of the Indian-Chinese Joint Working Group on the Border Issue were held between December 1988 and June 1993. Progress was also made in reducing tensions on the border via confidence-building measures, including mutual troop reductions, regular meetings of local military commanders, and advance notification of military exercises. Border trade resumed in July 1992 after a hiatus of more than thirty years, consulates reopened in Bombay (or Mumbai in the Marathi language) and Shanghai in December 1992, and, in June 1993, the two sides agreed to open an additional border trading post. During Sharad Pawar's July 1992 visit to Beijing, the first ever by an Indian minister of defence, the two defence establishments agreed to develop academic, military, scientific, and technological exchanges and to schedule an Indian port call by a Chinese naval vessel.

Substantial movement in relations continued in 1993. The sixth-round joint working group talks were held in June in New Delhi but resulted in only minor developments. However, as the year progressed the long-standing border dispute was eased as a result of bilateral pledges to reduce troop levels and to respect the cease-fire line along the India-China border. Prime Minister Narasimha Rao and Chinese premier Li Peng signed the border agreement and three other agreements (on cross-border trade, and on increased cooperation on the environment and in radio and television broadcasting) during the former's visit to Beijing in September. A senior-level Chinese military delegation made a six-day goodwill visit to India in December 1993 aimed at fostering confidence-building measures between the defence forces of the two countries. The visit, however, came at a time when press reports revealed that, as a result of improved relations between China and Burma, China was exporting greater amounts of military matériel to Burma's army, navy, and air force and sending an increasing number of technicians to Burma. Of concern to Indian security officials was the presence of Chinese radar technicians in Burma's Coco Islands, which border India's Union Territory of the Andaman and Nicobar Islands. Nevertheless, movement continued in 1994 on troop reductions along the Himalayan frontier. Moreover, in January 1994 Beijing announced that it not only favored a negotiated solution on Kashmir, but also opposed any form of independence for the region.

Talks were held in New Delhi in February 1994 aimed at confirming established confidence-building measures and discussing clarification of the line of actual control, reduction of armed forces along the line, and prior information about forthcoming military exercises. China's hope for settlement of the boundary issue was reiterated.

The 1993 Chinese military visit to India was reciprocated by Indian army chief of staff General B.C. Joshi. During talks in Beijing in July 1994, the two sides agreed that border problems should be resolved peacefully through mutual understanding and concessions. The border issue was raised in September 1994 when Chinese minister of national defence Chi Haotian visited New Delhi for extensive talks with high-level Indian trade and defence officials. Further talks in New Delhi in March 1995 by the India-China Expert Group led to an agreement to set up two additional points of contact along the 4,000-kilometer border to facilitate meetings between military personnel. The two sides also were reported as seriously engaged in defining the McMahon Line and the line of actual control vis-à-vis military exercises and prevention of air intrusion. Talks in Beijing in July 1995 aimed at better border security and combating cross-border crimes and in New Delhi in August 1995 on additional troop withdrawals from the border made further progress in reducing tensions.

Possibly indicative of the further relaxation of India-China relationsat least there was little notice taken in Beijingwas the April 1995 announcement, after a year of consultation, of the opening of the Taipei Economic and Cultural Center in New Delhi. The center serves as the representative office of Taiwan and is the counterpart of the India-Taipei Association in Taiwan both institutions have the goal of improving relations between the two sides, which have been strained since New Delhi's recognition of Beijing in 1950.

China's Foreign Policy

Although Chinese foreign policy since 1949 has had distinctive characteristics, the forces that shape Beijing's foreign policy and many of its overall goals have been similar to those of other nations. China has sought to protect its sovereignty and territorial integrity and to achieve independence of action, while interacting with both more powerful and less powerful countries. As with most other nations, Beijing's foreign relations have been conditioned by its historical experiences, nationalism and ideology, and the worldview of its leaders, as well as by the governmental structure and decision-making process. At times China's domestic policies have had wide-ranging ramifications for its foreign policy formulation.

Another characteristic Chinese foreign policy has had in common with that of many other countries is that the actual conduct of foreign relations sometimes has been at odds with official policy. Beijing's stress on principles in its official statements at times makes the contrast between statements and actions particularly noticeable. In addition, a nation's leaders must often make decisions in reaction to events and circumstances, rather than simply formulating a rational foreign policy based on their goals. The need to react to what has happened or what may happen adds an element of unpredictability to foreign policy decision making, as has been the case at several crucial junctures in Chinese foreign relation since 1949.

In addition to the aspects of foreign policy formulation and implementation that China has in common with other countries, China's foreign policy from 1949 has had these characteristics: contrast between practicality and adherence to principles fluctuation between militancy and peacefulness tension between self-reliance and dependence on others and contrast between China's actual and potential capabilities. These contradictory characteristics have at times created a confusing picture of Chinese foreign policy. Is China peace-loving or intent on fomenting unrest? Is China's ultimate goal to be self-sufficient or economically interdependent with the rest of the world? And is China basically a poor, developing country that is at most a regional power or actually a nascent economic and military giant deserving of superpower status?

The response to these questions is that since 1949 Chinese foreign policy has reflected all of these contrasting features. Beijing had emphasized principles and ideology above everything else in foreign relations, especially during the 1950s and 1960s, but Chinese leaders at times have also shown a practical side that gave them the flexibility to change policies, sometimes drastically, when they deemed it in China's best interest. One of the most dramatic changes was the shift from an alliance with the Soviet Union against the United States and Japan in the 1950s to an explicitly anti-Soviet policy and rapprochement with Japan and the United States in the 1970s. Since 1949 Chinese foreign policy has fluctuated between periods of militancy, for example during the Cultural Revolution (1966-76), when China called for worldwide revolution, and periods when Beijing has been a chief proponent of peaceful coexistence among nations, such as during the mid-1950s and again during the 1980s. How self-reliant or dependent on others China should become in order to modernize has been a constant dilemma in Chinese policy since the nineteenth century. As this policy fluctuated, Chinese foreign relations have alternated between a tendency toward isolation and periods of openness to foreign assistance and influence. Finally, the contradiction between China's actual capabilities since 1949 and its perceived potential has been another salient and distinctive feature of its foreign relations. China's tremendous size, population, natural resources, military strength, and sense of history have placed it in the unusual position of being a developing country that has often been treated as a major global power having a special relationship with the United States and, Russia, previously, the Soviet Union.

China's Policy towards India

China's Search for Power: The last century has been extremely difficult for China. The occupation by the Japanese in the 1930s and 1940s and the civil war, which brought Mao Zedong and the Chinese Communist Party to power in 1949, were extremely turbulent times in China's history. From this civil war the People's Republic of China (PRC) emerged. However, this was the beginning of another period of isolation where China attempted to revitalize itself. Under Mao, China was successful in becoming self-sufficient in nearly all resources and technologies, however, it was twenty to thirty years behind modern technical standards.

Following Mao's death in 1976, the new leader, Deng Xiaoping, commenced a series of reforms that radically changed China. Deng encouraged international trade and allowed foreign capital investment. The result has been China's phenomenal entry into world markets and a booming economy. The specific aim of these policies was to obtain large foreign exchange earnings, which would allow China to both modernize and become more independent. Following Deng's death in February 1997, Jiang Zemin, consolidated his political power base with the completion of the CCP's Fifteenth Congress in September 1997. Under Jiang's leadership it looks like economic reforms will continue, however, there seems to be little prospect for political change. This is exemplified by his call for stricter control of the press.

As China emerges as a global power it is important to understand what role it will play and the security perceptions it has of both Asia and the world. The most important issue for China today is political stability at home. Any attempt to influence the status quo is not welcome and is deemed to be interference in China's internal affairs. The economic reforms that were introduced by Deng Xiaoping in the late seventies have transformed the Chinese economy and produced a period of spectacular growth. China's Gross Domestic Product (GDP) grew at an average rate of 9.3 percent between 1979-1993. The world experienced a growth rate of 2.6 percent for the same period. China's GDP has also quadrupled over a period of only fifteen years. It has also improved its status as a trading nation, rising to eleventh position from number thirty-seven in ten years. Another important fact is that China has accumulated a large foreign currency reserve and is second in the world to Japan. China has also taken advantage of foreign investment and is also rated second in the world, after the US. It is important to realize that the above figures do not include any contribution from Hong Kong, which China regained as a possession in July 1997.

While China's performance has been impressive, it also has the potential to maintain this growth. It has a massive population, which represents not only a large domestic market but also a cheap labour source of some eight hundred million people. It is also a country that is blessed with vast natural resources. The current economic problems in Asia have not had a major impact on China, though there are predictions of slower growth. However, it is expected that China will become the world's largest economy, in terms of GDP, by 2010.

Chinese military strategy underwent a major change in the mid 1980s. The threat of a Soviet land attack had diminished and the attention of the People's Liberation Army (PLA) turned to the threat of regional disputes. Thus, the PLA started to focus on a strategy of limited war. However, with the downturn in relations with the West following the Tiananmen Square massacre, this strategy was revised. The Gulf War also had a significant impact on the Chinese leadership and the conflict was carefully studied. As a result, a new defence strategy emerged, based on fighting modern warfare using advanced technology. The Chinese have learned many lessons from the Gulf War. First, they have realized that electronic warfare and advanced weapons are decisive.

They have also learned the importance of strong air and naval power and that rapid response and fast deployment are a true measure of overall capability. Finally, they have realized that logistical support is as important as actual combat capability. These lessons learned have had a profound effect on the PLA's doctrine. First of all, the importance of ground forces has been reduced to allow additional focus on the air force and navy. Secondly, there has been a shift away from the philosophy that manpower is superior to machine power and that the offensive can be won by strength in numbers. Finally, there is a decreased reliance on the civilian population to fill the army's ranks as was required when the concept of the protracted people's war was in vogue. China has learned the lessons of the Gulf War and has doctrinally set a course to develop a modern and effective military with a power projection capability.

China's rise as an economic power, combined with its large-scale program to modernize its military, raises the question of how this power will be used. Associated with this new power has been an increase in the aggressiveness in China's territorial claims in the region. Externally, China's more assertive nationalism, territorial claims and modernizing military capabilities are causing some unease in the region. One of the main trouble spots concerns China's long standing territorial claims in the South China Sea. Two island groups, the Parcels and the Spratlys, have numerous claimants. Military conflicts with Vietnam in 1974 and 1988 and demonstrate China's resolve to use force if required. Although China has never challenged passage through this area, there are serious concerns about the security of this important sea- lane.

Taiwan is the most volatile issue concerning territorial claims and security in the region. The Chinese government sees Taiwan as a renegade province and treats any conflict between the two as an internal matter. Western countries have developed a policy of "one China" and officially recognize the regime in Beijing. However, at the same time they conduct a vibrant trade with Taiwan. The March 1996 crisis over Taiwan illustrates the tension concerning this issue. Concerned with the first free and democratic Taiwanese elections that were scheduled for 23 March 1996, China commenced live-fire naval and air exercises in the Taiwan Straits earlier that month. China conducted missile firings that disrupted shipping and refused to renounce the use of force to resolve the Taiwan issue. This action resulted in the US deployment of two carrier battle groups to the area. Chinese Prime Minister Li Peng warned the US to keep its ships out of the Taiwan Straits and earlier in the crisis there was a veiled threat by a Chinese official that China was prepared to use nuclear weapons, targeted on the US west coast, if the US intervened militarily. The crisis was resolved when the Taiwan's leader won a larger than expected victory, the Chinese ceased their exercise and the US ships left the area. The results of this crisis are uncertain. The Chinese lost diplomatic ground and were forced to back down for the moment. As China develops a more credible military force, any future confrontations of this sort will seriously test the will and ability of the US and the West to challenge China's actions.

A second area of concern is China's political stability. The Communist regime maintains firm control despite the huge challenges of running such a large and complex country. However, the main occupation of the regime is to stay in power. China perceives issues such as human rights and efforts to encourage democracy as an attempt to contain and interfere with internal affairs. The Chinese perspective is best described by the following:

In history, Chinese leaders have believed in force. Force worked in Tiananmen. It intimidated the intellectuals, and that paved the way for economic growth and political stability. It is realpolitik. And in the Chinese value system, sovereignty, national unification, and preserving the regime have always been higher than peace.

The strong economic attraction to China needs to be balanced by policies that will stand the strains that closer cooperation will place on it. The combination of a large and prosperous economy, a modernized and advanced military and a Communist regime determined to stay in power has the potential to offer considerable security challenges to the West early in the 21st century.

The final area of concern is related to the resources that will be required to ensure China's continued existence. China has twenty-two percent of the world's population, but only seven percent of the cultivatable land. The average cultivated land per capita is only one third of the world average and continues to shrink. Just feeding the population will require ninety million more tons of food by the year 2000 than it did in 1995. Construction reduces cultivated land by seven million hectares every year. While China is now an exporter of oil, its rapid industrialization could see it becoming an oil importer in the near future. The ability of the

Chinese government to manage this situation will play a key role in further territorial claims and the stability of the Communist regime. As China becomes a larger economic and military power the risk of failure in this regard will have a significant impact on Western interests in the region.

As China emerges as the next superpower, public opinion in the West seems split over how this event should be treated. A policy of openly engaging China encourages establishing a wide range of contacts with the hope of having some influence. However, it can also be viewed as giving concessions when a more firm policy is required. The contrasting option of containment implies a policy of distrust and suspicion. The ideal solution is an open and transparent China, which is both peaceful and stable. Unfortunately the secrecy of the regime, and the problems described above, do not provide a promising outlook. As the West engages China, it must be aware of the security threat China will potentially become in the future and ensure an appropriate security system is maintained to balance the power in the region.

China's history in the 20th century has been marked by occupation and civil war. This experience has fuelled its strong desire for Great Power status and at the same time put it decades behind the West in technological development. Under the leadership of Deng Xiaoping, China has undergone a transformation, which has produced a tremendous economic turnaround. China is now a major trading nation which has built up an impressive foreign currency holding and is predicted to be the world's largest economy by 2010. The Chinese leadership has recognized that economic reform is the only way to achieve the status it desires on its own terms.

It is clear that China's economic and military transformation has been aimed at challenging the balance of power that has existed in the region since World War Two. China has demonstrated hegemonic intentions through its territorial claims in the South China Sea and in its recent actions against Taiwan. A more aggressive and expansionist policy may occur as China faces more pressure to provide food and resources for one quarter of the world's population. If the current transformation continues, China will have, in the future, the economic and military might tô threaten both the countries in the region and the West. The closer ties with Russia have already resulted in a strategic relationship that is designed to counter the influence of the US. How long this relationship will be required is unknown. With its ongoing effort to develop a high technology economic system, China has set the foundation that will likely ensure that it is much stronger than the former Soviet Union and perhaps even more powerful than the US.

A communist government, that has demonstrated that it is unhappy with its status in the world, also rules China. While Western governments have devoted a great deal of time and thought on how to treat China, their policies have not had any effect on the current regime's respect for human rights or democracy. The fundamental issue is that the stability of the CCP itself represents a concern for both Asia-Pacific and world security. Any movement by the West to promote human rights and democracy in China represents a direct threat to the existing regime. The brutality of the Tiananmen massacre should serve as a warning of the importance the CCP places on maintaining power. China more and more sees itself as a counter to Western values and way of life. In its effort to emerge as a great power, China has changed its security strategy from defensive to offensive. If China wants to be a dominant world power, and chooses to act based on the example of the former Soviet Union, it will have the potential to seriously undermine the current world order.

Military Doctrine: Over the past decade, China has been engaged in a sustained drive to create a modern and professional military. How much military power does China ultimately desire? Although the answer is unclear, the ambiguity that surrounds China's motivations for the modernization of the People's Liberation Army (PLA) generates concern and even anxiety about the future of peace and stability in East Asia. Looking toward the future, several approaches might be used to determine how much military power China seeks to acquire. One option is simply to focus on the worst case and assume that all states, including China, want to develop as much military power as domestic resources and external constraints permit. The study of threat perceptions offers another approach, tracking changes in China's security environment to identify core drivers of military modernization and possible force structures.

China adopted its current military strategy in 1993. Following the normalization of relations with the Soviet Union and then the demonstration of precision-strike munitions in the Persian Gulf War, China's leaders instructed the PLA to prepare to fight "local wars under modern high technology conditions. The adoption of this military strategy stemmed from paramount leader Deng Xiaoping's judgment that small- and medium-sized local conflicts, not general or total wars, were the most likely threats that China would encounter in a world no longer characterized by intense competition between two superpowers. Chinese military writings portray these local conflicts as sudden, intense, and destructive, thus requiring China to develop new operational capabilities stressing joint operations, rapid response, and offensive strikes to deter such local wars from arising or to win them if they do erupt

China's multiple goals for the use of military power reflect the diversity of China's security challenges. Perhaps too crudely, China seeks to ensure the defence of a continental state, governed by an authoritarian political system, with growing maritime interests and several unresolved territorial disputes, especially over Taiwan. Yet, these goals defy simple categorization as status quo or revisionist, defensive or offensive. China's desire to secure its military homeland territory from attack is a defensive goal writings identify five pursued by all states, while its desire to alter the strategic goals for status quo across the strait through unification is its military power.

China's first goal, maintaining the Chinese Communist Party's monopoly on political power, distinguishes its armed forces from most other modern militaries in the world. Since becoming general secretary, Hu Jintao has stressed that the military falls under the absolute leadership of the party. This phrase highlights that internal security and defence of the CCP remains a top priority, as political unrest poses a stark challenge to the continued economic growth that underpins the party's legitimacy. Political Commissar of the Nanjing Army Command College Tian Bingren echoes Hu's view in a recent article, noting that the armed forces should provide important and powerful guarantees for the consolidation of the party's ruling position. Key sources of instability include ethnic violence, unemployment, income inequality, and cross-border criminal activity. The March 2008 demonstrations and riots in Tibetan areas only reinforce the view of one military scholar that threats to regime security such as ethnic unrest are a "strategic issue" that influences "national unification, social stability and economic development.

The second goal is securing China's territory from external threats, a basic mission for any country's armed forces. A study on army building states that "the safeguarding of a nation's territorial integrity must have a large and powerful armed force. Defending the homeland's territory, territorial waters and airspace ... is our army's duty bound responsibility." The end of the Cold War bolstered China's external security, as the collapse of the Soviet Union eliminated the largest land-based threat to China since 1949. In the 1990s, China further strengthened its border security through demilitarization and boundary agreements with its neighbours that reduced troop levels and resolved outstanding territorial disputes. Although China's territory is more secure than at any time since 1949, PLA sources still stress the importance of preparing for potential conflict along China's continental periphery that might threaten the country's territorial integrity. These concerns stem from the operational challenges of defending one of the longest land borders in the world, a task that is complicated by harsh environmental conditions and potential ethnic unrest in frontier areas. China also remains involved in one major territorial dispute on its land border with India. Although efforts to settle the dispute have progressed in recent years, resulting in a 2005 agreement on guiding principles, concerns remain that conflict could still erupt in the future.

A fourth goal that also attracts increasing attention is China's emphasis on defending its "maritime rights and interests" (haiyang quanyi). Today, China remains involved in maritime sovereignty disputes with many of its neighbours. Although it controls the Paracel islands claimed by Vietnam, it occupies only a minority of the features in the Spratlys in the South China Sea and none of the Senkakus disputed with Japan. With one exception, China has yet to reach maritime delimitation agreements with its neighbours and thus agree on the control of undersea resources, especially petroleum.

Chinese sources also reflect an increased sensitivity to military threats from the sea to China's wealthy coastal provinces, the need to exploit maritime resources for economic development, and, as a trading nation, the economy's dependence on sea lines of communication that could be disrupted in a conflict, especially one near China's coast. The NDU's study of military strategy, for example, notes the growing importance of "the rights and interests of our continental shelf and maritime exclusive economic zones, especially the threats facing strategic resource development and strategic passageways

A fifth goal is the need to maintain a stable external environment within which to continue economic development. In practice, this goal is linked with avoiding or deterring armed conflicts on China's periphery, lest they disrupt or potentially derail China's economic reforms. China prepares to achieve its strategic goals by strengthening or developing three general military capabilities: internal control, area denial around its periphery, and limited regional force projection. Reflecting the complexity of China's security challenges and the varied goals that it pursues, these capa- bilities also defy simple categorization. They support offensive and defensive campaigns, low-intensity and high-intensity operations, and the employment of force across the spectrum of the contemporary battle space on land, in the air, and at sea. To simplify the analysis, the discussion below examines only China's conventional military capabilities.

Internal control is the first capability required for China to achieve its strategic goals. It is key to ensuring regime security and contributes to maintaining territorial integrity by limiting domestic vulnerability to external pressure. Internal control enables the CCP to prevent the emergence of any political force that might challenge its rule and to limit any social unrest that might result in regime instability or even collapse by derailing the economic growth key to the CCP's continued legitimacy to govern China. Moreover, as highlighted by the demonstrations and riots in Lhasa and other Tibetan areas in March 2008, the potential for political unrest is likely to persist if not increase as China's authoritarian party-state seeks to cope with the social and institutional challenges of rapid growth in a multiethnic society. With the largest army in the world, China has already achieved an internal control capability. Nevertheless, as a form of policing and, at times, low intensity conflict, maintenance of this capability involves a significant number of personnel with the related financial, organizational, and logistical burdens of manpower-intensive military operations. Within China's armed forces, the People's Armed Police (PAP), a paramilitary organization, carries primary responsibility for internal control.

Within the PAP, internal security units, composed mostly of demobilized PLA infantry divisions, are trained to contain events that might upset political stability, including antigovernment demonstrations, riots, and potential rebellions. The PAP's internal security force consists of 660,000 troops deployed throughout the country and comes under the joint control of the State Council and the Central Military Commission. Other PAP units are assigned to secure border areas and checkpoints as well as critical infrastructure such as mines, dams, and forests. The leading role of PAP units in suppressing Tibetan unrest in March 2008 reflects the continued importance for the government of maintaining a robust internal control capability.

Although the PAP's establishment in 1982 reflected an effort to separate internal and external security missions for China's armed forces, internal security remains an important although secondary task for the PLA. In the early 1990s, for example, the original impetus for creating rapid-reaction units of high-quality troops came from a desire to suppress unrest quickly anywhere in the country.

China has achieved considerable progress in creating an area denial capability on the Asian continent around its land borders. China arguably first demonstrated such a capability in the mid-1960s, when concerns about potential Chinese involvement in the Vietnam War limited U.S. ground operations to areas below the 17th parallel. A key factor in China's continental denial capability is the strategic depth that large but sparsely populated frontiers within China create. This geography allows China to secure its population and economic centres from land-based threats by leveraging "defence-in-depth" against any attack, depth that raises significantly the costs for any potential adversary to coerce China through attacks on its homeland territory. The PLA's large ground force of more than 1.6 million troops complements this favourable geography, especially as it continues to modernize its weaponry and increase its mobility within the country. Taken together, the cost for any regional power to attack China on land would be high even if it were able to breach the border.

The number of troops within China's armed forces devoted to this mission reflects the continued importance of continental denial for China's military planners. Approximately 224,500 PLA and PAP troops are tasked with guarding China's land borders and maintaining internal security around ports of entry and adjacent areas. In wartime, these units also form the first line of defence in any attack against China's borders. In addition, almost one-half of the PLA's main force infantry and armoured units are based in provinces with an international boundary and are responsible in part for repelling any assault against Chinese territory or deterring an adversary from deploying large forces near its borders. This force structure, composed of light infantry units on the border and manoeuvre units in the interior, sustains a strong area-denial capability on its continental periphery.

Limited regional force projection is the third capability that China pursues. Force projection is the ability to deploy and sustain military forces beyond a country's borders, especially to conduct offensive operations. The capability that China pursues, however, is limited in the sense of projecting force in a well-defined area for a specific duration of time as opposed to all along China's coast and over all disputed areas. Regional force projection facilitates China's achievement of several of its strategic goals.

It is required to achieve national unification, as any coercive campaign against Taiwan to deter or prevent its formal independence would almost certainly require offensive operations against the island. It also plays a key role in maintaining regional stability, enabling China to deploy troops abroad to deter the spread of armed conflict or prevent a conflict from arising.

Force projection also allows China to maintain regional stability by playing a greater role in humanitarian relief, peacekeeping, and stability operations in East Asia. China has achieved even less progress toward acquiring capabilities to deploy and sustain forces far from its borders. Indeed, China's small role in regional disaster relief in the past several years demonstrates the limits of its ability to project military power. Following the December 2004 tsunami in Southeast Asia, for example, China lacked the ability to deliver aid rapidly to the region, a task completed by the aircraft carrier, and expeditionary strike groups deployed to Indonesia by the U.S. Navy.

When viewed through the lens of the security dilemma, China's military modernization in pursuit of conservative and nonexpansionist goals may nevertheless increase instability in East Asia. According to this theory, the dilemma exists because one state's efforts to increase its own security usually decrease the security of other states. Given the uncertainty created by anarchy in the international system, even if one state enhances its military power for what it sees as defensive reasons, other states are likely to see the same actions as offensive and threatening, resulting in security competition characterized by mistrust, suspicion, and spirals of tension. Such spirals are especially likely when a state increases its defence spending significantly and acquires force projection capabilities, two features of China's current military modernization effort.

By contrast, China sees its own military posture as defensive and nonthreatening. The strategic goals guiding China's military modernization are more certain than they might appear. Overall, the changes in China's force structure over the past decade are consistent with capabilities required for regime security, territorial integrity, national unification, maritime security, and regional stability. China is not pursuing broadly expansionist goals, nor is it investing heavily in forces that are inconsistent with its strategic goals.

Over time, of course, China's goals could change in ways that require new capabilities other than those outlined in this article. One possibility is that Chinese leaders could stress the need to protect China's economic interests not just in the region but around the world. Whether China will seek to move toward long-range force projection remains unknown. Nevertheless, changes in force structure and a substantial increase in the share of government spending on defence would provide a range of useful indicators to chart this type of shift. Potential indicators of such a shift include a significant expansion in the numbers of China's attack submarines for sustained patrols in distant waters; an increase in the number of large, multiproduct replenishment ships to support long-range patrols; the development of a robust, space-based ocean surveillance system; investments in large fleets of tanker and transport aircraft; and the development of a new type of bomber to replace China's aging H-6 fleet. The acquisition of multiple aircraft carriers would be another indicator of a move toward long- range force projection, but building just one such ship is likely to be pursued for the status that it conveys rather than the capability it generates.

India's Response to China's growing Influence in Central Asia: China has been a major player in South Asia for some time, maintaining its relationship with Pakistan to contain the power of India. The Sino-Indian relationship, marked by competition and cooperation, has come a long way since 1998, when India and Pakistan joined the exclusive nuclear weapons club. Today, China is wooing India to ensure that New Delhi does not join any political organization that may have an anti-Chinese purpose, including a closer relationship with Washington. To this end, New Delhi and Beijing agreed to cooperate on energy security and settled their long-standing border disputes, while increasing trade by 40 percent in 2005. China even supported India's bid for a U.N. Security Council seat.

The PRC also maintains continuing close ties with Pakistan in case Indian relations turn for the worse, and encourages Islamabad to deal with Islamic radicalism that might take root in China. The PRC increasingly values Pakistan for its location on the Arabian Sea. Much to India's displeasure, China is constructing a deepwater port at Gwadar on the Indian Ocean. The new port, like other Chinese-developed ports in Cambodia and Burma, will eventually allow the Chinese Navy to hedge against India's monopoly over major sea lanes.

Beijing has also agreed to help Pakistan construct a second nuclear reactor, and supports Islamabad's ballistic missile program. China is wooing other South Asia states, such as neighbouring Nepal and Bangladesh, to empower its regional influence as well. In 2005, China obtained observer status at the South Asian Association of Regional Cooperation meeting, a key regional institution over India's objections.

No country will shape the course of the 21st century for good or bad more than the PRC. Its international activism indicates that Beijing has ambitions that exceed China's historical East Asian sphere of influence. No major region of the world is untouched by China's growing presence.

These developments indicate that India's growing future role and alignments in Asia will be determined by the actions of the U.S. and China and their military involvement with Pakistan. If the U.S. is unable to influence Pakistan on dismantling terrorist infrastructure and facilitating transit facilities, and China continues to have close defence, nuclear and missile cooperation with Pakistan, India will have no option but to work closely with Russia and Iran instead to add value to its bilateral relations in Asia.

There are no indications of China- Pakistan relations weakening in the near future. In fact, when the Indian parliament was debating the India-U.S. nuclear deal, China signed two defence agreements with Pakistan.The U.S.-Pakistan equation is uncertain. So far, Pakistan is a declared major non-NATO ally. The U.S. is counting on Pakistani security forces to neutralize the Taliban and Al Qaeda and their associates who are operating from the Afghanistan-Pakistan border. While President Musharraf has co-operated to some extent in the operations to capture some activists of Al Qaeda, he has taken no action against the neo-Taliban. Although the Pakistani administration admits that some of the Al Qaeda leaders may be operating from their territory, they have denied the presence of any Taliban leaders, camps or activities in Pakistan. Policy makers in Pakistan were hoping that U.S. forces would leave Afghanistan after initial operations so that after their withdrawal, they could have strengthened and use the Taliban card again to attain "strategic depth" in Afghanistan.

With the possibility of an enduring U.S. presence, the neo-Taliban are trying to replicate the anti- Soviet Jihad of the 1980's through conventional strikes and terrorist acts. The target is not the Soviets, but the "Western infidels led by the U.S. and the UK" and their Afghan supporters. The objective is to tire and weaken the western forces. They hope that as a result of continuous bleeding, western forces may finally decide to quit. Once that happens, the Karzai government is bound to fall.

The Afghan government has repeatedly accusing Pakistan for harbouring the insurgents. In these circumstances, it will become increasingly difficult for the U.S. to keep defending President Musharraf, who is making the West pay for his domestic democratic deficit. While some institutions in Pakistan promote the ideology of terrorism, others provide training to carry it out. The possibility of another 9/11 with links to Pakistan against the West cannot be ruled out. There are reports that officials in the Pentagon are already rethinking the relationship with Pakistan. The June visit of Condoleezza Rice to Afghanistan and Pakistan seems to get the message across that America is "not leaving" and going to stay in Afghanistan for a "very, very long time to come." NATO is also formalizing its presence in Afghanistan to stay on a long term basis. Sensing these developments and in order to stay in power, President Musharaff may opt for cooperation in Afghanistan.

For India, the enduring U.S. presence in Afghanistan can be leveraged to push Pakistan into a cooperative direction. To assert its economic and strategic power, India would be able to reach Afghanistan and central Asia over land. This could also be a new beginning of India-Pakistan relations. While speaking at the launch of the Amritsar (India)- Nankana Sahib (Pakistan) bus service, the Indian Prime Minister said that "India and Pakistan must work together to open up new opportunities for economic cooperation, not only with South Asia, but also with West Asia and Central Asia. Cities like Lahore and Amritsar should once again become throbbing international commercial centres serving the entire region". On the other hand, China is also trying to improve its presence in Afghanistan through aid and other projects. If Pakistan is able to muster significant influence in Afghanistan, then triangular Pakistan- Afghanistan-China cooperation is also a possibility. After witnessing the Rose revolution in Georgia, the Orange revolution in Ukraine, the Tulip revolution in Kyrgyzstan and the violent protests in Uzbekistan, Central Asian states have clearly moved towards Russia and China. This has happened because of the U.S. dilemma in trying to balance two of its major foreign policy goals democratization and counterterrorism in Asia. Capitalizing on this U.S. quandary and it's overstretch in Iraq and Afghanistan,

Russia and China in cooperation with each other have consolidated their position in the region. So rather than reacting to events, India should have a clear-cut futuristic policy which supports all domestic and outside actors pushing for democracy and market reforms in the region. The

Indian government has been a more or less passive observer to these events. India was neither alarmed (like Russia and China), nor really excited (like many western governments) by these developments. The response to these developments is articulated by the Indian Defence Minister in his speech at Washington where he asserted that "by nature, India is not inclined to export ideologies, even ideologies it believes in and follows. India would rather promote democracy in the region by precept and example. Freer traffic between India and Asia would be a factor in favour of moderation and democracy there".

With the increasing profile of the organization, China's role is also becoming large within Asia. In the beginning, India showed interest in the SCO but the impression is that China never really wanted India in the grouping. India was welcomed as an observer in the SCO only when China was also admitted in SAARC as an observer. In addition, China also brought Pakistan into the grouping. The way the SCO has conducted itself in the last two years has further aggravated India's dilemma. India has a positive perception of the potential of the SCO as an instrument for promoting regional economic integration, trade and ensuring energy security. However, it has many reservations over the political direction of the SCO. Even with the main objective of fighting terrorism, it would be an uncomfortable position for India if the Dalai Lama and his followers, members of the Falungong and people asking for genuine democratic rights in Asian republics were clubbed together as terrorists/separatists/extremists.

India will find it difficult to digest these interpretations when it is also an important contributor to the UN Democracy Fund, whose purpose is to support democratization throughout the world. Furthermore, the objective of multi-polarity, as often raised by China, is constantly being used to counter the U.S. influence in Asia-Pacific. At a time when its relations with the U.S. are steadily moving forward, India would be cautious in its participation in the grouping.

As a result of these dilemmas, India was the only country among members and observers, which was not represented at the latest SCO Summit. The official position was that there was no need for the prime minister to attend the meeting as India was only an observer. The actual fact may be that India is giving serious thought to its involvement in the SCO. The way the organization is developing, some Indian analysts have already warned that it would "be imprudent for India to join the SCO". In my view, along with other partners, India should work for a separate regional organization. This new organization should include all countries which have legitimate interest in the region cooperating on a la carte basis. These include the five Central Asian countries, Afghanistan, China, India, Iran, Japan, Russia, Pakistan, Turkey and the United States. The idea is somewhat similar to Frederick Starr's "Greater Central Asia Partnership for Cooperation and Development" concept. Although the region has a history of over-engagement with regional organizations, so far none of the organizations is able to accommodate all major players. Moreover, many of them are only on paper.

Although SCO is already considered by some analysts as the de facto regional organization, there are many uncertainties. These include possible Russian uneasiness over increasing Chinese dominance and complications arising with future enlargements etc. In the absence of any other dynamic organization, India will continue to participate in the SCO to improve its standing in the region. In the long run, it will also further strengthen Russian position in the SCO. Despite very weak bilateral trade, which is about US$ 2 billion a year, India-Russia ties continue to be strong. Currently, about 75 percent of its weapons imports come from Russia. Although many Indian scholars have discussed the possibility of India-Russia cooperation in Central Asia in the past, concrete examples are emerging now. These include military cooperation in Tajikistan, the North-South corridor, joint exploration of oil and gas in Central Asia and Russian help with India's entry into the SCO.

Therefore, "as an increasingly powerful China asserts itself in Eurasia and America scrambles to deal with the consequences, Delhi and Moscow still hold many cards." Chinese expansion in Central Asia is watched very carefully in India. It is becoming clear that China is going to provide tough competition to India in both energy and trade. If Chinese expansion coincides with declining Russian influence, India will have no choice but to expand its political, economic and military capabilities in Central Asia. Simple realist logic would suggest close Indo-U.S. cooperation in Central Asia. These realities are fuelling India's "forward" Central Asia policy. There is also a feeling of urgency in policy circles to discover a strategy where India is able to reach the region over land.

The new U.S. thinking of linking South and Central Asia with possibilities of a wider new grouping could fit into Indian thinking. Improvements in India-Pakistan relations, however, would be a crucial input into this strategy. Sensing this alignment, China may try to accommodate some of India's security and economic concerns. If the U.S. is unable to influence Pakistan on dismantling terrorist infrastructure, India will continue to work with Moscow and Tehran to consolidate some control in Central Asia. Although policy makers in India do not believe in the policy of exporting democracy, they would be very sympathetic to political changes as they know that Indian interests would be served better by opening the region to further democratic changes and more economic reforms.

India's Policy towards China

Conventional Security: Pakistan is historically perceived to be India's main conventional threat, as evidenced by the military stand-off in late 2001 and early 2002. At the same time, India lost a war to China in 1962. China is also India's closest military equal, a fact made most clear when India pronounced that its 1998 nuclear tests were in response to the China risk.

India's military is rooting out internal militancy prevalent (in the northeast, in the east (among the Naxelite groups), and in Jammu and Kashmir.) Notably, however, there are no known Indian al Qaida or Taliban members. India is also located in a volatile neighbourhood, with ongoing wars, insurgencies and unrest taking place in Sri Lanka, Nepal, Pakistan, and Afghanistan, and a coup in Bangladesh.

Today everyone knows that in the coming century India has the intention and potential to enhance its wealth, prestige, and power. In this context, observers of world politics are wondering: How will India pursue those intentions? What will it do to realize its potential and assure its security? In the last year and half since the proposed Indo-US nuclear deal was announced, numerous experts have tried to induce answers to these questions from what is still a small universe of cases including India's attitude toward Iranian nuclear policy and energy (particularly pipeline) policy, toward US missile defence initiatives, toward the enlargement of the Shanghai Cooperation Organization, toward Chinese activity in South Asia. But, above all, observers have focused on a proposed deal between the US and India on nuclear cooperation. The dimensions and general features of the arena in which India will act are clear. It is a triangular space with China, India, and the US at the corners.

The view that a rising India will be the fulcrum of balance in Asia is now increasingly common. Steadily warming India-US relations have resulted in widespread attention to the geopolitics of Asia. It is difficult to predict whether or not India will become a strategic ally of the US or of China, but the sudden attractiveness of India will sooner or later alter the regional balance of power between the three countries.

In the real world, of course, actors are motivated and constrained by power, wealth, and prestige. Syncretic approaches such as the currently fashionable "analytic eclecticism" draw selectively on all three international relations traditions in rendering "explanatory sketches" of important international security questions such as the durability of US-South Korean alliance, the possible revisionist aspiration of a rising China, or whether it is international institutions rather than balance of power dynamics that are shaping strategy in South East Asia.

Explaining the future direction of Indian strategy within the China-India-US triangle is as analytically demanding a problem as one is likely to find in contemporary international relations. India is very unlikely to balance or to get on the bandwagon. Equipoise is the policy dictated by India's geography, power capabilities, identity, and potential to be a robust actor in global and regional politics. Like the old and now discredited Indian grand strategy of nonalignment, equipoise shuns formal alliances. The term draws on the realist balance of power idiom to identify an alternative stance neither balancing nor bandwagoning that is in dynamic equilibrium. That equilibrium is struck between domestic and international dynamics; balancing contradictory domestic cultural and political forces and international appeals and threats.

Economic Growth: For decades, India maintained what economists termed a "Hindu" rate of GDP growth between 1.5 and 3%. Following the 1991 economic reforms, growth tripled and has stabilized since 2006 at 8-9.5%. However, if India hopes to continue to lift up the 60% of its population in the rural sector and build infrastructure, it must increase its foreign financing significantly. Exchange with its neighbours has supported India's growth, from the "Look East" policy of the early 1990's to today's increasing engagement with ASEAN, BIMSTEC, and the new SAFTA agreement.

At the same time as it pursues regional agreements, India also engages bilaterally (with free trade agreements with Singapore and a possible bilateral investment treaty with the U.S.) and globally, taking a leadership position in the WTO Doha negotiations. India's growth has been bolstered by China, which has achieved annual growth of over 10% since 2000. However, the two countries will compete increasingly, as

India engages in China's traditional stronghold of manufacturing, and China focuses on the services market.

Energy Security: India currently imports 70% of its oil and 50% of its gas; it is projected to import 80% of its energy needs by 2025. While India holds that it should be allowed to expand energy consumption and emissions until its per capita levels correspond with those of Western countries, increasingly polls indicate that the Indian public is recognizing the importance of more attention to environmental concerns. India is increasingly exploring nuclear power as an alternative energy source (presuming the U.S.-India July 2005 civil nuclear agreement is completed); it is also one of the leading R&D venues for solar and wind power.

However, currently only 6% of potential non-conventional energy resources have been tapped. In an effort to ensure access to energy resources, India will continue to focus on the Middle East, particularly Iran (including the Iran-Pakistan-India oil pipeline). At the same time, India is expanding its search for energy resources into Africa and Latin America (though India typically loses bids to China).

Nuclear Capability: India's nuclear policy is shaped by its unstable relations with Pakistan and China, as well as the recent escalation of nuclear proliferation in the wider region. Its goal is to build a "credible minimum deterrent" through land-, air-, and sea-based capabilities. Since 2002, the India-Pakistan Composite Dialogue has significantly lowered tensions and resulted in several agreements to mitigate the chance of a mistaken nuclear attack.

If the U.S.-India civil nuclear agreement is completed (see India-Iran Relations briefing memo), India will be able to take a more active role in promoting non-proliferation directly, a goal that has long been touted as vital to India's national interest.

Leadership Roles: India has the second largest population in the world, and one of the youngest. Its economy, by purchasing power parity, is 4th in the world. India's soft power remains strong, and its military, economic and diplomatic reach is increasingly significant. India is a multi-ethnic and multi-religious democracy. While already a leader of the developing world, India now wants status in the developed world. Given South Asia's instability, there are ample opportunities for India to focus on helping to alleviate the conflicts in neighbouring Nepal, Sri Lanka and Bangladesh.

In so doing, India often confronts China's similar desire for regional leadership and seniority (such as China's desire to exclude India in 2005 from the newly formed East Asia Summit (EAS)). In addition to focusing on bilateral relationships, India engages in regional and ad hoc groups such as the 2004 Asian Tsunami Core Response Group, and enhancing its status in global groups (such as its bid to become a permanent member of the UN Security Council and interest in the G8).

The 21st century will be an Asian century. Simply by virtue of its breathtaking size and formidable exporting power, China is already transforming the economic map of Asia and the world. Yet China will not be alone in reshaping the global economic order. In India there is an economy with the potential to match it. In its likely impact on the global economy, India is the coming China.

The new India sometimes seems like the world in a single country. It combines first-world capabilities in information technology, pharmaceuticals and biotechnology with third-world levels of poverty.

The Tibetan Problem

Indian Prime Minister visited Arunachal Pradesh. While addressing a rally in Itanagar, he said that Arunachal Pradesh is India's land of the rising sun. China lodged its protest on Manmohan Singh's assertion over this claim of India. China has always said that Arunachal Pradesh is a part of China. Officials on the Indian side are numb since then over an issue, which has the potential to turn into a controversy. Pranab Mukherjee said, on 27 February, that China has claimed 9000 sq km of Indian territory including Tawang in Arunachal. China even denied a visa to IAS officer from Arunachal Pradesh when around 100 IAS officers were going for official visit to China, sometime back.

However, India did not react to that issue. China has been claiming Arunachal Pradesh as a part of its territory for a long time, but, the silence from New Delhi is definitely a concern. China officially claims 90,000 sq km of land in Arunachal Pradesh and Sikkim. But it is mainly interested in Tawang district. This district borders Tibet and Bhutan. China says that district belonged to Tibet and hence, wants India to return it in order to settle the border dispute. Coming to the current crisis in Tibet, the country has a history of at least 1300 years of Independence from China. In 821 A.D. both countries signed a treaty and recognized Tibet and China to be independent nations. During the 13th and 14th century, both

China and Tibet came under the influence of the Mongol Empire. Mongols conquered China while Tibetans and Mongols established the unique 'priest patron' relationship, also know as CHOYON.

The Mongol Empire ended in the mid 14th century. Mongolia became a separate country and by 15th century, political authority in Tibet passed into the hands of religious hegemonies and then, the institution of the Dalai Lama was formalized, and became a legitimate political representative of Tibet. In 1639, the fifth Dalai Lama established another CHOYON relationship with the Manchu Empire. Manchu occupied China and established the Manchu dynasty.

Manchu officials lived in Tibet from 1728 to 1911. In 1911, Sun Yat Sen, declared Manchus as foreigners and not ethnic Chinese and declared China as a republic. In 1914, China claimed Tibet but Tibet continued to be fully sovereign, until it was invaded by China. China claims that both China and Tibet came under influence of Mongols, so it is believed to be one nation. But this claim was not recognized for, which China carried on gross violations of human rights post 1949 invasion. This invasion marked the border dispute with India.

When Tibet declared itself as independent nation in 1912, the British rulers in India convened a meeting at Simla to ensure that violence in Tibet did not reach India, which lead to signing of Simla convention between China, India and Tibet. The accord gave China suzerainty over most of Tibet and boundary defined under this treaty know as McMahon line. However, later after signing the treaty, China reneged saying the 'provincial government' of Tibet had no right to sign such an accord. It then went on to stake claim to huge areas of land surrounding Tibet, which included Aksai Chin in Ladakh and Arunachal Pradesh in east.

After occupying Tibet, China occupied a large tract (approx. 38000 km) of Aksai Chin and build national highway 29, connecting it to eastern province of Xinjiang, which was considered as an illegal occupation by China. Tibet suffered after it was invaded by China. It made a plea to the United Nations (UN) but UN was unable to take any decision at that time. India also never protested against Chinese intrusion in Tibet. India now looks to maintain a healthy relation with China due to pressure from the business community and hence, the Tibet issue had taken a backstage.

The government must realise that they have some responsibility towards Tibet, and India has failed so far to exert any pressure on China. In November 2007, MPs from Arunachal Pradesh brought in notice to government of India that Chinese incursion into the state are becoming more frequent. The official figures quote 146 incursions in 2007. Chinese are even preventing locals from going up to regions where they had been going for years. China is pursuing the same policy it followed in Aksai Chin, 'claim-repeat the claim-grab-hold-let time pass'. China openly claims Arunachal Pradesh to be a part of their country. India today has no support or sympathy from the world when China made such claims. Indian government has not learnt any lesson from Aksai Chin. The silence from New Delhi can cost us Arunachal Pradesh. It even disturbs the local people on both sides ion the line of control, for which India needs to take bold steps.

The Border Dispute

Chinese President Hu Jintao's visit to India is the latest in a continuing series of high-level political exchanges between both countries. Political and economic relations have not been better since the 1962 war. Mutual economic dependence is growing stronger every year with bilateral trade increasing at a brisk pace.

However, despite prolonged negotiations at the political level to resolve the outstanding territorial and boundary dispute between the two countries, there has been little progress over this issue - one that will ultimately decide whether the two Asian giants will clash or cooperate for mutual benefit. China continues to be in occupation of and lays claim to large areas of Indian territory. At Aksai Chin in Ladakh, China continues to be in physical possession of approximately 38,000 square kilometres of Indian territory. In addition, Pakistan illegally ceded about 5,200 sq km of Indian territory in the Shaksgam Valley of Pakistan Occupied Kashmir, just north of the Siachen Glacier, to China in 1963 under a boundary agreement that India does not recognize.

Through this area, China built the Karakoram highway that now provides a strategic land link between Sinkiang, Tibet and Pakistan. China continues to stake its claim to about 96,000 sq km of Indian territory in Arunachal Pradesh. China's often stated official position is that the reunification of Chinese territories remains its sacred duty. It is not so well known that the Line of Actual Control (LAC) between India and China, implying de facto control after the 1962 war, is yet to be physically demarcated on the ground and reflected on military maps. The LAC is quite different from the disputed 4,100 km boundary along the McMahon Line.

The un-delineated LAC is a major destabilising factor as incidents such as the Nathu La clash of 1967 and the Wang Dung standoff of 1987 can recur. The only positive development has been that after over a dozen meetings of the Joint Working Group and the Experts Group, maps reflecting the respective versions of both forces have been exchanged for the least contentious Central Sector, that is, the Uttaranchal and Himachal Pradesh borders with Tibet, where no fighting had taken place in 1962. The fact that this has not opened the doors to similar exchanges in other sectors highlights how intractable the problem remains. Early in 2005, India and China agreed to identify guiding principles and parameters for a political solution to the five-decade old dispute. Many foreign policy analysts hailed it as a great leap forward. This is not the first time both countries have signed a feel-good agreement with each other.

The Border Peace and Tranquility Agreement (BPTA) signed with the Chinese in 1993 and the agreement on Confidence Building Measures in the military relations signed in 1996 were expected to reduce the operational commitments of the army from having to permanently man the difficult LAC with China. However, it has not been possible to withdraw a single soldier from the LAC thus far. In fact, despite the 1996 agreement, several incidents of Chinese intrusions at Asaphi La and elsewhere in Arunachal Pradesh have been periodically reported in the press and discussed in the Indian Parliament.

While no violent incident has taken place in the recent past, there have been occasions when Indian and Chinese patrols have met face-to-face in areas like the two fish-tail shaped protrusions in the north-east corner of Arunachal Pradesh. Such meetings have an element of tension and despite the best operating procedures, the possibility of an armed clash can never be ruled out. In the western sector in Ladakh, the LAC is even more ambiguous as the lack of easily recognizable terrain features on the Aksai Chin makes it difficult to accurately co-relate ground and map. Both sides habitually send patrols up to the point where they assume the LAC runs. These patrols leave tell-tale signs behind in the form of burjis (piles of stones), biscuit and cigarette packets and other similar markers in a sort of primitive ritual to lay stake to territory and assert their claim.

In this light, the Chinese government's unwillingness to exchange maps showing the alignment of the LAC in western and eastern sectors, while at the same time talking of lofty guiding principles and parameters to resolve the territorial and boundary dispute, is neither understandable or condonable. It can only be classified as another attempt to put off resolution of the dispute for future generations to resolve, as Deng Xiao Ping had reportedly told Rajiv Gandhi in 1988. The military gap between Indian and China is growing steadily. It would not be far-fetched to assume that China's strategy is to resolve the dispute when it is in a much stronger position in terms of comprehensive national strength so as to dictate terms at best, and maintain the status quo at worst.

It is the position of the Chinese People's Republic that the so-called McMahon Line named after the British General McMahon is illegal, null and void, and the result of a predatory, imperialist imposition of the British government in the year 1914. No Chinese government ever accepted the McMahon Line. Neither did the Imperial Government of China in 1914, nor the Chiang Kai-Shek government ever agree to it.

The very fact that even the Chiang Kai-Shek clique, which is nothing but a tool of U.S. imperialism, has not dared to dispute the Chinese People's Republic's position of the China-India border dispute, it in itself the most eloquent testimony to the correctness of the Chinese position. Nevertheless, the Chinese People's Republic has made every effort to achieve a reasonable and just settlement of the territory in dispute. It has consistently shunned the use of arms.

Although the border dispute is almost three years old now, and the Chinese have made innumerable other approaches to the Indian government to settle it on some amicable and acceptable basis the Nehru government has invariably turned them down. In the past two months alone the Chinese government made several proposals for negotiations. It made a notable effort on 4 August, and another one on 13 September. In neither of these proposals did the Chinese government lay down any preconditions for the negotiations. Nor did the Chinese government resort to the type of language which could in any way be construed as a threat to India. On the contrary, the diplomatic notes directed to the Indian government were couched in the most conciliatory language, and were calculated to effectuate a reasonable settlement which would safeguard the territorial integrity of China as well as India. The position of the London Times is of exceptional importance because it has always sided with India as against China. The London Times was obliged to make the above statement only after the Indian paper, Tribune, had reported that at a cabinet meeting the Indian government had decided to use armed force to deal with China.

As to what lies behind the aggressive attitude of the Nehru government, it must be borne in mind first of all that the imperialist world, particularly the U.S. would like nothing better than to see the two principal Asiatic powers, the two powers which hold the greatest revolutionary promise for mankind in the east, locked in military combat, shedding the blood of thousands, absorbing the resources and energies of millions of people, which should be used to construct a revolutionary way of life.

Since then, however, Beijing has upped the stakes by demanding major territorial concessions in populated areas of Arunachal Pradesh on terms that many in New Delhi see as humiliating and non-negotiable. Tawang, in particular, has emerged as a sticking point since the Chinese claim it to be central to Tibetan Buddhism given that the sixth Dalai Lama was born there. Ties between China and India were strained even further in May 2007 when the Chinese government refused a visa to an Indian official from disputed Arunachal Pradesh to visit China, and the Indian government's invitation soon thereafter to Taiwan's opposition Kuomintang (K.M.T.) party presidential candidate, Ma Ying-jeou, to visit India in June 2007 to hold talks with senior Indian officials. China voiced its opposition to Ma's visit and called on India to abide by the One China policy. Thereafter came media reports of the People's Liberation Army (P.L.A.) encroachments across the Line of Actual Control (L.A.C.) and Chinese small arms supplies to insurgents in India's volatile northeast via Bangladesh and Myanmar.

In this context, the rapid pace development of road, rail and military infrastructure in Tibet close to its borders with India and Nepal is seen as preempting any possible destabilization of Tibet post-Dalai Lama. Others, however, do not see any sinister designs in western China's development. Instead, they attribute the recent downturn in Sino-Indian relations more to domestic power struggles within the Chinese Communist Party (C.C.P.) than to the Dalai Lama succession issue or to Chinese concerns about India's growing tilt toward the United States. While there may be an element of truth in all these arguments, there are other more fundamental reasons behind the recent chill in Sino-Indian relations.

However, a number of negative developments, from Beijing's perspective, since early 2005; the Indian and Japanese bids for permanent seats on the U.N. Security Council, the formation of the East Asia Summit that includes India, Australia and New Zealand, the Indo-U.S. nuclear deal, India's ability to sustain a high economic growth rate of eight to nine percent and the strategic implications of India's Look East policy have apparently upset Chinese calculations.

Nonetheless, most see India as a future strategic competitor that would be an active member of an anti-China grouping due to the structural power shifts in the international system and advocate putting together a comprehensive contain India strategy based on both economic tools (aid, trade, infrastructural development) and enhanced military cooperation with pro-China countries.

In short, there is little or no sign of an early resolution to the conflicting claims, despite continuing negotiations and the recent upswing in diplomatic, political, commercial and even military ties between the world's two most populous countries. The border disputes have simmered in the background for more than 50 years, threatening to disrupt relations between Asia's two giants. With China insisting on the return of Tawang on religious, cultural, and historical grounds, Indians have a more powerful case for the return of the sacred Mount Kailash-Mansarovar in Tibet, since it is a sacred religious place associated with the Hindu religion.

Additionally, there is the contentious issue of the Shaksgam Valley that Pakistan handed over to China in 1963, which China's Foreign Ministry spokespersons now claim is a non-issue. Negotiating these issues will not be easy and will test diplomatic skills on both sides. It is worth noting that historically China has negotiated border disputes with neighbours in their moment of national weakness (Pakistan, Myanmar in the 1960s, and the Central Asian republics in the 1990s) or only after the overall balance of power had shifted decisively in China's favor and/or after they had ceased to be a major threat (land border settlements with Russia and Vietnam in the 1990s).

It has not, however, negotiated with those who are perceived as present rivals and future threats (India, Japan, Vietnam, the Philippines and Taiwan). In the meantime, both sides will have to learn to live without an early resolution to the dispute. Even if the territorial dispute were somehow resolved, India and China would still compete over energy resources, markets and for geostrategic reasons. A new potentially divisive issue for the future appears to be the ecological impact on the Indian subcontinent of Chinese plans to divert the rivers of Tibet for irrigation purposes in China. With China controlling the Tibetan plateau the source of Asia's major rivers there looms a potential conflict over depleting water reserves.

Water is increasingly becoming a divisive issue in India's bilateral relations with China. Simmering tensions over territory, Tibet, energy resources and rival alliance relationships ensure that Indian Prime Minister Manmohan Singh's assertion that there is enough geopolitical] space for the two countries to develop together will remain more a hope than a conviction. The relationship between the two rising Asian giants with overlapping spheres of influence and disputed frontiers will be characterized more by competition and rivalry than cooperation. Indeed, the possibility of confrontation cannot be ruled out completely.

India-China Relations in the Post-cold War Era: A study on India conducted in mid-2005 at the behest of the Chinese advocated that China take all measures to maintain its current strategic leverage, diplomatic advantages and economic lead over India. Although the evidence is inconclusive, the most plausible deduction is that this internal re-assessment of India lies behind the recent hardening of China's stance on the territorial dispute and a whole range of other issues in China-India relations. T

The Chinese are concerned that the U.S.-India nuclear deal and related agreements would bring about a major shift in the power balance in South Asia that is currently tilted in China's favour. The recent strengthening of China's strategic presence in Pakistan, Sri Lanka, Bangladesh, Myanmar and overtures to the Maldives should, therefore, be seen against this backdrop. Despite protestations to the contrary from India and the United States that New Delhi is unwilling and unlikcly to play the role of a closely aligned U.S. surrogate such as Japan or Britain, China's Asia strategy is based upon the premise that maritime powers such as the U.S., Japan, Australia, and India would eventually form an informal quadrilateral alliance to countervail continental China.

From Beijing's perspective, the responsibility for this negative development lies solely at New Delhi's door. In their writings, Chinese analysts seem upset over their southern neighbour's all-consuming passion to become a big power, and see the nuclear deal as its key to unlocking the door leading to the big league in world politics. Once the nuclear deal crosses all the big four hurdles (opposition from pro-Chinese Communist parties in India negotiations on I.A.E.A. safeguards approval by the Nuclear Suppliers Group (N.S.G.) and its passage by the U.S. Congress),

Beijing believes that it would end the nuclear symmetry between New Delhi and Islamabad (or, de-hyphenate the sub-continental rivals)

and put India on par with nuclear China (re-hyphenate China with India). This, from Beijing's perspective, is quite disconcerting because a major objective of China's South Asia policy has been to perpetuate parity between India and Pakistan. Add to this India's military exercises with the U.S., Japan and Australia, support for the concept of concert of democracies, and attempts to establish strategic ties with countries that fall within China's sphere of influence (Mongolia, South Korea, Vietnam, the Philippines, Taiwan, and Myanmar) all of these reinforce Beijing's fears about its containment. However, despite its strong disapproval of a pact that would narrow the power gap between India and China, Beijing would not want to take a stance that pushes India further into Washington's camp.

Most likely, Beijing would use its N.S.G. membership to further its own and its allies' interests by using the double standards argument to question Washington's commitment to non-proliferation goals in light of its decision to back India's nuclear industry while opposing the right to nuclear energy for Iran and Pakistan, by insisting that any changes to the N.S.G. guidelines to accommodate the deal must not be country specific but universal criteria-based so that all countries can benefit from the peaceful use of atomic energy under the I.A.E.A. safeguards, by using the deal to extract major concessions from Washington, including an end to the arms embargo and the lifting of bans on high-tech dual-use technology exports to China, by seeking new assurances that U.S.-India ties are not related to any contain China strategy. The fact of the matter is that China and India are locked in a classic security dilemma one country sees its own actions as self-defensive, but the same actions appear aggressive to the other.

India feels the need to take counter-balancing measures and launch certain initiatives to stay independent of China such as the Look East policy which are perceived as challenging and threatening in China. Like China, India is actively seeking to reintegrate its periphery with the framework of regional economic cooperation. Like China, India seeks greater international status and influence commensurate with its growing economic power.

However, like any other established status quo great power, China wants to ensure that its position remains strong vis-à-vis challenger India for strategic, economic and geopolitical reasons. Through closer strategic ties with India's neighbouring countries, China is warning India not to take any counter-measures to balance Beijing's growing might.

The Chinese government is fighting a defensive battle. It is only too well aware that U.S. imperialism is ready at all times to take advantage of any preoccupation that China may have with India to open another front against China wherever and whenever it finds it feasible, whether it be in the Pescadores, the Taiwan strait or new harassments over the air space of China. There are those who say China should give in give up what belongs to China in the interest of peace.

REFERENCES

Avedon, John F.: In Exile from the Land of Snows, New York, HarperCollins, 1997.

Barnett A. Doak: Communist China and Asia: Challenge to American Policy, Random House Inc., New York, 1960.

Bell, David V. J.: Resistance and Revolution, Boston, Houghton Mifflin Company, 1973.

Brown, Judith M.: Modern India: The Origins of an Asian Democracy, Oxford, Oxford University Press, 1994.

Ch'en Yi yen-lun hsüan (Selected Speeches of Ch'en Yi), Tz'u-lien ch'u-pan she, Hong Kong, 1967.

China and the Asian-African Conference (Documents), Foreign Language Press, Peking, 1955.

Craig, Mary: Tears of Blood: A Cry for Tibet, London, HarperCollins, 1992.

Dutt Vidya Prakash: China and the World: An Analysis of Communist China's Foreign Policy, Frederick A. Praeger, Inc., New York, 1964.

Edgerton, Franklin: The Beginnings of Indian Philosophy: Selections from the Rig Veda, Atharva Veda, Upanishads and Mahabharata, London, George Allen and Unwin, 1965.

Edin, Maria: Transition to Democracy in Exile - A Study of the Tibetan

Gandhi, M.K.: An Autobiography, or The Story of My Experiments with Truth, Ahmedabad, Navajivan Trust, 1927.

Government's Strategy for Self-Determination, University of Uppsala, Department of Government Minor Field Study, 1992.

Halpern A. M.: Policies Toward China: Views from Six Continents McGraw-Hill Book Co., for the Council on Foreign Relations, New York, 1965.

Harding Harry and Melvin Gurtov: The Purge of Lo Jui-ch'ing: The Politics of Chinese Strategic Planning, Report, The Rand Corporation, Santa Monica, California, February 1971.

Hinton Harold C.: Communist China in World Politics, Houghton Mifflin Co., Boston, Massachusetts, 1966.

Hudson G. F., Richard Lowenthal, and Roderick MacFarquhar: The Sino-Soviet Dispute, Frederick A. Praeger, Inc., New York, 1961.

Huntington, Samuel P.: 'Will More Countries Become Democratic?' in Political Science Quarterly, 1984.

Hutchinson, J. and Smith, A.D.: Nationalism, Oxford, Oxford University Press, 1994.

Inoki Masamichi: Japan's Future in Southeast Asia, Symposium Series II, Kyoto University, Center for Southeast Asian Studies, Kyoto, 1966.

Johnston Douglas M. and Hungdah Chiu: Agreements of the People's Republic of China, 1949-1967: A Calendar, Harvard University Press, Cambridge, Massachusetts, 1969.

Jones, Ken: The Social Face of Buddhism: An Approach to Social and Political Activism, London, Wisdom, 1989.

Klatt Werner: The Chinese Model. A Political, Economic and Social Survey, Hong Kong University Press, Hong Kong, 1965.

Lazar, E.: Tibet: The Issue is Independence, Berkeley, Parallax Press, 1994.

Lee Chae-Jin, "Chinese Communist Policy in Laos, 1954-1965," unpublished Ph.D. dissertation, University of California, Los Angeles, 1966.

Ling Nai-Min: Tibetan Sourcebook, Hong Kong, Union Research Institute, 1964.

Lopez, Donald S.: Prisoners of Shangri-La: Tibetan Buddhism and the West, Chicago, University of Chicago Press, 1998.

Nhat Hanh: Vietnam: The Lotus in the Sea of Fire, New York, The Fellowship of Reconciliation, 1967.

Ray, S.: Gandhi, India and the World: An International Symposium, Melbourne, Hawthorn Press, 1970.

5

Invasion of Tibet by China

Introduction

Often called "the roof of the world," Tibet occupies about 471,700 square miles of the plateaus and mountains of Central Asia. It is surrounded by the Chinese provinces of Tsinghai to the northeast, Szechwan to the east, and Yunnan to the southeast; Nepal, India, Bhutan, and Myanmar to the south; Jammu and Kashmir to the west. Lhasa is the capital of Tibet.

Virtually all of the Tibet is above 13,000 feet in altitude. Conditions in Tibet are primitive, and travel there can be particularly strenuous. Medical facilities are practically nonexistent. Tibet has maintained throughout its history a national identity distinct from that of China. In 1949, the People's Republic of China was officially announced in Beijing and the following year launched an armed invasion of Tibet. When China's People's Liberation Army invaded Tibet, Tibet was an independent state.

Under the 1951 Seventeen Point Agreement between the People's Republic of China and representatives of the Tibetan Government, which incorporated Tibet into China, China guaranteed no alteration of Tibetan political, cultural, and religious systems and institutions. The failure of the People's Republic of China to adhere to or uphold the Seventeen Point Agreement, and the imposition of so-called democratic reform, led to the March 1959 uprising in Lhasa. On March 10, 1959, the people of Lhasa assembled together and called for the Chinese to leave Tibet, thus marking the beginning of the uprising. The Chinese crackdown was harsh. An estimated 87,000 Tibetans were killed, arrested, or deported to labour camps. and flight to exile

Since the revolt against Chinese rule in Tibet that began in 1956 and through the end of the Cultural Revolution in 1976, an estimated 1,200,000

Tibetans were killed and more than 6,000 religious sites were destroyed. In 1959, 1960, 1964, and 1997 the International Commission of Jurists examined Chinese policy in Tibet, violations of human rights in Tibet, and the position of Tibet in international law.

The Simla Convention of 1914

The Chinese were disturbed by the success of the Russians in Mongolia, by the weakness of their own government, and by the fear that the British might open direct negotiations with Tibet. In January 1913, after an initial display of indignant resistance, they expressed their willingness to negotiate on the basis of the British Note of August 1912. They made strenuous efforts to have the discussions conducted in London or Peking rather than in India and they objected to entering a conference at which the Chinese representative would be on the same footing as the Tibetans. Nevertheless, in June, after some months of argument, the Chinese Government reluctantly agreed to a tripartite conference at Simla.

Even then their manoeuvring to secure, in advance, recognition of their claims to supremacy over Tibet did not cease until they had received a warning that unless the Chinese plenipotentiary arrived at Simla by 6 October, negotiations would be begun directly between the British and Tibetan Governments. Sir Henry McMahon was the British plenipotentiary and he had the assistance of Sir Charles Bell. China was represented by Ivan Chen and Tibet by Lonchen Shatra, a leading Tibetan minister, each of whom was a properly accredited plenipotentiary whose powers were accepted formally by the other participants in the Conference. Tibetan aims at the Conference were contained in a statement asking for acknowledgement of the independence they had reestablished by the eviction of the Chinese troops and officials. In furtherance of that, they wanted the Anglo-Chinese Convention of 1906 to be declared invalid and the Trade Regulations revised.

They also pressed for the acceptance of a frontier with China which would include all Tibetan peoples i.e. up to Tachienlu and the Koko Nor. The Chinese, in reply, put forward a claim to sovereignty over Tibet, resting it on the conquest by the Mongol Chingis Khan. They alleged that in the reign of K'ang Hsi the Tibetans had asked for the appointment of Ambans and they recalled the occasions on which Chinese armies had protected the Tibetans from foreign invaders.

They wanted a declaration of what had never been conceded before, that Tibet was an integral part of China and they claimed the right to station an Amban with 2,600 troops in Tibet and to control the foreign and military affairs of the country. In general, the Chinese Government aimed at a restoration of the political status under the Anglo-Chinese Convention of 1906. As for the frontier, they claimed a line running through Giamda, only some sixty miles east of Lhasa.

That would not only have restored the position won by the recent conquests of Chao Erh-fêng but would have improved on it considerably by making a great reduction in the area over which the Tibetan Government had hitherto exercised unquestioned jurisdiction and of which it was, at the time of negotiation, in full control. The Tibetans surprised both the other parties by the careful and voluminous documentation of their claims. They exhibited revenue records lists of houses, officials and headmen, charters, agreements, and other material relating to disputed districts. Against that, the Chinese could produce little but verbal statements including the above-mentioned allegation for which there is no historical foundation whatever that the Tibetans had asked for Ambans in the reign of K'ang Hsi.

The British plenipotentiary, Sir Henry McMahon, was, for much of the negotiations, in the position of mediator trying to find some common ground between two widely divergent extremes. In order to narrow the gap between irreconcilable claims to independence on the one hand and sovereignty on the other, he put forward the concepts of autonomy and suzerainty. A solution in those terms might, it was hoped, restore peace between Tibet and China on a basis similar to that existing before 1904 and allow the development of a stable Tibetan government free from outside influence, but in closer relations than before with the British Government.

The problem was to ensure the reality of Tibetan autonomy but still to leave the Chinese with a position of sufficient dignity. It might have been thought that the Chinese, having lost all authority at Lhasa, would agree without very great hesitation to accept formal suzerainty, at least as a first step. But considerations of face were important and Chinese consent to accept less than sovereign status was conditional on the acknowledgement that Tibet was an integral part of China. On the other side, the Tibetans, who had regained their complete independence, were strongly opposed to accepting Chinese overlordship under any name.

Their eventual assent to the concept of suzerainty was due to pressure from the British Government, which for many reasons disinclination to assume additional responsibilities being possibly the strongest was not prepared to support Tibet's claim to absolute independence. But such concessions as the Tibetans agreed to make were strictly conditional. They were one side of a bargain which would guarantee Tibet's freedom to conduct its own internal affairs and would put precise limits to the operation of Chinese suzerainty.

The Chinese, on their part, would have to agree not to send any officials into Tibet, except for one high officer with a suitable staff no Chinese troops were to be sent into Tibet except for a small escort for the high officer Tibet was not to be converted into a province of China or to be represented in any Chinese parliament. There was not even to be any stipulation that control of Tibetan foreign and military affairs should rest with China. One concession was resisted by the Tibetans with the utmost determination.

They fiercely disliked the proposed description of Tibet as an integral part of China and they finally prevailed, to the extent that this point was not mentioned in the main body of the agreement as eventually drafted but in notes which it was proposed to exchange. On another point, too, they advanced strong arguments. The Dalai Lama, who remembered how the Chinese had grasped their opportunity when the British withdrew from Lhasa in 1904. pressed for the appointment of a British official at Lhasa as a counterweight to the Chinese officer. That seemingly sensible proposal was rejected by the British Government because of its treaty obligations to Russia. The farthest the British plenipotentiary could go was an arrangement for a British officer to pay occasional visits to Lhasa to discuss matters arising out of the 1904 Convention. Even that was made contingent on Russian agreement in each instance. Such careful regard for the Anglo Russian Convention of 1907 seems over-scrupulous in view of Russian advances then taking place in Mongolia. It also tended to endanger the Tibetan position by leaving the field free at Lhasa for a Chinese representative to reassert his country's influence without the restraining presence of a British colleague. These questions of political status were difficult enough but further and even more intractable disagreements appeared in the matter of the frontier between Tibet and China.

There, both parties had opened their mouths very wide. The Chinese claim to a line running through Giamda, within almost sixty miles of Lhasa, had no basis in history beyond being included in the grandiose projects of Chao Erh-feng. The Tibetan counter demand for a frontier which would include the Koko Nor and Tachienlu, although having the justification that the majority of the population there was of Tibetan stock and that there were many monasteries in direct relations with the Dalai Lama and some states recently under the administration of the Lhasa Government, extended to large areas where it could not be shown that the Tibetan Government had, in the past thousand years, exercised actual jurisdiction.

An obvious compromise was the historic boundary, running roughly along the upper waters of the Yangtse, which had existed at least since the time of the Manchu dynasty but there was a case for saving Tibet's interest in the states and monasteries of Tibetan origin, lying to the east of that line, in country which had never been dominated by the Chinese before the recent campaigns of Chao Erh-fwng and where, since the Revolution, Chinese influence was tenuous and uncertain.

To bridge the conflicting claims McMahon devised the idea of Outer and Inner Tibet. Outer Tibet was to be the wide area, to the west of the historic Yangtse frontier, over which the Tibetan Government had for many centuries exercised complete jurisdiction. That was the Tibet where all the restrictions on the proposed suzerainty of China were to apply. Inner Tibet was to be the broad peripheral area, extending in the north to the Altyn Tagh range and in the east to the old provincial borders of Kansu and Szechwan, in which the population was mainly Tibetan by race and religious affinity.

There was to be no bar to the appointment of Chinese officials or the sending of troops there but Inner Tibet would be included in the ban against the conversion of Tibet into a Chinese province. Acceptance of those frontiers, which were shown in a map attached to the proposals, would have meant the surrender by the Chinese of the important town of Chamdo and a strip of territory between the Salween and upper Yangtse which had only recently been seized out of the direct control of Lhasa by Chao Erh-feng and where the Chinese position was already precarious.

It would also have meant that considerable areas outside the historic boundaries of the Eighteen Provinces, which the Chinese had been gradually claiming as new territories, would be described as falling in Tibet Inner Tibet. In those regions there would be no restrictions on Chinese activities although in theory China would be suzerain rather than sovereign. On the Tibetan side it would have meant the exclusion from direct administration by Lhasa of the valuable districts of Derge and Nyarong, lying to the east of the upper Yangtse, over which they had extended their authority in 1860.

In effect, there would have emerged two regions with differing status. Outer Tibet would have been something like a self-governing dominion of China, while Inner Tibet would have been the subject of peaceful contention in which the better or more attractive administration could be expected to win. British concern was primarily with Outer Tibet and, in addition to the political security expected from the clauses regulating the status of Tibet, British interests were to be secured by the cancellation of the virtual monopoly of economic and commercial concessions which the Chinese had obtained through Article III of the Anglo-Chinese Convention of 1906, by the grant of most-favoured-nation treatment and by suitable arrangements for trade between India and Tibet. After negotiations lasting six months the various proposals were embodied in a draft tripartite convention. Summary of its main points is;

1. The Conventions of 1890, 1904, and 1906 were to stand, except in so far as they might be modified by or repugnant to the present Convention.
2. Britain and China to recognize that Tibet is under Chinese suzerainty, and to recognize also the autonomy of Outer Tibet to respect its integrity and to abstain from interference in its internal affairs.
3. China not to send troops or station officials in Outer Tibet except for an Amban and his escort of 300 men. Britain to be similarly bound except for the British Trade Agents and their escorts.
4. China and Tibet not to negotiate about Tibet with one another or any other power except as provided in the 1904 and 1906 treaties.
5. Article III of the 1906 Convention, which virtually gave China a monopoly of all concessions with regard to Tibet, to be cancelled but China's position to be safeguarded by the understanding that the term 'foreign power' in Article IX of the 1904 treaty did not include China. British trade to have most-favoured nation treatment.
6. New Trade Regulations to be negotiated between Britain and Outer Tibet.

7. The British Trade Agent at Gyantse might visit Lhasa in connection with matters arising out of the 1904 Treaty.
8. Inner and Outer Tibet defined in a map, attached to the Convention.
9. The English text of the Convention to be authoritative.
10. Disputes arising from the Convention, between China and

Notes were also to be exchanged providing, among other things, for the recognition that Tibet forms part of Chinese territory and forbidding the representation of Outer Tibet in any Chinese parliament. Up to the last moment Ivan Chen continued to press for further concessions but when it appeared that no further modification would be considered he joined the other two plenipotentiaries in initialling the draft.

His action was immediately repudiated by the Chinese Government which declined to accept the Convention. The sole reason given then, and to be repeated later, was the unacceptability of the provisions regarding the Sino-Tibetan frontier. It may be doubted whether that was the whole story. The territory in Outer Tibet which would have had to be given up was of no great extent and had been acquired by force only four years earlier. As for Inner Tibet, as a practical issue there was nothing to prevent the Chinese Government as they were, in time, to prove from making their influence effective there, by whatever name it was called.

But the formal surrender of territory, however acquired, and the prohibition against making Inner Tibet a provincc may have seemed too great an affront to Chinese pride. There may also have been the fear that once the border area had been given the name of Tibet Inner Tibet the British might help the Lhasa Government to occupy it. Even so, the intensity with which the Chinese sustained their dislike of the Simla Convention suggests that indignation about the frontier was the symptom of a deeper resentment against the whole basis of the proposals.

Invasion of Tibet

Tibet's demise began shortly after the Communist Party in China gained control and formed the People's Republic of China (PRC) in 1949, when China began reporting its belief that the People's Liberation Army must liberate all Chinese territories, including Tibet, Xinjiang, Hainan and Taiwan. Partially in reaction to the PRC's threats, but also to solve a long-time border controversy with its newly communist neighbour, the Tibetan Government wrote to China's leader, Mao Zedong, just two months after the PRC was formed, suggesting talks to resolve all boundary feuds. This document was also delivered to the governments of India, Great Britain and the United States, and even though these countries were and are fully against the expansion of Communism, they still supported Tibet's negotiations with the PRC in order to prevent military action.

Two high ranking Tibetan representatives, Tsepon Shakabpa and Tsechag Thubten Gyalpo, traveled to confer with PRC officials on neutral ground in a third nation. The first direct negotiations commenced in Hong Kong between the Tibetan representatives and the PRC's new Ambassador to India. During the talks, the PRC's ambassador insisted that Tibet agree to a two-point proposal, which said that henceforth, China would control Tibet's national defence and that Tibet would be acknowledged as an official part of China.

The Tibetan Government refused to comply to this and the discussions were terminated. These failed negotiations led to hard times in which the Tibetan people wanted a youthful, unimpeachable leader, but the Dalai Lama didn't agree, believing he was not yet ready for the throne.The Tibetan People had called for His Holiness to be formally pronounced ruler before the appropriate age. This did not happen yet though, but only followed with another disastrous event that rocked Tibet. On 7 October, 1950, the enemy attacked the Tibetan frontier in six places simultaneously.

These forty thousand soldiers from China's Red Army easily overwhelmed Tibet's small territorial army of eight thousand in merely two days, killing more than half of Tibet's troops and detaining the Regional Governor. The shear hostility of the PRC left Tibet's neighbouring ally, India, stunned and outraged. Many other nations shared this belief, and powerful countries, like the United States and Britain, conveyed their support of India's opinion. Although, other information shows that this attack, unlike the Chinese invasion in 1910, was done with control and toleration. Tibetan's which were apprehended and dismissed remarked at the good treatment they had received. Just a month after China's first attack on Tibet, the Tibetan National Assembly called together an urgent meeting. In this session, following news from the Dalai Lama's eldest brother on China's full plans, a then sixteen year old Dalai Lama was beseeched to take on the title and total command of Head of State, and abandon his home in Tibet's capital, Lhasa, and settle close to Tibet's shared border with India in Dromo, in order to remain safe. Also following China's assault, Tibet pleaded with the globe to put a stop to China's outrageous actions.

A statement delivered simultaneous to the fourteenth Dalai Lama being made Head of State made the following cry for help appealing to the world for peaceful intervention in (the face of this) clear case of unprovoked aggression. The same month, in November, a letter from Tibet's Government was sent to the Secretary General of the United Nations, requesting aid and intervention from the group. In this message, Tibet explained that it understood that a peaceful nation like itself could never alone resist China's hostility, and that their government recognized that the UN would halt any further assault on Tibet. This topic had been refused at its proposal by India, who even declared a non-violent resolution that would aid all involved nations. The UN disregarded this plea even after the Tibetan Government wrote a second time to the UN in December of that year, 1950. With China's seizure of Tibet's eastern and northern regions, the devastation of Tibet's inadequate army, the invasion of many more Chinese soldiers into central Tibet, and with no major foreign aid or intervention, the long-time peaceful country of Tibet had no other choice but to negotiate with their malicious Communist neighbour.

In April of 1951, a five-man team of Tibetan representatives travelled to China's capital to re-open negotiations. These officials were instructed to explain Tibet's beliefs and to hear out China's opinions. However, this negotiation team was specifically not given the plenipotentiary authority to conclude an agreement, and was told to submit any significant subjects to the Tibetan Government. The negotiations began in late April. They began with a series of rejected proposals put forth by China, which caused the communist nation great frustration. It could easily defeat its weaker neighbour, and would not stand for this refusal. China firmly explained that the then present proposal was final. During this, the Tibetan officials were verbally offended, intimidated with violent threats and almost literally held captive.

All negotiations were ended, and the Tibetan officials were restricted from referring with their government on the situation, opposite to what Chin has alleged. The delegation was bestowed with the impossible task of deciding whether to agree to the present arrangement on its own, or face the burden of sentencing its capital, Lhasa, to Chinese invasion. The five-member team of Tibetan officials finally cracked under the tremendous strain, and signed the Agreement of the Central People's

Government and the Local Government of Tibet on Measures for the Peaceful Liberation of Tibet. However, because the representatives were specifically withheld the power to make any major decisions alone, their authorization of the agreement was unofficial and did not bind either His Holiness or Tibet's government.

The Tibetan officials cautioned the Chinese of this fact, but it had no effect. The knowledge that the signing was unofficial was no problem to China. The PRC continued on with the ceremonial signing and revealed to the world that the Peaceful Liberation of Tibet was successful with the conclusion of a treaty between both parties. The main terms of the seventeen-section contract allowed the Chinese military forces to occupy Tibet and enabled the PRC to control Tibet's foreign dealings. However, the agreement also assured that the present Tibetan Government would remain and Tibet would have independence both religiously and politically.

On 27 May, 1951, what is now called the Seventeen-Point Agreement was announced in full on Radio Beijing. Amazingly enough, this was the first point in time that both the Tibetan Government and its leader, the Dalai Lama, learned of this revolutionary agreement. Less than a month after the agreement was signed by the Tibetan official, the Dalai Lama travelled back to his former home, Lhasa, with the desire to renegotiate a more beneficial arrangement with China. Neither His Holiness nor the Tibetan Government revealed Tibet's denial of the present treaty. The historic day of 9 September, 1951, will forever be remembered to many as the beginning of the end for Tibet. On this day, approximately three thousand soldiers from China's Red Army entered Tibet's capital, Lhasa, with an additional twenty thousand troops trailing. At that point, the People's Liberation Army had conquered every major city in Tibet and had much more of its forces throughout Western and Eastern Tibet, making Tibet almost completely under the power of China's strong military. With this large increase in power by China, the communist nation decided to reject any further attempt at negotiation, thus no change in the current treaty could be made and Tibet could do nothing.

Although, during the invasion and occupation of Tibet, many Tibetan's were confused at the positive promises and actions of the Chinese. Assurances of religious freedom, new educational and medical facilities, and more astounded the Tibetan's. The good treatment of captured Tibetans was also surprising. However, only nine months later, China's true colours were shown with its negative actions. This fully turned the Tibetan people against the Chinese and started the first resistance. Following Tibet's Liberation, Mao Zedong immediately established the Seventeen-Point System, which totally eliminated Tibet's past independence. Since then, almost one and a half million people in Tibet have been slain, and over six thousand religious buildings have been demolished. Tibet, now officially the Tibet Autonomous Region, makes up nearly one fifth of China's total area, yet the people of Tibet constitute only a fraction of China's six percent minority population.

Even in their own country, the people of Tibet are being made a minority. Because of support by the Chinese Government for Chinese Han, China's largest race, to move to the region of Tibet, there is now only one Tibetan to every ten Han. The PRC is now filling Tibet with thousands of Chinese businessman and workers, and is investing billions of Yuan in order to improve Tibet's poor economy. The events that led to Tibet's invasion by China and the actions following the invasion have deeply changed and hurt Tibet. When examining all of this, one of the most important things is the number of times China broke international law. Although, even with all the damage done to Tibet, China continues to deny any wrongdoing. The PRC keeps steadfast in its belief of its right to remain in control of Tibet, as so many other countries have done to weaker nations in the past. China acted wrongly, but even worse is that no other country was willing to stand up against these injustices. This problem and many other occurrences will only continue unless the world is able to say no and put a stop to this crude violation of international law.

Indo-China Facedown in Tibet

Soon after the Communist victory against the Guomindang and the founding of the PRC on 1 October, 1949, Radio Beijing began to announce that the People's Liberation Army must liberate all Chinese territories, including Tibet, Xinjiang, Hainan and Taiwan. Partly in response to this threat, and in order to resolve long-standing border disputes with China, the Foreign Office of the Tibetan Government, on 2 November, 1949, wrote to Mao Zedong proposing negotiations to settle all territorial disputes. Copies of this letter were sent to the Governments of India, Great Britain and the United States.

Although these three Governments considered the spread of Communism to be a threat to the stability of South Asia, they advised the Tibetan Government to enter into direct negotiations with Chinese

Government as any other course of action might provoke military retaliation. The Tibetan Government decided to send two senior officials, Tsepon Shakabpa and Tsechag Thubten Gyalpo, to negotiate with representatives of the PRC in a third country, possibly the USSR, Singapore or Hong Kong. These officials were to take up with the Chinese Government the content of the Tibetan Foreign Office's letter to Chairman Mao Zedong and the threatening Chinese radio announcements still being made about an imminent liberation of Tibet they were to secure an assurance that the territorial integrity of Tibet would not be violated and to state that Tibet would not tolerate interference.

When the Tibetan delegates in Delhi applied for visas to Hong Kong, the Chinese told them that their new Ambassador to India was due to arrive in the capital shortly and that negotiations should be opened through him. In the course of negotiations, the Chinese Ambassador, Yuan Zhong-xian, demanded that the Tibetan delegation accept a Two- point Proposal i) Tibetan national defence will be handled by China and ii) Tibet should be recognized as a part of China. They were then to proceed to China in confirmation of the agreement.

On being informed of the Chinese demands, the Tibetan Government instructed its delegates to reject the proposal. So negotiations were suspended. On 7 October, 1950, 40,000 Chinese troops attacked Eastern Tibet's provincial capital of Chamdo, from eight directions. The small Tibetan force, consisting of 8,000 troops and militia, were defeated. After two days, Chamdo was taken and Kalon (Minister) Ngapo Ngawang Jigme, the Regional Governor, was captured.

Over 4,000 Tibetan fighters were killed. The Chinese aggression came as a rude shock to India. In a sharp note to Beijing on 26 October, 1950, the Indian Foreign Ministry wrote, Now that the invasion of Tibet has been ordered by Chinese government, peaceful negotiations can hardly be synchronized with it and there naturally will be fear on the part of Tibetans that negotiations will be under duress. In the present context of world events, invasion by Chinese troops of Tibet cannot but be regarded as deplorable and in the considered judgement of the Government of India, not in the interest of China or peace.

A number of countries, including the United States and Britain, expressed their support for the Indian position. The Tibetan National Assembly convened an emergency session in November 1950 at which it requested the Dalai Lama, only 16 at that time, to assume full authority as Head of State. The Dalai Lama was then requested to leave Lhasa for Dromo, near the Indian border, so that he would be out of personal danger. At the same time the Tibetan Foreign Office issued the following statement "Tibet is united as one man behind the Dalai Lama who has taken over full powers."

They have appealed to the world for peaceful intervention in (the face of this) clear case of unprovoked aggression. The Tibetan Government also wrote to the Secretary General of the United Nations on 7 November 1950, appealing for the world body's intervention. Letter said that Tibet recognizes that it is in no position to resist the Chinese advance. It is thus that it agreed to negotiate on friendly terms with the Chinese Government. Though there is little hope that a nation dedicated to peace will be able to resist the brutal effort of men trained to war, Tibetan government understand that the United Nations has decided to stop aggression wherever it takes place. On 17 November, 1950, El Salvador formally asked that the aggression against Tibet be put on the General Assembly agenda. However, the issue was not discussed in the UN General Assembly at the suggestion of the Indian delegation who asserted that a peaceful solution which is mutually advantageous to Tibet, India and China could be reached between the parties concerned.

A second letter by the Tibetan delegation to the United Nations on 8 December, 1950 did not change the situation. Faced with the military occupation of Eastern and Northern Tibet, the defeat and destruction of its small army, the advance of tens of thousands of more PLA troops into Central Tibet, and the lack of active support from the international community, the Dalai Lama and the Tibetan Government decided to send a delegation to Beijing for negotiations with the new Chinese leadership.

Different Points of View on Occupation of Tibet

It must be noted that the interpretation of Tibetan history and contemporary affairs has become highly politicized. Facts provided by the Chinese government on the one hand, and by the Dalai Lama and human rights groups in the West often show great discrepancies. Both sides need to be looked at closely. At present, a major propaganda war is still raging over the nature of the relationship between China and Tibet.

Chinese Viewpoint: A classic case of this conflict of values can be seen in the Chinese occupation of Tibet. Although this involved some erosion of Tibetan religion and culture, and the bloody suppression of revolts, these actions must be interpreted in the light of Chinese

Communist views on feudalism and the repressive function of religion. Also important were the traditional connections between the Tufans of the Qinghai-Tibet Plateau and the culture of the Tang dynasty, the need to gain firmer control of Buddhist institutions and the various historical cases of Tibet being forced to recognize Chinese suzerainty in 1652, the 1720's and 1905. Quite simply, the Chinese government has not accepted the political legitimacy of the Tibetan state or of its religious leadership, and stress that the Tibetans are one nationality among many in their multi-national state.

From the Chinese viewpoint, being a nationality does not automatically infer the right to statehood. Once this has been understood, it is easy to see that concerns for the unity of China, as well as pragmatic military and economic gains, have been allowed to overtake measures to preserve the autonomy of Tibet. The main arguments maintained by China (PRC) include the following:

Ancient China's view of itself was based on two central conceptions. The first of these was China was the Middle Kingdom (or central kingdom), which as an advanced and long-enduring civilization had a rightful place of supremacy in East Asia. This was in part due to a cosmological conception of the Chinese Emperor as supreme under Heaven, and therefore having a leading moral and political role in ordering world affairs.

A related historical conception was that beyond the frontiers of China there were only partly civilised regions, viewed as the 'wild' domains of 'barbarians', especially to the north and west. Imperial China saw her role here as protecting her civilised heartland, and creating a zone of peace and tranquillity adjacent to her borders. This was done both through the export of her superior Chinese culture, but also through what has come to be called the tribute system of international relations. The tribute system refers to traditional patterns of diplomatic relations and deference between stronger and weaker powers, in which the weaker power gains direct material benefits.

This was the way Chinese sources liked to conceive of ancient Chinese relations with tribes and nations on its borders, and implied in many cases positive economic benefits for the weaker power in the relationship, while enhancing the status and prestige of imperial China, whose emperor was viewed in some sense as a 'world-arranger'. Once a state entered the tribute system, it might find itself at least partially protected under the place it had now found as a respecter of Chinese cultural values. At the least, it would find trade and diplomatic relations much easier. In fact, from the 3rd century B.C. onwards, Chinese emperors tended to declare all forms of trade 'tribute', a fact which resulted in nationalities as far distant as the Roman Empire being at times declared part of the tribute system. Silk, as well as other valuable trade goods (including porcelain) became part of this economic and political relationship.

One assertion that is often made is that via the tribute system China could never deal with other states as equals, but only as part of a subordinate group. Two systems were used for this. The first was the tribute system, with the recipients being clearly subordinates. A second way involved less subordination, but still involved hierarchy, by using matrimonial alliances to bring other countries into a family of nations. China, of course, was interpreted as the head of this family, and therefore provided leadership and could expect adequate respect. This foreign policy was made attractive to the barbarians by the wealth China offered, and raising their ambitions by allowing them to marry Chinese princesses. The fact that sometimes they passed off Chinese commoners as daughters of the Emperor was viewed as irrelevant. Both methods relied on the barbarians' greed, and were a means to convert the sons and grandsons of enemies into loyal servants by linking them into subservient roles within the pattern of Chinese international relations. In 706 A.D. the Chinese passed of one such false princess to the Tibetan king of the time. However, the Tibetans then turned the tables by then repeatedly demanding an alliance (meng) and the status of an equal state.

This statement of universal inequality in dynastic Chinese international relations is not quite true. At times, China has been willing to negotiate on an equal basis with other major powers, e.g. the Xiongnu barbarians on their northwest in 193 B.C. in the early 9th century, and with the Russian Empire in the 17th century, while in the 20th century China has had to recognize the reality of Russian and American power. However, the tribute-relationship was held to apply to relations with Tibet, and therefore justified (in Beijing's eyes) its absorption into the modern state of China. The tribute system, though officially defunct once China lost Korea as a tributary ally in 1895, nonetheless still has some bearing on modern Chinese conceptions. Modern Chinese diplomacy is still concerned with the recovery of what Chinese leaders see as China's proper place in Asia and in world affairs generally. This conception has direct implications for Chinese relations with Vietnam, Taiwan, the two Koreas, and in the long-term, perhaps more problematically, with Japan. This conception of China's rightful place is more significant than straightforward border claims in mapping potential future conflict in Northeast Asia. Tribute in the past inferred recognition of status. Today, though no physical tribute is required, recognition of what China considers its legitimate role in Asia is a major issue for Beijing.

Furthermore, the imperial Chinese tended to conceive of a heartland (the Central Kingdom), surrounded by outer areas which had to be pacified either by protective walls, by tributary relationships with pacified tribes, or by the creation of military colonies which allowed them to seize and control enemy lands by a process known as 'can shi, a policy of gradually consuming alien territory] as the silk worm consumes leaves.

All major nations of the world, including U.S., Britain and India have recognized that Tibet is part of China's sovereign territory, and none of these nations have given official recognition of the government-in-exile status to the Dalai Lama. In April 1954 the Indian government made an agreement with China not to intervene in each other's internal affairs, explicitly recognising that Tibet was part of China, a view based on the fact that the Indian leader Nehru hoped for friendly relations with an adjacent socialist country, and wished to avoid border wars which would destabilise the new (and still poor) Indian state. Thus, when the Dalai Lama travels the world, he is received as a religious and moral leader, not as a head of state.

After 1950 the Dalai Lama's government signed a Seventeen-Point Agreement with China which recognized Chinese sovereignty.

PRC claims that the population of the Tibetan Autonomous Region, outside of military forces, still remains more than 95% Tibetan, with a total population of 2.02 million of whom 1.93 million are Tibetan. Furthermore, during the 1980s, there was no official policy of mass migration into the country, and only elite cadres were brought in to complete special projects in the country. However, there was an attempt to reduce even these cadres in the period 1980-84, but thereafter extra officials and skilled workers were brought in. However, overall in the 1980s, there was an effort to reduce 'political' cadres.

Prior to 1950 Tibet had one of the most old-fashioned and oppressive serf societies in the world. After rioting in the 1980s, Chinese authorities sought to remind the world of this earlier 'slave society' by publishing a picture in the People's Daily of a Tibetan peasant whose eyes had been gouged out as a punishment under the old system.

China has tried to modernize Tibet and improve it materially. This has been demonstrated by large areas of government investment, (1) the development of industry, and the training of Tibetan children, some of the best of whom are sent into China for further education. China has also build dozens of schools in Tibet, including 64 middle schools, 14 secondary technical schools, and three institutes of higher learning. China has also developed large farming and irrigation projects, e.g. The Three River Project, costing upward of US $ 362 million dollars. It has also built major road and new rail links into the country, linking it economically and strategically to China's western regions.

Since 1980, though Chinese is taught in schools, Chinese authorities have allowed the use and study of Tibetan language, even among students studying in China. In 1987, probably in an attempt to mollify Tibetan resistance and world opinion, Tibetan for the first time was made the official language in Tibet, with even Chinese cadres being encouraged to learn it. At the same time, university and technical level education still relies on Chinese, and to some extend English.

Since 1960s the Chinese have attempted various proactive policies to improve their situation in Tibet. From the 1960s they called for the return of the Dalai Lama, though at first they suggested he should live in Beijing, not Lhasa. Later on, it was suggested he could live in Lhasa, though there would need to be division between political and secular administration. In particular, he would need to accept that Tibet is an integral part of China, a view re-emphasised in 1988. From 1979 talks opened between delegates of the Dalai Lama and those of the Chinese government. The Dalai Lama came close to accepting central Chinese demands in the 1988, when he declared that he would accept that complete independence for Tibet was impossible, but asked for internal autonomy, with China looking after defence and foreign affairs issues.

This proposal did not seem ridiculous, bearing in mind the autonomy promised by the PRC to both Hong Kong and Taiwan (one country, two systems) if they unified with China. Indeed, a Chinese academic has recently argued that complete internal autonomy under the 'one-country, two-systems' approach is the best way to resolve real problems in Tibet. However, visits by Tibetan delegates to Tibet were met by huge massed crowds supporting the Dalai Lama, indicating how Chinese social programs had not won the loyalty of Tibetans.(2) Furthermore, continued riots in Lhasa from 1987-1989 indicated that the formula of internal autonomy might be a dangerous one. Other impediments included the site for talks China chose Beijing, the Dalai Lama Geneva, though in 1989 he proposed Hong Kong as an alternative.

Behind the scenes contact continued through 1985-1995, but did not bear fruit, perhaps in part due to the crack down of liberal-forces in China from 1989 onwards. In 1995 the Dalai Lama once again called for the resumption of talks, this time adding that he would being willing to talk anywhere. Through the late 1990s downs to 2002, the Dalai Lama continued an active international political campaign, but was met by repeated criticism in PRC media, which has continued to portray him as a 'splitist', or 'separatist'. Only in late 2002 were contacts made again between Beijing and the Dalai Lama, via the envoy Lody Gyari, based on the idea of an autonomous Tibet within China.

At the same time, some problems continue within Tibet, with dissidents still being arrested and imprisoned. However, through early 2003, China lifted most travel restrictions for tourists, indicating its secure control of the region. The Chinese also released the former Panchen Lama in 1978, after some 10 years in jail and re-education, while in 1980 the Chinese leader Hu Yaobang publicly recognized that the Cultural Revolution of the 1960s had a very destructive effect on China and had a strong negative impact on Tibet, arguing that a broad economic reform and localization policy was needed to improve conditions. In the 1980s, 60% of all leadership cadres included 40-60% Tibetans, though this did not include military posts. Unfortunately, Hu Yaobang was himself discredited for being too liberal in 1987.

Tibetan's Viewpoint: The presentation of pre-1950 Tibet as nothing more than a harshly oppressive feudal society with a large number of parasitic priests supported by the labour of virtual slaves is a distorted image. This view has been challenged both by the religious view of monks providing a real source of enlightenment, education and health care for the community, as well as by Western sociological analyses. It has been suggested that most Tibetan monasteries (aside from the big three around Lhasa) were quite small, with only 50-200 monks, and that they met the educational and religious needs of nearby communities.

That the feudal system in Tibet, though harsh, was in fact moderated by the principle of compassion, which was central to Buddhist religion.

At the same time, even the Dalai Lama would come to admit that certain Tibet institutions ground down the poor, e.g. the system of inheritable debt. However, the Dalai Lama argues that Tibetan serfdom was in fact less oppressive than that found in Imperial China, and that the Chinese confuse the Tibetan feudal system with their own past.

The peoples of Tibet are ethnically, racially and culturally distinct from the Chinese, and do not even use the same writing script.

That with the expulsion of Chinese forces from China in 1912, Tibet confirmed its position as an independent sovereign state, both in international law and in fact, a view published by the International Commission of Jurists in 1959.

That the systems of collective farms introduced by the Chinese, along with types of grain (winter wheat instead of barley) were not suited to Tibetan climate, resulted in famine and thousands of deaths during the first two decades of Chinese occupation.

That the special status of Tibet as an Autonomous Region is largely undermined by the strong presence of the PLA (People's Liberation Army) in the country, and that during the early period Tibet was in fact effectively governed by the PLA.

That the invasion of Tibet was not based on Marxist principles, nor on a desire for justice for poor Tibetans (these were later rationalizations). In fact, the invasion was driven by Chinese nationalism and Han chauvinism.

That the Chinese security forces have engaged in arbitrary arrests, executions, torture and degradation of their political opponents in Tibet, a view first published by the International Commission of Jurists in 1960, but sustained today by International Organizations such as Amnesty International, and of course by the U.S. State Department. Many of these groups argue that the harshness of the Chinese occupation was such that it can be viewed as either genocide, or cultural genocide. This was certainly true during the period of the Cultural Revolution, during which Maoist Red Guards tried to destroy all forms of religion and superstition in Tibet.

The Dalai Lama suggests that 1.25 million Tibetans have lost their lives since 1959. Of more than 1,500 functioning temples and monasteries, only 26 were functioning in 1987. Other articles speak of up to 6,254 monasteries destroyed. Part of this destruction of monasteries may have been a traditional Chinese fear of the Buddhist monasteries being centres of subversion, a trend which emerged within China itself as early as the Tang dynasty. Furthermore, in so far as religion seems an essential part of traditional Tibetan values, this was also a strong attack on Tibetan identity.

That political suppression continues in Tibet, with torture and imprisonment for political reasons common. Showing the Tibet flag, singing songs about an independent Tibet, or even having a picture of the Dalai Lama, can result in arrest, though this policy may have been softened in 1995-7. Increased tensions over religious organizations within the PRC generally re-emerged by 1999-2002, though there was the release of some prisoners during this part in order for China to improve the perception of its human rights record. At least through September 2002 China seemed to be tightening its hold on Tibet.

In contradiction to the more lenient policy used for many Western minorities in China (for the Kazakhs for example), a two child per couple policy has been imposed on Tibet since 1990.

There has been a massive immigration intake of Chinese, prompted by more open economic policies. Even if not officially planned, it results in more Chinese than Tibetans in the entire region that used to be the 'kingdom' Tibet. Overall, exile sources argue that 7.5 million Han Chinese have entered historically defined Tibet, compared to 6 million Tibetans. The discrepancy with Chinese official figures is partly a product of changing borders. Here part of the issue is that large parts of north and eastern Tibet were incorporated into the nearby Chinese provinces of Szechwan, Kansu and Qinghai - it is possible that much of the Chinese immigration has been into these areas, though the Chinese presence in Lhasa is also growing. The Dalai Lama suggests that in Qinghai province (once Amdo province of Tibet), there are 2.5 million Chinese and only 750,000 Tibetans. However, the Tibetans in exile also claim that even in the Tibetan Autonomous Region, Chinese already outnumber Tibetans, an interpretation strongly disputed by the Chinese authorities.

The supposed Seventeen-Point Agreement was in reality forced upon Tibet by the invasion, and that since China had since broken many clauses of the agreement, the Agreement is in any case invalid.

The Tibetan government-in-exile has modernized itself, set up democratic system of voting to create a parliament of regional representatives, established a constitution which even allows for the electoral take over of executive functions of the Dalai Lama (on the basis of a two-thirds majority in the new National Assembly), and also encouraged the involvement of women in state affairs. In other words, it is no longer a feudal system. As of 2002, the 'Tibetan community had its first direct election for a prime minister as a step toward forming a government that could function separately from the Dalai Lama'.

That although the Chinese have allowed the rebuilding of some monasteries, these are largely show pieces for tourists and done for propaganda reasons. Serious study and teaching of religion is still limited, while the intake of new monks has also been extremely limited, especially since 1993. Although ordinary religious practises are allowed, any that are too political are declared against public order. Clampdowns on monasteries and rebellious monks, as well as attempts at Chinese patriotic indoctrination, have continued through 1994-1998 and into 2001.

That although the Chinese have tried to modernize Tibet and improve the economy, most of this wealth comes back to Chinese (Han) nationals. This was demonstrated by the fact that through the 1980s the average pay for Tibetans was half that of an urban worker in eastern China, and that his life span is 10-14 years less than that of the Chinese. This situation has only been slightly improved in the 1990s.

Seventeen Point Agreement

The Tibetan nationality is one of the nationalities with a long history within the boundaries of China and, like many other nationalities, it has done its glorious duty in the course of the creation and development of the great motherland. But over the last hundred years and more, imperialist forces penetrated into China, and in consequence, also penetrated into the Tibetan region and carried out all kinds of deceptions and provocations. Like previous reactionary Governments, this government continued to carry out a policy of oppression and sowing dissension among the nationalities, causing division and disunity among the Tibetan people.

The Local Government of Tibet did not oppose imperialist deception and provocations, but adopted an unpatriotic attitude towards the great motherland. Under such conditions, the Tibetan nationality and people were plunged into the depths of enslavement and suffering. In 1949, basic victory was achieved on a nation-wide scale in the Chinese people's war of liberation the common domestic enemy of all nationalities the reactionary government was overthrown and the common foreign enemy of all nationalities the aggressive imperialist forces was driven out.

On this basis, the founding of the People's Republic of China and of the Central People's Government was announced. In accordance with the Common Programme passed by the Chinese People's Political Consultative Conference, the Central People's Government declared that all nationalities within the boundaries of the People's Republic of China are equal, and that they shall establish unity and mutual aid and oppose imperialism and their own public enemies, so that the People's Republic of China may become one big family of fraternity and cooperation, composed of all its nationalities. Within this big family of nationalities of the People's Republic of China, national regional autonomy is to be exercised in areas where national minorities are concentrated, and all national minorities are to have freedom to develop their spoken and written languages and to preserve or reform their customs, habits, and religious beliefs, and the Central People's Government will assist all national minorities to develop their political, economic, cultural, and educational construction work. Since then, all nationalities within the country, with the exception of those in the areas of Tibet and Taiwan, have gained liberation.

Under the unified leadership of the Central People's Government and the direct leadership of the higher levels of People's Governments, all national minorities have fully enjoyed the right of national equality and have exercised, or are exercising, national regional autonomy. In order that the influences of aggressive imperialist forces in Tibet may be successfully eliminated, the unification of the territory and sovereignty of the People's Republic of China accomplished, and national defence safeguarded in order that the Tibetan nationality and people may be freed and return to the big family of the People's Republic of China to enjoy the same rights of national equality as all other nationalities in the country and develop their political, economic, cultural, and educational work, the Central People's Government, when it ordered the People's Liberation Army to march into Tibet, notified the local government of Tibet to send delegates to the Central Authorities to hold talks for the conclusion of an agreement on measures for the peaceful liberation of Tibet.

At the latter part of April, 1951, the delegates with full powers from the Local Government of Tibet arrived in Peking. The Central People's Government appointed representatives with full powers to conduct talks on a friendly basis with the delegates of the Local Government of Tibet.

The result of the talks is that both parties have agreed to establish this agreement and ensure that it be carried into effect.

1. The Tibetan people shall be united and drive out the imperialist aggressive forces from Tibet that the Tibetan people shall return to the big family of the motherland - the People's Republic of China.
2. The Local Government of Tibet shall actively assist the People's Liberation Army to enter Tibet and consolidate the national defences.
3. In accordance with the policy towards nationalities laid down in the Common Programme of the Chinese People's Political Consultative Conference, the Tibetan people have the right of exercising national regional autonomy under the unified leadership of the Central People's Government.
4. The Central Authorities will not alter the existing political system in Tibet. The Central Authorities also will not alter the established status, functions and powers of the Dalai Lama. Officials of various ranks shall hold office as usual.
5. The established status, functions, and powers of the Panchen Lama shall be maintained.
6. By the established status, functions and powers of the Dalai Lama and of the Panchen Lama is meant the status, functions and powers of the 13th Dalai Lama and of the 9th Panchen Lama when they were in friendly and amicable relations with each other.
7. The policy of freedom of religious belief laid down in the Common Programme of the Chinese People's Political Consultative Conference will be protected. The Central Authorities will not effect any change in the income of the monasteries.
8. The Tibetan troops will be reorganized step by step into the People's Liberation Army, and become a part of the national defence forces of the Central People's Government.
9. The spoken and written language and school education of the Tibetan nationality will be developed step by step in accordance with the actual conditions in Tibet.
10. Tibetan agriculture, livestock raising, industry and commerce will be developed step by step, and the people's livelihood

shall be improved step by step in accordance with the actual conditions in Tibet.

11. In matters related to various reforms in Tibet, there will be no compulsion on the part of the Central Authorities. The Local Government of Tibet should carry out reforms of its own accord, and when the people raise demands for reform, they must be settled through consultation with the leading personnel of Tibet.
12. In so far as former pro-imperialist and pro-Kuomintang officials resolutely sever relations with imperialism and the Kuomintang and do not engage in sabotage or resistance, they may continue to hold office irrespective of their past.
13. The People's Liberation Army entering Tibet will abide by the above-mentioned policies and will also be fair in all buying and selling and will not arbitrarily take even a needle or a thread from the people.
14. The Central People's Government will handle all external affairs of the area of Tibet and there will be peaceful co-existence with neighbouring countries and the establishment and development of fair commercial and trading relations with them on the basis of equality, mutual benefit and mutual respect for territory and sovereignty.
15. In order to ensure the implementation of this agreement, the Central People's Government will set up a military and administrative committee and a military area headquarters in Tibet, and apart from the personnel sent there by the Central People's Government it will absorb as many local Tibetan personnel as possible to take part in the work. Local Tibetan personnel taking part in the military and administrative committee may include patriotic elements from the Local Government of Tibet, various district and various principal monasteries the name list is to be prepared after consultation between the representatives designated by the Central People's Government and various quarters concerned, and is to be submitted to the Central People's Government for approval.
16. Funds needed by the military and administrative committee, the military area headquarters and the People's Liberation Army entering Tibet will be provided by the Central People's

Government. The Local Government of Tibet should assist the People's Liberation Army in the purchases and transportation of food, fodder, and other daily necessities.

17. This agreement shall come into force immediately after signatures and seals are affixed to it.

In March 1959 the Dalai Lama fled from Tibet. On 20 June, he made a statement to a press conference in Mussoorie, India. On this first opportunity that he had had to address the free world, he made it clear that he and his government were denouncing the Seventeen-Point Agreement because it had been signed under duress and the terms had been broken by the Chinese authorities. The extract below gives the details.

Consequences

As the international community takes an increasingly keen interest in the question of Tibet, the demand for information grows. The world is no longer obsessed with the political ideological conflict between the two superpowers of the Cold War period, so that Governments and non-governmental actors can, once again, turn to other burning problems, such as the situation in Tibet. Many Governments are in the process of reviewing their foreign policy on many fronts. They should also thoroughly review their Tibet policy in line with the post-cold war international reality. Initiatives by parliaments and conferences in different parts of the world to address the human rights situation in Tibet and its underlying political cause as well as moves by a growing number of countries to take up the issue again at the United Nations have met with strong resistance from the Government of the People's Republic of China.

One of the results have been a stream of propaganda booklets, following the Stalinist and Maoist tradition, intended to convince foreign readers of China's right to rule Tibet and the great benefit it brought to the people of Tibet. The Present document, Tibet Proving Truth from Facts, is intended to respond to the new demand for concise information on key points of the Tibetan question, and at the same time, to serve as a response to the Chinese propaganda, particularly the one issued by State Council under the title of Tibet Its Ownership and Human Rights Situation, and published as White Paper.

The Tibetan Government-in-Exile does not have the resources to respond to each misrepresentation of the Tibetan situation which appears in the Chinese propaganda. This publication touches upon many areas of concern the fundamental question of the status of Tibet, the validity of China's claim to ownership of it and Tibetan people's right to self-determination the 17-Point Agreement and its effect on Tibet's status the events surrounding the resistance to Chinese rule and the Dalai Lama's flight to India the Tibetan social system before the Chinese occupation and democratic reforms initiated by the Dalai Lama human rights conditions in occupied-Tibet deprivation of religious freedom socio-economic conditions and colonialism population transfer and control the state of Tibet's environment issues related to the militarization of Tibet and the efforts that have been undertaken to find a solution to the question of Tibet. One aspect of the Tibetan situation has been insufficiently highlighted in the past, even though it is fundamental to understanding the context of much of what is happening in Tibet today. This is the profoundly colonialist nature of Chinese rule in Tibet.

Resistance to the Chinese occupation started to take on organized forms as early as 1952, reached massive proportions in 1959, and has continued, primarily underground, ever since. Despite the Dalai Lama's efforts to find a modus vivendi with the Chinese Government once it became evident that effective international response to the Chinese aggression was not forthcoming, the cycle of resistance and violent repression was not to be prevented. As refugees were pouring into Lhasa from Eastern Tibet with accounts of Chinese atrocities there, and as the Chinese presence throughout the country became increasingly oppressive, the Tibetan people rose up against all odds, in desperation and hope, in March 1959.

The uprising was brutally put down by the PLA, which claimed to have killed over 87,000 Tibetans between March 1959 and October 1960 in Central Tibet alone. The Dalai Lama fled the country under the protection of Tibetan guerilla forces only hours before the compound where he had stayed was shelled by Chinese artillery, killing thousands of Tibetan people who had gathered around the palace to protect him. Neither the uprising, nor the Dalai Lama's escape was planned. All the facts show that the Dalai Lama did all he could to prevent an open confrontation between Tibetans and the mighty Chinese army.

The consequences of the confrontation which occurred were devastating the Chinese troops massacred thousands of people tens of thousands were taken to concentration camps or labour camps where most died Tibetan cultural and religious institutions were destroyed and the population was subjected to terror campaigns and massive re-education efforts which the Chinese in China experienced only years later during the Cultural Revolution.

China has always tried to justify its policy in Tibet by painting the darkest picture of traditional Tibetan society. Tibetan society before the Chinese invasion was, by no means, perfect. That was the reason why the Dalai Lama initiated far-reaching reforms soon after he assumed full temporal authority in the early fifties. Whatever be the case, no country can invade, occupy, annex and colonize another country just because its social structure does not please it. In terms of social mobility and wealth distribution, traditional Tibet compared favourably with most Asian countries.

Every administrative posts below the Dalai Lama was held by an equal number of monk and lay officials. Although lay officials hereditarily held posts, those of the monks were open to all. Monasteries offered equal opportunities to all to rise to any height through their own scholarships. All land belonged to the state which granted estates, to monasteries and to individuals who had rendered service to the state.

The present Dalai Lama attempted to introduce land reforms by proposing that all large estate holdings of monasteries and individuals be acquired by the state for distribution amongst peasants. He created a special reform committee which was authorised to hear and redress complaints by individuals against the state authorities. Famine and starvation were unheard of in independent Tibet.

However, from 1950 onwards, the Chinese military and civilian personnel were fed on the state buffer stocks. They forced the Tibetan populace to sell their personal stock of grains at nominal prices. Soon after his arrival in India, the Dalai Lama organized the Tibetan Government-in-Exile. A series of democratic changes were initiated. A popularly-elected body of people's representatives, known as the Assembly of Tibetan People's Deputies, was constituted and a draft constitution for future Tibet promulgated.

The constitution even contained a clause whereby the executive powers of the Dalai Lama could be curtailed by a majority of two-thirds of the total members of the National Assembly. In 1990, the Assembly of Tibetan People's Deputies was expanded and its authority strengthened. The Assembly now elects the council of ministers, who were formerly appointed by the Dalai Lama. A Tibetan Supreme Justice Commission was also set up to act as the judiciary. In 1992, the Dalai Lama announced a Guideline for Tibet's future polity. It provided that the future government of Tibet would be elected by the people on the basis of adult franchise. The Dalai Lama said he himself would not play any role in the future government of Tibet, let alone seek the Dalai Lama's traditional political position.

The guidelines said Future Tibet shall be a peace-loving nation, adhering to the principle of ahimsa (non-violence). It shall have a democratic system of government committed to preserving a clean, healthy and beautiful environment. Tibet shall be a completely demilitarised nation.

The Chinese occupation of Tibet has been characterised by systematic and gross violations of human rights. This has resulted in the death of over 1.2 million Tibetans (one-sixth of the population) between 1951 and 1979, and exile of some 80,000. Although, today, the Chinese Government argues that Tibetans enjoy freedom and human rights, all evidence points to continuation of gross violations of human rights.

Organizations, such as the Amnesty International, Asia Watch, Unrepresented Nations and Peoples Organization, the International Commission of Jurists, Pax Christi, SOS Torture and France Libertes have documented and reported widespread and systematic abuses against individual Tibetans and against the Tibetan people, their culture and religion. A number of governmental delegations to Tibet, such as those from Australia, Austria, and Switzerland, confirmed the seriousness of these charges. Human rights violations in Tibet are inextricably linked to China's colonial policy in Tibet, which cannot tolerate any form of opposition to Chinese absolute rule over this territory.

In 1991 the United Nations Sub-Commission on Prevention of Discrimination and Protection of Minorities adopted a resolution on the situation in Tibet, calling attention to the violation of human rights and fundamental freedom of the Tibetans which threaten the distinct cultural, religious and national identity of the Tibetan people. The UN Secretary General prepared a note for the UN Commission on Human Rights containing numerous detailed reports of human rights violations in Tibet, and since then, these United Nations bodies have continued to hear and consider evidence of such rights abuses in Tibet, and international concern for the situation in Tibet is growing.

During his visit to Tibet in 1980, Chinese Communist Party Secretary Hu Yaobang publicly admitted that Tibetans had not under the Chinese rule. Few other Chinese leaders have had the courage to admit the failure of Chinese rule in Tibet. Instead they boast in typical colonial manner about the great social and economic benefits China has brought to the backward Tibetans. It is true that under Chinese rule, roads, airfields, power stations and bridges have been built in Tibet. In recent months the country has also been opened to foreign investment for a faster economic development.

Yet, as most travellers to Tibet recognize, this limited development will primarily benefit the Chinese colonialists, Government and military rather than the Tibetan people. The Tibetan population is still among the poorest in the world, the literacy rate of Tibetans in Tibet (as opposed to those in exile) is shockingly low, unemployment among Tibetans (as opposed to Chinese settlers) in Tibet is growing fast, and in all walks of life, Tibetans are subjected to discrimination.

It is clear that if the Tibetan people are left to run their own affairs as they have been for the past 34 years in exile, their economic, social and cultural situation will definitely improve significantly.

Buddhism flourished in Tibet in the seventh century. Receiving royal patronage, it spread throughout Tibet. With the assumption of power by the Dalai Lamas in 1642, the era of harmonious blend of religion and politics was established in Tibet. Buddhism has not been a mere system of belief to the Tibetans it encompasses the entirety of Tibetan culture and civilization and constitutes the very essence of Tibetan lives. Of all the bonds which defined Tibetans as a people and as a nation, religion was undoubtedly the strongest.

Tibetan national identity became indistinguishable from its religion. Monasteries, temples and hermitages were found in every village and town throughout Tibet. By 1959, there were a total of 6,259 monasteries and temples with about 592,558 resident monks and nuns. Soon after their invasion of Tibet, the Chinese authorities began to undermine the traditional social system and religion of Tibet.

By the middle of the fifties, monasteries, temples, and cultural centres were systematically looted and destroyed in eastern Tibet. The physical desecration and destruction was accompanied by public condemnation of religion and humiliation and ridicule of religious persons. Contrary to official Chinese assertions, much of Tibet's culture and religion was destroyed between 1955 and 1961, and not during the Cultural Revolution (1966-1976) alone. By 1976 only eight monasteries and nunneries had escaped Chinese destructions. Since 1979, some superficial religious freedom was allowed.

This included selective renovation of places of worship and allowing people to indulge in rituals like prostrations, circumambulations, etc. But the propagation of the teachings of the Buddha is discouraged and strictly controlled. The essence of Buddhism lies in mental and spiritual development achieved through intensive study with qualified lamas, understanding and practice. But the Chinese authorities discourage this in their campaign to misrepresent Tibetan religion.

Contrary to Chinese claims, most of the renovation work of the places of worship, including the state-sponsored ones, came through the initiative of the Tibetan public who contributed their labour and money. The assistance given by the Chinese government only forms a fraction of the total costs. The Chinese authorities, even now, do not let the functioning units of the monastic universities to continue their traditional religious practices.

Admission to monasteries are controlled, number of monks limited and political indoctrination is undertaken in the monasteries. The management of monasteries is placed in the hands of a maze of state bureaucracies. Though China no longer bombs or sends Red Guards to destroy Tibet's monasteries, its aim still remains the same as before total elimination of Tibetan religion and culture.

China's assault on the Tibetan religion, culture and national identity is nearing its terminal and irreversible phase through the implementation of China's final solution to the Tibetan problem absorption of the Tibetans through sheer force of numbers. In many regions of Tibet and in the urban areas, Tibetans are already greatly outnumbered by Chinese settlers and administrators. All instruments of political, economic, social and even cultural power in Tibet are in the hands of the Chinese, so that any talk of autonomy by Beijing is mere window dressing. In reality, Tibetans are fast being marginalised and becoming a second-class citizens in their own country. Exact figures for the Chinese and Tibetan populations of Tibet are not available. Chinese population statistics are unreliable with respect to Tibet and hide the magnitude of the Chinese population transfer going on.

Those statistics are also entirely inconsistent with other statistics released by the Chinese Government for the region. The Tibetan Government-in-Exile, on the other hand, is not permitted by the Chinese authorities to carry out scientific surveys of the situation, and must, therefore, rely on clandestine reports and estimates from a variety of observers. Despite the lack of exact figures, and despite Chinese denials, the evidence points to a deliberate and long-standing population transfer policy.

The policy is carried out largely with the help of Government incentive programs for Chinese from various Chinese provinces to relocate in Tibet. Higher wages, special housing, business and pension benefits are but some of the incentives provided. China's fourth population census in 1990 put the Chinese population (including a small number of Mongols) in the Tibetan provinces of Kham and Amdo at 4,927,369.

However, it is said that there is at least one un-registered Chinese against every two registered ones. The actual Chinese population, both registered and unregistered, in these areas should be about 7.5 million. In the recent years, China is reported to have stepped up the transfer of its population to the TAR also. The policy and practice of population transfer is not only violative of the Fourth 1949 Geneva Convention, which prohibits the transfer of civilian population into occupied territory, unless it is done with full and informed consent, it also constitutes a violation of the human rights of the people into whose territory the settlers are being transferred. This is evident from the United Nations Sub-Commission on Prevention of Discrimination and Protection of Minorities Resolutions, and from the results of the UNPO Conference on Human Rights Dimensions of Population Transfer. In Tibet, population transfer presents the greatest threat to the survival of the Tibetan people and culture and is therefore a form of ethnic submersion and cultural genocide.

For centuries Tibetans lived on their sparsely populated plateau in harmony with nature. Respect for all forms of life and for nature is a basic tenet of Buddhism, and in Tibet's plateau environment maintenance of the delicate ecological balance is vital for the survival of animal, plant and human life. The Chinese occupation and militarization of Tibet, the large influx of Chinese settlers and the colonial exploitation of Tibet's natural resources in total disregard of environmental consequences is having devastating effects on the environment.

Tibet has lost most of its rich forests, causing alarming desertification of vast areas, degradation of grasslands or their conversion into agriculture for Chinese settlers. This has also caused irreparable damage to many of Tibet's precious nomadic pasture lands. Nuclear testing and weapons production, uranium mining, and dumping of hazardous waste is having predictably dangerous effects on human and animal life in some parts of Tibet.

Chinese control in Tibet has been and continues to be maintained by a large military force. The number of the PLA troops and other security forces in Tibet varies, and so do the independent estimates of their strength. In the entire area of Tibet there are, at any rate, several hundred thousand well armed and equipped men. In the north of Tibet China has nuclear installations and testing grounds, and recently it has developed the capability of fast deployment of troops by air from military bases anywhere in China. The heavy militarization of Tibet is evident to any visitor to Lhasa and other important places in Tibet.

Lhasa is virtually surrounded by military camps and the inner city has a heavy presence of special armed police and under-cover security personnel. Several dozen nuclear warheads are believed to have been stationed in Tibet. The first nuclear weapon was brought onto the Tibetan plateau in 1971 and stationed in the Tsaidam basin, in northern Amdo. As China's ground-based nuclear missiles can be transported and fired from trailers, efforts to locate and count missiles in certain areas remain difficult. China's primary weapon research and design facility, known as the Ninth Academy is located in Dhashu (Haiyan) in the north-eastern Tibetan province of Amdo.

The facility is the most secret organization in China's entire nuclear programme and remains today an important and high security military weapons plant. It was responsible for designing all of China's nuclear bombs through the mid-seventies. It also served as a research centre for detonation development, radiochemistry and many other nuclear weapons related activities. In 1988, China carried out in Tibet what the Jiefangjun Bao of 16 September, 1988 called chemical defence manoeuvres in the high altitude zone to test newly-developed equipment.

China has been conducting nuclear tests in several areas of Tibet in order to determine the radiation levels among the people living in those parts. The militarization of Tibet not only represents an oppressive burden on Tibetans and a source of fear and, in many cases, terror, but it is also a source of instability and potential conflict in the region. In 1962, it led to the first Sino-Indian war in history, and tension on the border has remained high since then.

The Dalai Lama and his Government have repeatedly made efforts to find a negotiated solution to the grave situation in Tibet. In 1979,

China's supreme leader Deng Xiaoping stated that anything except total independence of Tibet could be discussed and resolved. This has remained the stated position of the Chinese government, but China has consistently behaved contrary to that position. In reliance upon Deng Xiaoping's statement, the Dalai Lama made a number of proposals, both bi-laterally and publicly, to the Chinese Government for negotiations. Sadly, these overtures were not reciprocated by China. In 1980, the Dalai Lama proposed sending teachers to Tibet from among well educated Tibetan refugees to help improve the education of young Tibetans.

In 1987, the Dalai Lama announced a Five-Point Plan and a year later elaborated on that plan in a speech delivered in Strasbourg. The Strasbourg Proposal, as it later came to be known, contained far reaching concessions which fully responded to China's declared interests in Tibet. Despite the fact that all these initiatives fell well within China's stated policy, that anything except total independence could be negotiated and resolved, the Chinese Government refused to come to the negotiating table. Early this year, the Dalai Lama and the Tibetan Government in exile proposed to send a high level delegation to Beijing to deliver a letter and note of the Dalai Lama to China's leaders and, once again, to attempt to open an official dialogue.

The Dalai Lama's desire to seek a peaceful negotiated solution is well known and has earned him the Nobel Peace Prize and numerous other awards. But it takes two to negotiate, and despite China's insistence that it is willing to talk, it always raised obstacles or sets conditions that cannot be met. The Tibetan Government welcomes the efforts of many concerned governments who have called on China to agree to negotiations without preconditions.

It is hard to understand China's reluctance to do so, unless it believes in achieving a solution to the Tibetan question through a combination of force and population transfer or ethnic submersion. Hope for the survival of Tibet and its people and culture now lies in the ability of the International community to persuade China that it should act with moderation, respect the Tibetan people's rights, and enter into earnest negotiations with representatives of the Dalai Lama and the Tibetan people in order to seek a peaceful and mutually acceptable solution, in keeping with the legitimate rights and aspirations of the Tibetan people.

REFERENCES

Andrugtsang, Gompo Tashi: Four Rivers, Six Ranges: Reminiscences of the Resistance Movement in Tibet, Information and Publicity Office of His Holiness the Dalai Lama, 1973.

Ardley, Jane: Resistance, Religion and Politics: the Tibetan Independence Movement in Comparative Perspective, Keele University, 1999.

Bell, David V. J.: Resistance and Revolution, Boston, Houghton Mifflin Company, 1973.

Bondurant, Joan V.: Conquest of Violence: The Gandhian Philosophy of Conflict, Princeton, N.J., Princeton University Press, 1958.

Conner, Victoria and Robert Barnett: Leaders in Tibet: A Directory, London, Tibet Information Network, 1997.

Donnet, Pierre-Antoine: Tibet: Survival in Question, London, Zed Books, 1994.

Edgerton, Franklin: The Beginnings of Indian Philosophy: Selections from the Rig Veda, Atharva Veda, Upanishads and Mahabharata, London, George Allen and Unwin, 1965.

Goldstein, Melvyn C.: 'The Circulation of Estates in Tibet: Reincarnation, Land and Politics' in Journal of Asian Studies, 1973.

Humphreys, Christmas: Buddhism, London, Penguin, 1951/1990.

International Commission of Jurists: The Question of Tibet and the Rule of Law, Geneva, ICJ, 1959.

Mao Tse-tung: The Selected Works of Mao Tse-tung, 5 vols., International Publishers Co., Inc., New York, 1954.

Mozingo David: China's Foreign Policy and the Cultural Revolution, Interim Report No. 1, IREA Project, Cornell University, Ithaca, New York, March 1970.

Purcell Victor: The Chinese in Southeast Asia, 2nd ed., Oxford University Press, London, 1965.

Robinson Thomas W. et al.: The Cultural Revolution in China, University of California Press, Berkeley, 1971.

Schurmann Franz: Ideology and Organization in Communist China, University of California Press, Berkeley, 1966.

Ten Glorious Years, Foreign Language Press, Peking, 1960.

Van Lyman P. Slyke: Enemies and Friends: The United Front in Chinese Communist History, Stanford University Press, Stanford, California, 1967.

Williams Lea E.: The Future of the Overseas Chinese in Southeast Asia, McGraw-Hill Book Co., for the Council on Foreign Relations, New York, 1966.

6

Tibetan Resistance

Introduction

When the Communist Chinese government ordered its so-called People's Liberation Army (PLA) to march into Tibet in 1949, the people of Tibet's eastern region were the first to experience the threat of Chinese invasion. The people of Kham and Amdo rose up and confronted the Chinese army at the onset of the invasion of our motherland. Pitched battles were fought under the command and banner of local chieftains. However, there was no proper organization and strategy, no unity, and only uncoordinated efforts to combat the common enemy were made. By 1957 a large number of volunteer defenders from various parts of the eastern region of Tibet had gathered around Lhasa, the capital of Tibet.

The initial People's Republic of China's military invasion of Tibet in 1950 met with high resistance in the heart of the country. The 14th Dalai Lama, on the urging of his elder brother, Gyalo Thondup, proposed reforms, including limitations on the land holdings of the monasteries, abolishing of debt bondage, and other government and tax reforms as a response to the invasion. These were designed to forestall expected revolutionary initiatives of the Communists. However, these ideas found little support among the entrenched Tibetan power structure. The Chinese leadership was skeptical of being able to control Gyalo, but had decided to support him as a way to colonize the region. Their plan was to indoctrinate him in Beijing. Foreseeing the eventual cultural submersion of his people, the Dalai Lama fled to India in 1959, eventually settling in Darjeeling near Kalimpong on the Tibetan border.

The Dalai Lama has said that he appealed to the Nationalist Chinese and the United States for aid in resisting the Communist Chinese occupation and together with others in the Darjeeling/Kalimpong area formed a small independence group. Other leaders included Tsepon W.D. Shakabpa, who participated in the 1947 trade delegation and Khenchung Lobsang Gyaltsen, a monk who was the Tibetan trade representative in Kalimpong. The CIA, whose contacts in the area were through the Royal family of Sikkim, is skeptical about Gyalo's claims but was in contact with him in August, 1952. Gyalo was also in contact with B. N. Malik, director of India's intelligence agency, the Intelligence Bureau from 1953 on.

The United States, which was engaged in the Korean War with the Chinese, began to aid the Tibetan independence movement. In the summer of 1956, several independence protests broke out in Amdo and Kham, and the CIA began to aid the Dalai Lama. This was ruthlessly suppressed. In early 1957 Dalai Lama selected eight candidates from the group for CIA training for scouting missions into Tibet in order to assess the nature of Tibetan independence movement. They were trained at the CIA's training facility on Saipan, the Saipan Training Center, and dropped in two groups by parachute back into Tibet in 1958. The first group, dropped near Lhasa, travelled there and requested that the Dalai Lama request aid from the United States for their movement. That request was refused by the Dalai Lama but the CIA continued their support. The second group was inserted near Litang in Kham and made contact with a Tibetan resistance group. However that group was soon attacked and all but one of the inserted group killed. The survivor managed to find his way to central Tibet where freedom fighters were mobilizing.

The Tibetans' tendency was to form large groups, complete with their herds and families, and so were easy targets for the People's Liberation Army Air Force. They also fought vigorous battles with large groups of Chinese soldiers in which they suffered heavy casualties. Thus, they were unsuccessful in conducting traditional guerrilla warfare. This failure led to their ultimate retreat into India in 1959 after the Lhasa rebellion.

The First Phase

By 1957 a large number of volunteer defenders from various parts of the eastern region of Tibet had gathered around Lhasa, the capital of Tibet. The Khampas felt the need to form a united organization to confront the Communist Chinese aggression. But by that time, the Chinese had started to exert pressure and our government's position was rather helpless. Meanwhile the Khampa volunteer leaders were having secret meetings, busy in laying out future plans and strategies. As a result of their common efforts it was finally and unanimously decided to form a united resistance organization against the common enemy, the Communist Chinese aggression. The leaders then signed a statement pledging their commitment to risk everything to resist the Communist Chinese. It was the first time that all the regions of Kham and the Khampas of all regions came together under one organization and fought under one banner since the splitting up of Tibet during the reign of the last King.

Soon after the creation of the organization, comprehensive plans were made to face the Chinese at various fronts. Assignments had been directed, locations to be scouted had been assigned, and monasteries, estates and provincial Dzongs to contact for assistance had been identified. A 27-point military law governing the conduct of the volunteers had been made.

Knowing that an official request required by the CIA for assistance to the resistance had been ignored by the Tibetan authorities and also knowing that it would take a long time, even if one would ever be forthcoming, General Andruk Gonpo Tashi, with a rather large division of selected men and horses under his command, started moving towards Shang Gaden Chokhor to get weapons and ammunition from the Tibetan government depot there. The rest of the volunteer troops were detailed in small groups of 50-100 to various places to scout and to ambush the Chinese movements. After quite a few encounters with the Chinese troops and several ambushes of Chinese convoys by the volunteers, the Lhokha area, south of Tsangpo was free of Chinese presence except for Tsethang, where a Chinese garrison with underground tunnels was occupied by a Chinese army force of about 2,000 which could not be driven out despite repeated attacks by the volunteers.

Meanwhile, General Gonpo Tashi's troops took all the arms and ammunition from Shang Gaden Chokhor and headed back south but, as a result of many serious encounters with Chinese soldiers who blocked all the routes, they could not penetrate through the Chinese army to cross Takdru Ka and return to the South, but had to move towards the North and further northeast from Nemo Shang. Hence the division became known as the Northern Regiment. They passed through Jang Yangpachen and Jang Namtso towards Jang Lharigo, then proceeded through Gyasho Bengal to Sarteng and Chakra Pelber in the area of Shota Lhosum.

On their way the volunteers had to fight numerous battles and suffered heavy casualties. In a serious encounter with the Chinese army in Dre-Gung Mashung, General Gonpo Tashi was wounded by shrapnel and bullets and later in exile, despite months of medical treatment in England, he died of these old wounds in Darjeeling in September 1964. As the number of recruits increased, a few more commanders were named in Chakra Pelber, which then served as temporary headquarters of the Northern Regiment, and a number of scouting forces were sent from Pelber to Powo Tamo, Naksho Tsogu, Lho Dzong area and to Tsawa Pesho to recruit new volunteers, to scout and to obtain as many arms and as much ammunition as possible from government depots.

In 1957, before the return of the team of trainees from the U.S., General Andruk Gonpo Tashi asked Phala for a formal request so the Tibetan resistance would not be left short of arms and ammunition. Again in 1958, through a radio message to Athar and Lotse, the CIA asked to obtain a request from the Tibetan Authority. This was relayed to the concerned authority accordingly, but the Tibetan authorities, for reasons better known to them, did not bother to send one. However, because of the urgency of the situation of the freedom fighters in Tibet, the Eisenhower administration approved the CIA providing the support requested by the guerillas, including resupply drops as well as additional training of Tibetans by the CIA. So the log-awaited and the first resupply drop was made in August 1958 without formal request from the Tibetan government.

To combat the Communist threat, Chushi Gangdruk asked the CIA through radio message for more supply and training of more Tibetans in addition to a pilot group of six Khampas, including Mr. Athar, who were already trained and had been parachuted into Samye Lhokha and Lithang, Kham. A large number of volunteers were sent to Colorado for guerilla training and about 40 of them later airdropped into the Domshung area of Amdo Toma, Markham and Chakra Pelber in Kham between 1952 and 1962; the rest of them came back to India and were detailed to positions along the Indo-Tibetan frontier lines for various intelligence works.

In the beginning of autumn 1958, just before the first resupply drop was made, the headquarters of the resistance organization were shifted from Tsona to Lhagyari, from which all the resistance troops were detailed to carry out raids on the Chinese until 1959 when the headquarters was in the process of moving.

In September 1958 the Tibetan government in Lhasa sent a second delegation to Lhagyari. This delegation consisted of two fourth-ranking government officials, namely Tekhang Khenchung Thupten Samchok and Tsepon Namseling. Their mission was to dissuade the Khampas from their activities. They had the Kashag's letter in their hands saying that the Khampas were reactionaries and their activities were against the law of the land and therefore they should surrender their arms peacefully to the authorities. After discussion with the volunteer leaders, the representatives agreed with our cause and chose to join the volunteer force rather than return to Lhasa.

In the beginning of 1959 the resistance headquarters at Lhagyari called a meeting of top leaders to discuss various important matters of the organization. It was resulted then in the meeting that a team of three delegates would go to India to make contacts with the world outside for assistance and also to raise funds from the Khampa traders in India who could not join the resistance force. Subsequently Jago Namgyal Dorjee of Derge, Sadhu Lobsang Nyandak of Tehor and Jangza Chozak of Lithang were chose in the meeting to form the delegation. Not knowing what was to happen in Lhasa in a month or so, the delegation left Lhagyari secretly for India via Bhutan. Not very long after they reached India, the news of the Dalai Lama's escape was in the headlines of all the newspapers in India.

Lhasa Uprising

The 1959 Tibetan uprising, or 1959 Tibetan Rebellion began on 10 March, 1959, when an anti-Chinese and anti-Communist revolt erupted in Lhasa, the capital of Tibet, which had been under the reign of the Communist Party of China since the Invasion of Tibet in 1950. Although the major event marked by the 14th Dalai Lama's flight occurred in 1959, armed campaign between Tibetan rebellion force and Chinese army has started in 1956 in Kham and Amdo regions which were subjected to social reform. The guerrilla warfare later spread to the rest of Tibet region and lasted through 1962. The anniversary of the uprising is observed by many Tibetan independence groups as Tibetan Uprising Day (or Tibetan National Uprising Day). The Office of Tibet, which disseminates information on behalf of the Tibetan Government in exile, has given its account of the uprising and the aftermath. In the late 1950s, opposition to Chinese presence in Tibet had grown within the city of Lhasa.

Armed revolt by Tibetans in Kham and Amdo provinces began in 1956, resulting in the deployment of additional Chinese military forces to eastern Tibet. Punitive strikes were carried out by the Chinese government against Tibetan villages and monasteries. Threats to bomb the Potala Palace and the Dalai Lama were reportedly made by Chinese military commanders in an attempt to intimidate the revolting guerrilla forces into submission. On 1 March, an unusual invitation to attend a theatrical performance at the Chinese military headquarters outside Lhasa was extended to the Dalai Lama.

The Dalai Lama- at the time studying for his lharampa geshe degree- initially postponed the meeting, but the date was eventually set for 10 March. On March 9, the head of the Dalai Lama's bodyguard was visited by Chinese army officers. The officers insisted that the Dalai Lama would not be accompanied by his traditional armed escort to the performance, and that no public ceremony for the Dalai Lama's procession from the palace to the camp should take place, counter to tradition. Word of the invitation reached Tibetans in Lhasa, sparking fears that plans were being laid for a Chinese abduction of the Dalai Lama.

On 10 March, an estimated 300,000 Tibetans surrounded the Dalai Lama's palace to prevent him from leaving or being removed. This event marked the beginning of the uprising in Lhasa, though Chinese forces had skirmished with guerrillas outside the city in December of the previous year. The Chinese government has stated that the riots were initiated by the Dalai clique. On that day, according to China Daily, a senior lama, Pagbalha Soinam Gyamco, who worked with the PRC as a member of the Preparatory Committee of the Tibetan Autonomous Region, was killed and his body was dragged by a horse in front of the crowd for two kilometers. On 12 March, protesters appeared in the streets of Lhasa declaring Tibet's independence. Barricades went up on the streets of Lhasa, and Chinese and Tibetan forces began to fortify positions within and around Lhasa in preparation for conflict.

A petition of support for the armed rebels outside the city was taken up, and an appeal for assistance was made to the Indian consul. Chinese and Tibetan troops continued moving into position over the next several days, with Chinese artillery pieces being deployed within range of the Dalai Lama's summer palace, the Norbulingka. On 15 March, preparations for the Dalai Lama's evacuation from the city were set in motion, with Tibetan troops being employed to secure an escape route from Lhasa.

On 17 March, two artillery shells landed near the Dalai Lama's palace, triggering his flight into exile. Open conflict began on the night of 19 March, including the shelling of the Norbulingka and Lhasa's major monasteries. Combat lasted only about two days, with Tibetan forces being badly outnumbered and poorly armed. Before peaceful liberation in 1951, Tibet was under a feudal serfdom characterized by the dictatorship of upper-class monks and nobles. The broad masses of serfs in Tibet eagerly wanted to break the shackles of serfdom. After the peaceful liberation, many enlightened people of the upper and middle classes also realized that if the old system was not reformed, the Tibetan people would never attain prosperity. In light of Tibetan history and the region's special situation, the central people's government adopted a very circumspect attitude toward the reform of the social system in Tibet. The 17-Article Agreement stipulated that the central government would not use coercion to implement such reform and that it was to be carried out by the Tibetan local government on its own. During his visit to India in January 1957, Premier Zhou Enlai of the State Council handed a letter from Chairman Mao Zedong to the Dalai Lama and Bainqen Lama and the accompanying Tibetan local government senior officials.

The letter informed them of the decision of the central authorities that reform would not be conducted during the Second Five-Year Plan period (1958-62) whether reform should be conducted after six years would still be decided by Tibet according to its own situation and conditions then. However, some members of the Tibetan ruling class were hostile to reform and wanted to preserve the serfdom forever so as to maintain their own vested interests. They deliberately violated and sabotaged the 17-Article Agreement and intensified their efforts to split the motherland. Between March and April 1952, Sicab Lukangwa and Losang Zhaxi of the Tibetan local government gave secret support to the illicit organization the people's conference to oppose the 17-Article Agreement and create disturbance in Lhasa, demanding that the PLA pull out of Tibet. In 1955, Galoin Surkang Wangqen Geleg of the Tibetan local government and others secretly plotted an armed rebellion in the Tibetan-inhabited area of Xikang Province. Rebellion broke out in that area in 1956 and the rebels besieged the local government institutions and massacred hundreds of government staff as well as common people.

In May 1957, with the support of Galoins Neuxar Tubdain Tarba and Xainga Gyurme Doje, a rebel organization named four rivers and six ranges and later the rebel armed forces named religion guards were founded. They raised the slogan of Tibetan Independence and opposition to reform and further intensified their rebellious activities. The armed rebels harassed Qamdo, Dengqen, Heihe and Shannan. The then Tibetan local government admitted that many Tibetan people lodged complaints against the rebels with it. In August 1958 alone, there were more than 70 complaints. The central people's government, in the spirit of national unity, repeatedly urged the Tibetan local government to punish the rebels to maintain public order. Meanwhile, it told the Galoins of the Tibetan local government, The central government will not change its decision on postponing reform in Tibet and in the future, when the reform is conducted, the policy to be followed will still be one of peaceful reform.

However, the reactionary clique of the upper social strata in Tibet took the extreme forbearance of the central government as a sign of weakness and easiness to bully. The armed rebellion in Tibet was supported from the beginning by foreign anti-China forces. In 1957 the CIA culled six young men from among Tibetans residing abroad and sent them to Guam of the United States to receive training in map-reading, radio transmission, shooting and parachuting. Subsequently, the United States trained 170 Kamba guerrillas in batches in Hale Camp, Colorado. The trained Kamba guerrillas were air-dropped or sneaked into Tibet to launch an effective resistance movement to oppose the Chinese occupation. An article entitled The CIA Tibetan Conspiracy in the Hong Kong-based Far Eastern Economic Review disclosed in its September 5 issue of 1975 that in May 1958, two agents trained by the Americans in the first batch brought a transceiver to the headquarter set up by the rebel leader Anzhugcang Goinbo Zhaxi in Shannan to make contact with the CIA.

Before long, the United States air-dropped arms and ammunition, including 20 sub-machine guns, two mortars, 100 rifles, 600 hand-grenades, 600 artillery shells and close to 40,000 bullets, to the rebels in the plateau called Chigu Lama Thang. During the same period, the United States clandestinely shipped large amounts of arms and ammunition overland to the rebels entrenched in the Shannan area. With the collusion of the Tibetan serf-owners bent on retaining serfdom and the foreign anti-China forces, the rebellious activities soon became rampant.

The climax was the elaborately planned armed rebellion in Lhasa on March 10, 1959. On February 7, the Dalai Lama took the initiative and said to Deng Shaodong, deputy commander of the Tibet Military Area Command, and other officers, after its return from studies in the hinterland, the Song and Dance Ensemble under the Tibet Military Area Command has a very good repetoire he would like to see its show. Deng and the other officers expressed immediate readiness and asked the Dalai Lama to fix the time and place for performance. They also conveyed the Dalai Lama's wish to Surkang and other Galoins of the Tibetan local government and Paglha Tubdain Weidain, adjutant general of the Dalai Lama. On March 8, the Dalai Lama said he would go to the performance in the Tibet Military Area Command Auditorium at 3 pm on 10 March.

The Tibet Military Area Command carefully prepared for the occasion. But on the evening of 9 March, the Miboin (mayor) of Lhasa provoked citizens by saying tomorrow the Dalai Lama will go to the Military Area Command for a banquet and a performance the Hans have prepared a plane to kidnap the Dalai Lama to Beijing every household should send people to Norbu Lingka, the residence of the Dalai Lama, to petition him not to attend the performance in the Military Area Command. The next morning, the rebels coerced more than 2,000 people to mass at Norbu Lingka, spreading the rumor that the Military Area Command is planning to poison the Dalai Lama and shouting slogans such as Tibetan Independence and Away with the Hans. The rebels hit and wounded Sampo Cewang Rinzin, a former Galoin of the Tibetan local government and then a deputy commander of the Tibet Military Area Command. They stoned to death Kainqoin Pagbalha Soinam Gyamco, a progressive patriot and member of the Preparatory Committee for the Tibet Autonomous Region. His body was tied to the tail of a horse and dragged through downtown as a warning. Subsequently, the rebel leaders convened the so-called people's congress and people's conference of the independent state of Tibet, intensifying their efforts to organize and expand armed rebellion.

They brazenly tore up the 17-Article Agreement and declared the independence of Tibet, launching a full-scale armed rebellion against the motherland. Although Norbu Lingka was controlled by the rebels and it was hard to make contact with the Dalai Lama, acting representative of the central government Tan Guansan managed to send three letters to the Dalai Lama on 10, 11 and 15 March through patriots. In them, Tan expressed his understanding of the Dalai Lama's situation as well as his concern for the latter's safety. He pointed out that the rebels were making reckless military provocations and demanded that the Tibetan local government immediately work to stop them. The Dalai Lama penned three letters in reply to Tan on 11, 12 and 16 March. In his letters, the Dalai Lama wrote, he is taking measures to calm things down. The unlawful activities of the reactionary had made Dalai Lama worry. As to the incidents which were brought about under the pretext of ensuring Dalai Lama safety and have seriously estranged relations between the central people's government and the local government, Dalai Lama made every possible effort to deal with them.

In the letter of March 16, he said that he had educated and severely criticized officials of the Tibetan local government. He also expressed the desire to still go to the Military Area Command a few days later. All three letters of the Dalai Lama have been photographed by reporters of the Xinhua News Agency and published, and are still well preserved. However, on the evening of March 17, Galoins Surkang, Neuxar and Xaisur and other rebel leaders held the Dalai Lama under duress and carried him away from Lhasa to Shannan, the base of the armed rebel forces. When the armed rebellion failed, they fled to India. After the Dalai Lama left Lhasa, about 7,000 rebels gathered to wage a full-scale attack on the Party, government and army institutions before dawn on March 20. The PLA, driven beyond its forbearance, launched under orders a counterattack at 10 am the same day.

With the support of patriotic Tibetan monks and lay people, the PLA completely put down the armed rebellion in Lhasa within two days. Before long, the PLA suppressed the armed rebellion in Shannan, where the rebels had been entrenched for a long time. Armed rebel forces who fled to other places were dissolved. The PLA was highly disciplined in the course of quelling the rebellion and this won the wholehearted support of Buddhist monks and laymen. They took the initiative to help the PLA in putting down the rebellion.

Various self-defence, joint-defence, livestock protection and other forms of joint-defence teams sprang up in various places to build roads, provide transport, dispatch mail, serve as guides, boil tea, send water, stand sentry and give first-aid to wounded PLA soldiers, effectively isolating the rebels

Final Phase of Resistance: In the middle of 1960 the Khampas decided to relocate to Mustang in north-west Nepal, because it would be easier to receive arms and ammunition from abroad if they were based outside Tibet. Guerrillas began to arrive in Mustang in late 1960, under the command of General Baba Yeshi. By the summer of 1962 the Chinese had successfully regained control of Lhoka, but there were by then over 6,000 troops in Mustang. Khampa operations persisted in Mustang until 1974. Mustang was chosen for several reasons. Culturally it was convenient because although politically part of Nepal, to all intents and purposes it was Tibetan by religion and language. Furthermore, its geographical location was ideal: a 15,000-foot high plateau overhanging the strategic Lhasa-Xinjiang highway, and surrounded by Tibet on three sides.

Due to this position the tactics employed by the guerrillas in Mustang consisted of raids into Tibet conducted by small units of guerrillas, who focused on ambushing PLA convoys. These operated with varying degrees of success; the most successful was in 1966 when a convoy on the Lhasa-Xinjiang road was destroyed. Those killed in this ambush included the head of the PLA's western command and all his staff. More importantly, the raid provided the guerrillas with documents including information on the Cultural Revolution, and Chinese figures showing that 87,000 Tibetans had been killed in the aftermath of the Lhasa Uprising.

As well as carrying out raids, the guerrillas in Mustang also established an espionage network throughout Tibet, with the result that the local communist party unknowingly employed many spies as party cadres. Tibetan guerrillas were also responsible for recording the details of China's vast military build-up along Tibet's Himalayan frontier, and also of the relocation of China's main nuclear base from Lop Nor in Xinjiang to Nagchuka, north of Lhasa. Despite the strategic achievements and advantages of Mustang, however, the operations there formed the last phase of the Tibetan guerrilla movement. Many problems and forces combined to destroy the guerrillas in Mustang.

Although the CIA aid to the guerrillas had not been their sole means of support and supply, when it was withdrawn, the future of Mustang was jeopardised. India had previously provided aid to the guerrillas because Tibetans had made up the staff of the Special Frontier Force, which was formed to guard India's northern borders. By the 1970s the SFF had matured into an independent force, so the Indians felt they no longer had to sustain the previous levels of aid to the guerrillas.

A further external pressure on the guerrillas came from the Nepalese government. As Nepal was a neutral country and was understandably fearful of China, it disapproved of the Khampas entering Mustang, but realised that the Khampas could only be opposed by force. Some of the local people in Mustang feared the Khampas and resented their actions, but resigned themselves to the guerrillas because they felt their presence was the wish of the Dalai Lama. However in 1972 Kathmandu launched a propaganda campaign aimed at discrediting the Khampas by branding them rapists, bandits and murderers. This campaign - for which there does not appear to be any supporting evidence - culminated in a Nepalese army attack on Mustang's bases in 1974, after Mao Zedong personally put pressure on King Birendra of Nepal, with threats of direct action if the guerrilla bases were not destroyed.

By the 1970s many guerrillas had already been fighting for over ten years, and were now in their forties and fifties. Unfortunately they could not be a match for the younger PLA troops, and age, rather than battle, was responsible for the majority of deaths.

Reasons behind Failure of Resistance

In the last resort of fighting in Mustang, there were too many factors against the Khampas. The PLA in Tibet amounted to around 25,000 when they invaded in 1950 and has steadily increased to at least 600,000 in the early 1990s. A different source says that in the summer of 1962 there were only 6,000 Khampas in Mustang. If it is accurate, then the guerrillas were not only limited by their remote position in Mustang, but also by numbers. Lack of weapons was one of the problems besetting the Khampas from the outset, as well as the size of their units, which seriously hampered their progress.

Khampas grew weaker with time, and there was never any evidence of the establishment of political organization within the guerrilla movement. Also there was lack of discipline within the ranks of those who identified themselves with the guerrilla movements. Their main advantage was their popular support. They were resisting the Chinese for the same reasons that the Chinese presence was generally resented everywhere in Tibet. Khampa guerrillas did not enjoy the public support of the Dalai Lama and the Tibetan government in exile, because they practiced violence. The Tibetan government in exile, established in the aftermath of the Lhasa Uprising, has always chosen to emphasize the non-violent aspects of the Tibetan independence movement.

Foreign Involvement

The United States funded training and arms for the guerrillas in Tibet and the United States prior to the uprising and for several years following. From 1959 to 1964, Tibetan guerrillas were secretly trained at Camp Hale by the CIA. The Tibetan project was codenamed ST Circus, and it was similar to the CIA operation that trained dissident Cubans in what later became the Bay of Pigs Invasion. In all, around 259 Tibetans were trained at Camp Hale. Some were parachuted back into Tibet to link up with local resistance groups (most perished) others were sent overland into Tibet on intelligence gathering missions and yet others were instrumental in setting up the CIA-funded Tibetan resistance force that operated out of Mustang, in northern Nepal (1959-1974). In the early 1950s, the U.S. invaded Korea and threatened to invade revolutionary China itself.

Meanwhile, the Central Intelligence Agency (CIA) worked day and night to gather reactionary forces into its spy networks and to develop covert teams that could wage secret war against the new people's power in China. In April 1949 U.S. Secretary of State Dean Acheson cabled his Ambassador in New Delhi that the U.S. rulers would like to see Tibetan military capacity resist quietly strengthened. Tibet historian writes In the summer of 1950 instructions were given to the Office of Policy Coordination, the bureaucratic arm officially in charge of covert operations, to initiate psychological warfare and paramilitary operations against the Chinese Communist regime. Top feudal forces around the Dalai Lama offered themselves as eager agents first to the reactionary Kuómintang (KMT) forces led by Chiang Kai-shek on Taiwan and soon to the U.S. directly.

The Dalai Lama's two older brothers, the incarnated lama Thubten Jigme Norbu and Gyalo Thondup, emerged as key Tibetan CIA agents. According to the historians, George Patterson was intimately involved as a translator and go-between in these negotiations. He reported that in 1953 Thubten Norbu contacted the CIA and was told to take his case to the KMT (from whom he was already receiving covert aid). Patterson also recalled an encounter two years later between Ragpa Pangdatsang and representatives from the Indian and American governments. At this time the United States was supposed to have suggested a ten-year plan of revolt, the aim of which was the eventual overthrow of China's control in Tibet. One of the recent book can be considered the 'official' version of the Dalai Lama view of history, contends that Gyalo Thondup made an agreement with the CIA as early as 1951.

It was initially an intelligence-gathering arrangement upgraded to guerrilla warfare in 1956. Within a short space of time the United States had eclipsed the KMT as the rebel's prime source of military aid. In opening these arrangements with the U.S. imperialists, Thubten Norbu carried a letter authorizing him to negotiate on behalf of the Dalai Lama. In 1958, the CIA started using air bases in Bangkok, Thailand to airdrop guns and ammunition into the ethnic-Tibetan regions of Kham. It was Gyalo Thondup who arranged the first CIA training missions, picking six Tibetans for that purpose. A secret CIA training camp was soon set up for Tibetan agents at Camp Hale, high in the Colorado Rockies.

The CIA intrigues encouraged an armed uprising in March 1959, as feudal forces tried to expel the revolutionary army from Tibet. Despite cries of innocence on the part of the Dalai Lama, officials in Washington were planning for the events months before that fateful March in 1959.

In March 1959, the feudal Tibetan forces were quickly defeated. The Dalai Lama was whisked into exile in India by a covert CIA operation. CIA-trained agents in the Dalai Lama's caravan laid out special airdrop targets in the snow to guide a U.S. military C130 aircraft that had been specially modified to fly in the thin Tibetan air. Halfway to India, a radio operator joined the Dalai Lama's group so the whole operation could be directly monitored from the CIA station in Dacca, East Pakistan.

The CIA immediately set up a Tibetan contra force among the exiles. Ten Tibetan contra camps were set up in the tiny principality of Mustang on the Nepal-China border. The CIA had three more C130s modified for high altitude airdrops. This major recruiting effort yielded 14,000 Tibetans and some additional tribal people in the field, entirely dependent on long-range transport and infiltration, and armed, equipped and fed by the Agency. In 1961 the Dalai Lama said the only weapons that the rebels possess are those they've managed to capture from the Chinese. Some reports say the Dalai Lama personally picked the contra field commander in Mustang.

At this time, the Indian government was preparing a border war with revolutionary China, and their direct involvement in the Tibetan contra army picked up. At a secret Indian base in Orissa, U.S. agents, Indian officials and Tibetan contras met weekly to coordinate their activities. The first Tibetan contra raid into China was staged in late 1961, just before war broke out between India and China. CIA study from this period with detailed information on how Tibet's unique weather might affect the use of aerial, chemical and biological warfare. Meanwhile, the top Tibetan clergy rented tens of thousands of Tibetan refugees to the Indian government to build military roads in northern India for the coming war against the Chinese revolution. When war broke out between India and revolutionary China in 1962, India's forces were quickly defeated by the People's Liberation Army. While the Tibetan exiles were helping India attack China, powerful revolutionary forces *inside* India were taking inspiration from the Maoist revolution. Internationalist Indian revolutionaries took the side of China. Soon, revolutionary communists led by Charu Mazumdar formed a new Maoist vanguard party in India and in 1967 started a great armed struggle among the peasants of Naxalbari in the same Darjeeling district where so many Tibetan feudals had entered India.

The Tibetan contra border raids continued through the 1960s. The CIA money that Gyalo Thondup received for these operations increased. The CIA hoped these Tibetan contras could maintain networks of agents, conduct sabotage, and generally harass the revolutionary forces. But, overall, this whole Tibetan contra operation was a failure. As the revolution deepened in Tibet, the border was more and more successfully sealed. Revolutionary militias of the People's Communes made up of former Tibetan serfs joined the People's Liberation Army in hunting down and killing these hated feudal saboteurs and spies.

Meanwhile, the people in Nepal increasingly demanded that these armed camps be removed. In the last known raid in 1969, a Tibetan contra raiding party was completely wiped out by revolutionary forces. By the early 1970s, the U.S. ruling class was tied down in Vietnam and was preparing to open relations with the People's Republic of China. A corrupt, ineffectual, armed Tibetan contra movement no longer suited U.S. imperialist plans. The CIA simply cut the Tibetan contras loose. In 1975 the Dalai Lama ordered the remnants of the contra forces in Nepal to lay down their arms. When CIA funding dried up, the Tibetan contras simply had no basis for continuing their guerrilla war from exile.

Consequences

According to the Tibetan Government in Exile an estimated 86,000 Tibetans died in the events surrounding the 1959 uprising. The Norbulingka was struck with an estimated 800 shells, killing an unknown number of Tibetans within and camped around the palace. Lhasa's three major monasteries- Sera, Ganden, and Drepung- were seriously damaged by shelling, with Sera and Drepung being damaged nearly beyond repair. Members of the Dalai Lama's bodyguard remaining in Lhasa were disarmed and publicly executed, along with Tibetans found to be harboring weapons in their homes.

Thousands of Tibetan monks were executed or arrested, and monasteries and temples around the city were looted or destroyed.

According to western sources, the 1959 uprising did not succeed because it lacked support from the Tibetans. Even western sources never estimated that more than 20,000 were involved. This number might however be underestimated since according to chinese sources, PLA killed 86,000 Tibetans the days after the Dalai Lama's flight. The radio teams were experiencing major resistance from the population inside Tibet. The CIA trained Tibetans from 1957 to 1972, in the United States, and parachuted them back into Tibet to organize rebellions against the PLA. But with little support from fellow Tibetans they often fell to the hands of the PLA quickly. In one incident, one agent was immediately reported by his own brother and all three agents in the team were arrested.

They were not mistreated. After less than a month of propaganda sessions they were escorted to the Indian border and released. Many prominent Tibetan leaders did not support the 1959 rebellion. In April 1959, the 19 years-old 10th Panchen Lama, second most important spiritual leader in Tibet residing in Shigatse, would have sent a telegram to Beijing expressing his support for suppressing the 1959 rebellion. He also called on Tibetans to support the Chinese government. However, after a tour through Tibet, in May 1962, he met Zhou Enlai to discuss a petition he had began writting end of 1961, criticizing the situation in Tibet. The petition was a 70,000 character document that dealt with the brutal suppression of the Tibetan people during and after the Chinese invasion of Tibet. In this document, he criticizes the suppression that the Chinese authorities had orchestrated in unjust retaliation of the 1959 Tibetan uprising.

Government in Exile

Government in exile is also a method of political resistance. The Tibetan government in exile is the official face of the Tibetan independence movement. It is not officially recognized by any other government or international political organization. While the previous government in Tibet was made up of nobles who had inherited their seats, and an equal number of monastic officials, in 1960 the Dalai Lama established the Assembly of Tibetan People's Deputies.

The first election was held in September 1960. Membership is based upon two criteria: the regional origin of the candidate, and the religious affiliation. The Tibetan government in exile seeks to be the representative body of all Tibetans, so the inclusion of the excluded regions is a politically symbolic gesture.

The important step taken by the Tibetan government in exile has been the implementation of the Charter of Tibetans-in-exile. This is a series of guidelines for the organization and functioning of the government, and it effectively replaced the constitution. The legislature, constitution and charter have all been seen as major steps towards the full implementation of democratic principles in Tibetan government. Whether true democracy does exist or not in the Tibetan government in exile is of vital importance for the independence movement, and will be addressed below.

Although the Tibetan government in exile has not directly encouraged or incited political resistance in Tibet, it still plays an important role. Protest during the late 1980s has strengthened Tibetan loyalty to the Dalai Lama, and has kept the issue of Tibetan independence alive. The Dalai Lama's tireless campaigning around the world has meant that Tibet is not forgotten. The exile government also produced a Tibetan-language copy of the United Nations Universal Declaration of Human Rights for circulation inside Tibet, which is, inevitably, banned by the Chinese.

The Tibetan government in exile has of course also been forced to accommodate refugees from Tibet, numbers of whom have increased following renewed unrest in the late 1980s. While the Tibetan people may have shown their commitment to a violent struggle, the Dalai Lama has remained fully opposed to violence as a means to liberate Tibet from the Chinese. He believes that violence can only ever make any existing disagreement far worse, and that non-violence is the natural act of compassion.

REFERENCES

Adams, Vincanne: Tigers of the Snow and Other Virtual Sherpas. Princeton, Princeton University Press, 1996.

Ahmad, Zahiruddin, trans.: A History of Tibet by the Fifth Dalai Lama of Tibet. Bloomington, Ind.: Research Institute for Inner Asian Studies, 1995.

Alexander, Andre: The Old City of Lhasa: Report from a Conservation Project. Berlin, Tibet Heritage Fund, 1998.

Allan, Michael, ed.: Anthropology of Nepal: Peoples, Problems, and Processes. Kathmandu, Mandala Book Point, 1994.

Aris, Michael: Report on the University of California Expedition to Kutang and Nubri in Northern Nepal in Autumn 1973. Contributions to Nepalese Studies 2 (2): 45–87, 1975.

Aris, Michael: Bhutan: The Early History of a Himalayan Kingdom. Warminster, Eng.: Aris and Phillips, 1979.

Aris, Michael: Hidden Treasures and Secret Lives: A Study of Pemalingpa (1450–1521) and the Sixth Dalai Lama (1683–1706). Shimla, Indian Institute of Advanced Study, 1988.

Aris, Michael: The Raven Crown: The Origins of Buddhist Monarchy in Bhutan. London, Serindia Publications, 1994.

Atkinson, Robert: The Life Story Interview. Thousand Oaks, Calif. Sage, 1998.

Attenborough, R.: The Population of Stongde, Zangskar. In Himayalan Buddhist Villages, ed. J. Crook and H. Osmaston, Bristol, University of Bristol Press, 1994.

Avedon, John F.: In Exile from the Land of Snows. New York, Vintage Books, 1986.

Axinn, William G., Thomas E. Fricke, and Arland Thornton: The Microdemographic Community Study Approach. Sociological Methods and Research, 1991.

Aziz, Barbara: Tibetan Manuscript Maps of the Dingri Valley. Canadian Cartographer, 1975.

Aziz, Barbara: Tibetan Frontier Families. New Delhi, Vikas, 1978.

Baker, Ian A., and Romio Shrestha: The Tibetan Art of Healing. San Francisco, Chronicle Books, 1997.

Barnett, Robert: Resistance and Reform in Tibet. London, C. Hurst, 1994.

Basu, Alaka Malwade, and Peter Aaby: The Methods and Uses of Anthropological Demography. Oxford, Clarendon Press, 1998.

Batchelor, Stephen: The Awakening of the West: The Encounter of Buddhism and Western Culture. Berkeley, Parallax Press, 1994.

Beall, Cynthia M., and Melvyn C. Goldstein: Work, Aging, and Dependency in a Sherpa Population in Nepal. Social Science and Medicine, 1982.

Beckwith, Christopher I.: The Tibetan Empire in Central Asia. Princeton, Princeton University Press, 1987.

Beckwith, Christopher I.: Medieval Tibeto-Burman Languages. Leiden, E. J. Brill, 2002.

Beer, Robert.: The Encyclopedia of Tibetan Symbols and Motifs. Boston, Shambhala, 1999.

Bell, Charles: The People of Tibet. Delhi, Motilal Banarsidass, 1992.

Bellezza, John V.: Divine Dyads: Ancient Civilization in Tibet. Dharamsala, Library of Tibetan Works and Archives, 1997.

Benedict, Paul K.: Sino-Tibetan, a Conspectus. Cambridge, Cambridge University Press, 1972.

Bentor, Yael.: Tibetan Tourist Thankas in the Kathmandu Valley. Annals of Tourism Research 20: 107–137, 1993.

Bernbaum, E.: The Way to Shambhala. New York, Anchor Press, 1980.

Bishop, Naomi H.: Himalayan Herders. Fort Worth, Texas, Harcourt Brace, 1998.

Bishop, Peter D.: The Myth of Shangri-La: Tibet, Travel Writing, and the Western Creation of Sacred Landscape. London, Athlone Press, 1989.

Bishop, Peter D.: Dreams of Power: Tibetan Buddhism, Western Imagination. Rutherford, N. J., Fairleigh Dickinson University Press, 1993.

Bishop, Peter D.: Reading the Potala. In Sacred Spaces and Powerful Places in Tibetan Culture, Dharamsala, Library of Tibetan Works and Archives, 1999.

Bista, Dor Bahadur: People of Nepal. Kathmandu, Ratna Pustak Bhandar, 1967.

Dommen Arthur J.: Conflict in Laos: The Politics of Neutralization, Pall Mall Press, London, 1964.

Insor D., Thailand: A Political, Social, and Economic Analysis, Frederick A. Praeger, Inc., New York, 1963.

Keyes Charles F.: Isan: Regionalism in Northeastern Thailand, Cornell University, Dept. of Asian Studies, Ithaca, New York, 1967.

Lamb Alastair: Asian Frontiers: Studies in a Continuing Problem, Frederick A. Praeger, Inc., New York, 1968.

McCabe Robert Karr: Storm Over Asia: China and Southeast Asia, Thrust and Response, New American Library of World Literature, Inc., New York, 1967.

Modelski George: SEATO: Six Studies, University of British Columbia, for the Australian National University, Vancouver, 1962.

Skinner G. William: Chinese Society in Thailand. An Analytical History, Cornell University Press, Ithaca, New York, 1957.

Thompson Virginia and Richard Adloff, The Left Wing in Southeast Asia, Wm. Sloane Associates, under the auspices of the International Secretariat, Institute of Pacific Relations, New York, 1950.

Toye Hugh, Laos: Buffer State or Battleground, Oxford University Press, London, 1968.

Trager Frank N.: Marxism in Southeast Asia: A Study of Four Countries, Stanford University Press, Stanford, California, 1959.

7

Chinese Intrusion and Sino-Indian War

Introduction

Every war can be traced back to its roots deep in the chronicles of history; they are the result of a series of steps that inevitably lead to the war. The Sino-Indian war of 1962 was no exception; its roots can be traced back to the Chinese takeover of Tibet wherein the first seeds of war were sown. After Indian independence in 1947, India had maintained missions in Lhasa and Gyangtse. Due to the close relations that existed between India and Tibet, going back centuries beyond the British trade treaties and also because of the unsettled conditions of a China enwrapped in a bitter civil war, Tibet's transactions with the outside world were conducted mainly through India.

China also had a mission in Lhasa, emphasizing the point that Tibet was nominally independent. On July 8, 1949, following the defeat of Chiang Kai Shek's Nationalist Government in the Chinese civil war, the Tibetan Government asked the Chinese mission to vacate, calling upon its rights as an independent country to request the expulsion of diplomats. Tibetan records show that they had planned this expulsion of the Chinese agents for more than a year. China invited Tibetans early in the 1950s to accede peacefully and backed up this emphatic plea by stationing an army near the city of Chamdo in East Tibet.

An anxious Tibetan delegation hurriedly agreed to go to Peking to talk to the PRC themselves in an effort to defuse the sudden tension. On October 7, 1950, the day the Tibetan delegation was scheduled to arrive, 80,000 soldiers of the People's Liberation Army (PLA) of China attacked Tibet and announced its peaceful liberation. The Dalai Lama was forced to sign the 17-Point Agreement of May 23, 1951, surrendering to the

Chinese attack. Imposed on the Tibetan government, the Agreement, the PRC claims, shows that Tibetans not only agreed to, but actually invited Chinese Communist troops to liberate Tibet. This action, and the systematic devastation of the Tibetan people and culture, naturally, took both Tibet and India completely by surprise.

Nehru complained that he had been led to believe by the Chinese Foreign Office that the Chinese would settle the future of Tibet in a peaceful manner by direct negotiation with the representatives of Tibet. The legality, or lack thereof, and account of the PRC's invasion of an independent Tibet, though entwined in history with the '62 war, will be omitted in this project. The huge public outcry in India protesting the Chinese invasion mainly dealt with the political and cultural facets of this issue.

Prior to Indian independence, the British had earmarked Tibet as a neutral buffer zone in view of British India's defence environment vis-à-vis the similar imperialistic leanings of China and Russia. Barring a few people with acute perception, most Indian politicians, along with the common man, failed to anticipate the strategic ramifications of the Chinese aggression and the loss of this buffer. Jaharwalal Nehru, the Prime Minister of the newly independent India, following his foreign policy of trying to establish its mutual, non-aligned relations on the international scene, held the view that India could ill afford a confrontation over Tibet at a nascent point in India's history, and especially so during the ongoing Korean War.

On November 18, 1950, Jawaharlal Nehru wrote to the Home Minister, Sardar Vallabhbhai Patel stated India could not save Tibet, as India should have liked to do, and India's very attempt to save it might well bring greater trouble to it. It would be unfair to Tibet for us to bring this trouble upon her without having the capacity to help her effectively. It may be possible, however, that India might be able to help Tibet to retain a large measure of her autonomy. Indeed, India' under Nehru's leadership, went to great lengths to insure and assure that friendship with China was the keystone of India's foreign policy, and that India along with China could mutually hold the non-aligned balance of power in Asia.

While high-minded, this impractical view was to result in disastrous, unforeseen consequences for India. Nehru's two closest advisors at the time were the socialist-leaning Krishna Menon and India's then Ambassador to China during the Communist Revolution, K. M. Panikkar.

They were largely responsible for Nehru's decision to recognize Chinese sovereignty over Tibet. Panikkar had strong Communist leanings - so much so that he successfully wished his daughter's marriage to a leading Communist labour leader. Panikkar, when called upon by Nehru, went so far as to fib that there was a lack of confirmation of the presence of Chinese troops in Tibet and argued that to protest the Chinese invasion of Tibet would be an interference to India's efforts on behalf of China in the UN.

It would be instructive to examine the Chinese claims on Tibet in brief at this juncture, since the dispute over the McMahon Line that demarcated the border between India and China owes its origins to these claims. The ostensible reason given by China when the PLA entered Tibet was to liberate three million Tibetans from imperialist aggression, to complete the unification of the whole of China, and to safeguard the frontier regions of the country. Cutting through the propaganda reveals the underlying truth in this statement - the safeguarding of China by proactive engagement in the 'engagee' in this case being the Kingdom of Tibet.

It is generally surmised that the reason behind China's invasion was to gain control of the highly strategic crossroads of Tibet that lead to the heart of Western, Central, South and South East Asia, and can be used as a springboard for engaging the same. In 1842, the autonomous Tibetans and the Dogra rulers of the kingdom of Jammu and Kashmir signed a non-aggression pact on respecting the old, established frontiers. The boundary was not specified. To clarify this, in 1847 the British delineated a boundary from the Spiti river up to the Pangong lake. The area further north up to the Karakoram Pass was left out. The first boundary alignment here was recorded in 1865 when W. H. Johnson of the Survey of India trekked across the Aksai Chin and drew a map including this in Jammu and Kashmir. Johnson was soon appointed Kashmir's commissioner in Ladakh.

The Foreign Office came to be of the view that the border should be pushed further to the Kuen Lun range to absorb Aksai Chin and to put a British controlled buffer in between to forestall the presumed Russian advance, as the British did with Afghanistan, though nothing came of this. In 1892 the Chinese put a boundary marker at the Karakoram Pass and told the British officer and adventurer, Capt. Young, that Chinese territory began there and that the boundary ran along the Karakoram range.

The reasons given for this was that Askai Chin is an integral and sacred part of Tibet, which the Chinese claim.

Sadly, the claim has no credible historical, or legal, backing while Tibet has always had varying degrees of freedom historically, and at various times it was autonomous, at other times it was integrated into a larger China, or allied with Indian kingdoms. Indeed, Tibet was also a tributary to the Mughal Empire in the subcontinent. Regardless, it was noted by both the British and the Chinese, even then, that the boundary marker could not be regarded as having any legal value in international law because the boundary was not demarcated jointly. In 1904, a British military expedition was sent to China under the leadership of Colonel Young to prevent China from falling under the influence of foreign powers. An Anglo-Tibetan treaty was signed with China that granted Britain trading rights and marked the origin of direct British influence in and of Tibet.

An Anglo-Chinese treaty of 1906 followed up the previous treaty. Treaties not withstanding, the Chinese tried to capture Tibet many times until 1913, but failed to make headway against the British. In 1913, Tibet declared independence, and a conference was held in 1914 in Simla regarding Tibetan independence. The Simla Conference was agreed to be a tripartite one, in which the Tibetans were an equal partner in the talks with the Chinese and British. Legalities of the Tibetan independence notwithstanding, this casts much doubt on the nature of Chinese position that states Tibet was merely a Chinese province. Tibet demanded recognition of their de facto sovereignty - a proposal intolerable to the Chinese, as China did not wish to give up their claim to Tibet, though they did not actually control it. It was decided that Tibet was to be divided into an Inner- and an Outer-Tibet.

Eventually it was agreed that Outer-Tibet would accept Chinese suzerainty if its autonomous status were recognized, but in the end China refused to sign the treaty because of disagreements over the China- inner Tibet border - not the Tibet-India border - based on vague and ephemeral historical boundaries. When this happened, China lost the opportunity to be recognized as suzerain over Tibet in international law. Tibet was at the time functionally independent, as its government's participation in the border talks shows, and by no treaty had it agreed to accept Chinese suzerainty. In the end, the only legally binding outcome of the 1914 conference was that Britain and Tibet, represented by Sir Henry McMahon and Lonchen Shatra respectively, reached an agreement of a border settlement binding between themselves, bringing McMahon Line into being. To this meeting, the Chinese delegate was not invited, as the McMahon line was the agreement on the official demarcation of the border between Tibet and India this highlights the fact that all the parties -China included- recognized that Tibet had full authority to negotiate its boundary with India.

It is of crucial importance to note that the McMahon line legally had nothing to do with China. To this date, the Chinese claim to the Indian areas is based upon the non-recognition of the McMahon Line, regardless of the recognition of Tibetan autonomy and Tibet's acceptance of the McMahon Line, which is is based on their illegal claim to Tibet. Seizing the opportunity to expand in the late 50s, they played upon quirky logic that would've been legally binding had Tibet been legally been part of China

The first, (again, assuming Tibet is legally Chinese) is that the Tibetans, as a province of China, could not legally be signatories to the Simla Convention. Though the understood agreement that a Tibetan delegate was present, and the fact that Chou Enlai himself assured Nehru of Tibetan autonomy when the Chinese Prime Minister visited India in 1954. Also, the Chinese were never actual signatories to the Simla Convention, which was agreed to between the Tibetans and the British. Because a unilateral (solely British, since the Tibetan signature is not legally binding) agreement on a border demarcation is not valid, the whole McMahon line demarcation, which India inherited, comes into question. Had these historical facts been put proactively forward by the Indian government in during the Chinese invasion of Tibet in 1950, rather than dismissed out of apprehension of the geo-political situation, the world would have been appraised of the situation and the Indian locus stand would have been strengthened.

Instead Mr. Nehru preferred a policy of appeasement and surrender to China and accepted this mammoth change in status quo. Regardless of vehement public outcry and hurt, the Indian government went so far as opposing the discussion of Tibet's appeal to the UN General Assembly of 23rd Nov 1950. Thus, the prescient in policy established was to cultivate Chinese friendship by buying it off. As events were to prove later, this was a most disastrous road to take. Nehru had failed to take into account that China had always tried to expand its territories at the expense of its neighbours, and a time would come when Indian territory would have to be defended against the Chinese dragon.

Background

The cause of the war was a dispute over the sovereignty of the widely-separated Aksai Chin and Arunachal Pradesh border regions. Aksai Chin, claimed by India to belong to Kashmir and by China to be part of Xinjiang, contains an important road link that connects the Chinese regions of Tibet and Xinjiang. China's construction of this road was one of the triggers of the conflict. Arunachal Pradesh is also claimed by both nations although it is roughly the size of Austria, it is sparsely inhabited by numerous local tribes due to its mountainous terrain.

The Johnson Line: The western portion of the Sino-Indian boundary originates in 1834, with the Sikh Confederation's conquest of Ladakh. In 1842 the Sikh Confederacy, which at the time ruled over much of Northern India (including the frontier regions of Jammu and Kashmir), signed a treaty which guaranteed the integrity of its existing borders with its neighbours. The British defeat of the Sikhs in 1846 resulted in transfer of sovereignty over Ladakh, part of the Jammu and Kashmir region, to the British, and British commissioners contacted Chinese officials to negotiate the border.

The boundaries at its two extremities, Pangong Lake and Karakoram Pass, were well-defined, but the Aksai Chin area in between lay undefined. In 1865, British surveyor W H Johnson came to an agreement with the Maharaja of Kashmir, in whose service he was employed, on a proposed Johnson Line which placed Aksai Chin in Kashmir. China rejected the arrangement, and the British government also harboured doubts, so decided to take up the issue in an attempt to reach a settlement. However in 1892, before the issue had been resolved, China erected boundary markers at Karakoram Pass on the ancient caravan route between Xinjiang and Ladakh (which were disputed by the British Indian Government). Throughout most of the 19th century Great Britain and the expanding Russian Empire were jockeying for influence in Central Asia, and Britain decided to hand over Aksai Chin to Chinese administration as a buffer against Russian invasion.

The newly-created border was known as the MacCartney-MacDonald Line, and both British-controlled India and China now began to show Aksai Chin as Chinese. In 1911 the Xinhai Revolution resulted in power shifts in China, and by 1918 (in the wake of the Russian Bolshevik Revolution) the British no longer saw merit in China's continuing possession of the region. On British maps the border was redrawn as the original Johnson Line, but despite this reversion the new border was left unmanned and undemarcated. According to Neville Maxwell, the British had used as many as 11 different boundary lines in the region, as their claims shifted with the political situation By the time of Indian independence in 1947, the Johnson Line had become India's official western boundary. On 1 July, 1954, Indian Prime Minister Jawaharlal Nehru definitively stated the Indian position.

He claimed that Aksai Chin had been part of the Indian Ladakh region for centuries, and that the border (as defined by the Johnson Line) was non-negotiable. According to George N. Patterson, when the Indian government finally produced a report detailing the alleged proof of India's claims to the disputed area, the quality of the Indian evidence was very poor, including some very dubious sources indeed. At the time, Chinese officials issued no condemnation of Nehru's claims or made any opposition to Nehru's open declarations of control over Aksai Chin. In 1956, Chinese Premier Zhou Enlai stated that he had no claims over Indian controlled territory. He later argued that Aksai Chin was already under Chinese jurisdiction, implying that there was therefore no contradiction with his earlier statement since China did not regard the region as Indian controlled, and that since the British hand-over China had regarded the McCartney MacDonald Line as the relevant border.

Zhou later argued that as the boundary was un-demarcated and had never been defined by treaty between any Chinese or Indian government, the Indian government could not unilaterally define Aksai Chin's borders. During the 1950s, China constructed a road through Aksai Chin, connecting Xinjiang and Tibet, which ran south of the Johnson Line in many places. Aksai Chin was easily accessible to the Chinese, but access from India, which meant negotiating the Karakoram mountains, was more problematic. Consequently India did not even learn of the existence of the road until 1957 finally confirmed when the road was shown in Chinese maps published the following year.

The McMahon Line: In 1826 India and China gained a common border, including the area of what is now called Myanmar, following British annexations in the Anglo-Burmese Wars. In 1913, representatives of Great Britain, China and Tibet attended a conference in Simla regarding the borders between Tibet, China and India. Whilst all three representatives initialled the agreement, Beijing later objected to the proposed boundary between the regions of Outer Tibet and Inner Tibet and did not ratify it. The details of the Indo-Tibetan boundary was not revealed to China at the time. The foreign secretary of the Indian government, Henry McMahon, who drew up the proposal, decided to bypass the Chinese (although instructed not to by his superiors) and settle the border bilaterally by negotiating directly with Tibet.

According to later Indian claims, this border was intended to run through the highest ridges of the Himalayas, as the areas south of the Himalayas were traditionally Indian. However, the McMahon Line lay south of the boundary India claims. India's government held the view that the Himalayas were the ancient boundaries of the Indian subcontinent, and thus should be the modern boundaries of India while it is the position of the Chinese government that the disputed area in the Himalayas have been geographically and culturally part of Tibet since ancient times Months after the Simla agreement, China set up boundary markers south of the McMahon Line. T O'Callaghan, an official in the Eastern Sector of the North East Frontier, relocated all these markers to a location slightly south of the McMahon Line, and then visited Rima to confirm with Tibetan officials that there was no Chinese influence in the area.

The British-run Government of India initially rejected the Simla Agreement as incompatible with the Anglo-Russian Convention of 1907, which stipulated that neither party was to negotiate with Tibet except through the intermediary of the Chinese government. The British and Russians cancelled the 1907 agreement by joint consent in 1921. It was not until the late 1930s that the British started to use the McMahon Line on official maps of the region. China took the position that the Tibetan government should not have been allowed to make a such a treaty, rejecting Tibet's claims of independent rule.

For its part, Tibet did not object to any section of the McMahon Line excepting the demarcation of the trading town of Tawang, which the Line placed under British-Indian jurisdiction. However, up until World War II, Tibetan officials were allowed to administer Tawang with complete authority. Due to the increased threat of Japanese and Chinese expansion during this period, British Indian troops secured the town as part of the defence of India's eastern border.

In the 1950s India began actively patrolling the region. It found that, at multiple locations, the highest ridges actually fell north of the McMahon Line. Given India's historic position that the original intent of the Line was to separate the two nations by the highest mountains in the world, in these locations India extended its forward posts northward to the ridges, regarding this move as compliant with the original border proposal, although the Simla Convention did not explicitly state this intention. Indian military historian V.K. Singh argues that the basis of these boundaries, accepted by British India and Tibet, were that the historical boundaries of India were the Himalayas and the areas south of the Himalayas were traditionally Indian and associated with India.

China also cited traditional boundaries as justification for its claims on areas south of the McMahon Line (then part of the North East Frontier Agency). However, according to Singh, these claims were unsupported by anyone other than China. Both sides allege that the other's claims are founded on former imperial demarcations. The Chinese government regards Indian territorial claims as a continuation of imperialistic claims made by British India. Singh notes that India does not claim all areas which were previously under Indian Imperial Rule, such as those lands conquered by the Mauryans or Cholas.

Panchsheel: The Five Principles of Peaceful Coexistence or Panchsheel are a series of agreements between the People's Republic of China and India. After the Central Chinese Government took control of Tibet, China came into increasing conflict with India. However, both nations were newly-established and interested in finding ways to avoid further conflict. Therefore in 1954 the two nations drew up the Five Principles of Peaceful Coexistence:

1. Mutual respect for each other's territorial integrity and sovereignty
2. Mutual non-aggression
3. Mutual non-interference in each other's internal affairs
4. Equality and mutual benefit
5. Peaceful co-existence

The Five Principles of Peaceful Coexistence were first put forth by Premier Zhou Enlai of China at the start of negotiations that took place in Beijing from December 1953 to April 1954 between the Delegation of the Chinese Government and the Delegation of the Indian Government on the relations between the two countries with respect to Tibet.

Later, the Five Principles were formally written into the preface to the "Agreement Between the People's Republic of China and the Republic of India on Trade and Intercourse Between the Tibet Region of China and India" concluded between the two sides. Since June 1954, the Five

Principles were contained in the joint communiqué issued by Premier Zhou Enlai of China and Prime Minister Jawaharlal Nehru of India, and have been adopted in many other international documents. As norms of relations between nations, they have become widely recognized and accepted throughout the world.

Despite the existence of the Panchsheel, continued differences between the two nations led to the Sino-Indian War in 1962. Indian historians have claimed the Panchsheel to be a naïve diplomatic document. Nehru's motivation was that in the absence of either the resources or a policy for defence for the Himalayan region, Indian hope seemed to rest on the premise that establishing a physiological buffer between India and the People's Republic of China would act in place of a physical buffer zone. Thus the catch phrase of India's diplomacy with China in the 1950s was "Hindi-Chini bhai-bhai" which means, in Hindi, "Indians and Chinese are brothers"

Events Leading up to War

Tibet Controversy: Numerous changes occurred in the late 1940s. With the creation of the Republic of India and the separate Islamic Republic of Pakistan in 1947, and the establishment of the People's Republic of China in China in 1949. One of the most basic policies for the Indian government was that of maintaining cordial relations with China. The Indian government wished to revive its ancient friendly ties with China. When the PRC was declared, India was among the first countries to give it diplomatic recognition. After coming to power, the PRC announced that its army would be occupying Tibet. India sent a letter of protest to China proposing negotiations on the Tibet issue. The newly formed PRC was more active in posting troops to the Aksai Chin border than the newly formed Indian republic was.

India decided to take moves to ensure a stable Indo-Chinese border. In August 1950, China expressed its gratitude to Indian attempts to stabilize the Indo-Chinese border.To clear any doubts or ambiguities, Prime Minister Nehru stated in Parliament in 1950 that Indian maps show that the McMahon Line is Indian boundary and that is indian boundary India stand by that boundary and India will not let anyone else come across that boundary.

China expressed no concerns at these statements. By 1951, China had extended numerous posts within Indian claimed territory in Aksai Chin. The Indian government, on the other hand, concentrated its military efforts on stopping Ladakh from being taken by Pakistani troops and did not establish itself in Aksai Chin. On various occasions in 1951 and 1952, however, the government of China expressed the idea that there were no frontier issues between India and Chinese Tibet to be worried about. Later, in September 1951, India declined to attend a conference in San Francisco for the conclusion of a peace treaty with Japan because China, which India viewed as an important factor in this treaty, was not invited because of its status as an international pariah.

In the coming years India strived to become China's representative in world matters, as China had been isolated from many issues. India vigorously pressed, since the start of the 1950s, for the PRC to be included within the UN. The People's Liberation Army defeated the Tibetan army in a battle at Chamdo in 1950 and Lhasa recognized Chinese sovereignty over Tibet in 1951. The Indian army asserted control of Tawang at this time, overcoming some armed resistance and expelling its Tibetan administrators. In 1954, the China and India concluded the Five Principles of Peaceful Coexistence under which India acknowledged Chinese sovereignty in Tibet. Indian negotiators presented a frontier map to the Chinese that included the McMahon Line and the Chinese side did not object.

At this time, the Indian government under Prime Minister Nehru promoted the slogan Hindi-Chini bhai-bhai (India and China are brothers). In 1 July, 1954 Nehru wrote a memo directing that the maps of India be revised to show definite boundaries on all frontiers, where they were previously indicated as undemartcated. The new maps also revised the boundary in the east to show the Himalayan hill crest as the boundary.

In some places, this line is a few kilometres north of the McMahon Line. These new maps also revised the maps to show the countries of Bhutan and Sikkim as part of India. Beginning in 1956, the CIA used Indian Territory to recruit Tibetan guerrillas to fight Chinese troops, with a base in Kalimpong, India. The Indian public was outraged when it learned in 1958 that China had built a road between Xinjiang and Tibet through Indian-claimed territory in Aksai Chin. In 1956, Nehru expressed conern to Zhou Enlai that Chinese maps showed some 120,000 square kilometres of Indian territory as Chinese.

Zhou responded that there were errors in the maps and that they were of little meaning. He stated that the maps needed revising from previous years where such ideas were considered to be true. In November

1956, Zhou again repeated his assurances that he had no claims based on the maps. Tibet disagreements were a major reason for the Sino-Indian conflict. According to John W. Garver, Nehru's policy on Tibet was to create a strong Sino-Indian partnership which would be catalyzed through agreement and compromise on Tibet. Garver believes that Nehru's previous actions (befriending China on such issues as war in Korea, the PRC's U.N. admission, the peace treaty with Japan and transfer of Taiwan to the PRC, Indochina, and decolonization and the Afro-Asian movement) had given Nehru a confidence that China would be ready to form an Asian Axis with India.

Much misunderstanding between the two nations led to diplomatic spats over Tibet, with Nehru's move to accommodate the Dalai Lama overshadowing his other actions and opinions on Tibet, including the opinion that an armed resistance movement in Tibet would be suicidal and counterproductive. While China treated India's concerns with Tibet as expansionist, India's concerns were in fact sentimental and culturally-linked, as Buddhist Tibet had been under influence of Indian culture for many years. Top leader Mao Zedong was humiliated by the reception the Dalai Lama obtained in India when he fled there in March 1959.

The Tibet disagreements heightened in the Chinese media, with Mao himself asking Xinhua News Agency on 19 April, to produce commentary on unknown Indian expansionists operating in Tibet. Mao decided on April 25 to openly criticize Nehru for his Tibet policy. Tensions steadily increased between the two nations when Mao implied that the Lhasa rebellion in Tibet was caused by Indians. On 6 May, 1959, Mao published The Revolution in Tibet and Nehru's Philosophy where he accused Nehru of openly encouraging Tibetan rebels. This publication was evident of China's perception of India has a threat to its rule of Tibet, which became an underlying reason for triggering the Sino-Indian War.

India had become the imperialist enemy, with Nehru and his big bourgeoisie striving to prevent China from exercising full sovereignty over its territory of Tibet to form of a buffer zone. On the same day, Zhou Enlai lashed out at Nehru's class nature. Zhou Enlai stated that Nehru and people from the Indian upper class oppose reform in Tibet, even to the extent of saying that reform is impossible. Tibet to remain for a long time in a backward state, becoming a 'buffer state' between China and India.

This is their guiding mentality, and also the center of the Sino-Indian conflict. India continued negotiations about Tibet. According to the Indian official history, India wished to express goodwill to China and stop the claims of it having a hostile design in Tibet. In August 1959, the Chinese army took an Indian patrol prisoner at Longju, which falls north of the McMahon Line coordinates drawn on the Simla Treaty map (27°44'30''N), but claimed by India to lie directly on the McMahon Line.

There was another bloody clash in October at Kongka Pass in Aksai Chin in which 9 Indian frontier policemen were killed. Recognizing that it was not ready for war, the Indian Army assumed responsibility for the border and pulled back patrols from disputed areas. On October 2, Nikita Khrushchev defended Nehru in a meeting with Mao. The Soviet Union's siding with Nehru, as well as the United States' influence in the region, gave China the belief that it was surrounded by enemy forces.

On 16 October, General Lei Yingfu reported on Indian expansionism on the Thagla Ridge. On 18 October, the Chinese government approved the PLA's plan of a self-defensive counterattack against India because of its actions in Tibet. However, Mao decided against further escalation because he feared that India would retaliate by permitting the U.S. to station U-2 surveillance aircraft on its territory.

This would allow the CIA to photograph China's nuclear test site at Lop Nor in Xinjiang. A few days after Kongka Pass, Chinese Prime Minister Zhou Enlai proposed that each side withdraw 20 kilometres from a Line of Actual Control. He defined this line as the so-called McMahon Line in the east and the line up to which each side exercises actual control in the west. Nehru responded with a proposal to turn the disputed area into a no man's land.

Chinese studies of the 1990s still maintain that India was planning aggression in Tibet. Most Chinese scholars agree that the root cause of the war was India's plan to seize Tibet and turn it into a protectorate or colony of India. The official Chinese history of the war states that Nehru was planning to create a great Indian empire.

It was also insisted that there were right wing nationalist forces that influenced Nehru to pursue the goal of controlling Tibet. Zhao Weiwen, of the Chinese Ministry of State and Security, places emphasis on Nehru's dark mentality. China's policy on Tibet did much to heighten the conflict and tensions between the two nations. The perceptions of India as a capitalist expansionist body intent on the independence of Tibet to create a buffer zone between India proper and China was fundamentally erroneous. The negative rhetoric led to what Zhou himself called the Sino-

Indian conflict. Because of these false fears, China treated the Indian Forward Policy of the 1960s, which India admits as a fundamental mistake, as the beginning of Indian expansionism into Tibet.

Early Incidents: Various border conflicts and military incidents between India and China flared up throughout the summer and fall of 1962. In May, the Indian Air Force was told not to ready itself for war, although it was assessed as being a feasible way to repel the unbalanced ratio of Chinese to Indian troops. In June, a skirmish caused the deaths of dozens of Chinese troops.

The Indian Intelligence Bureau received information about a Chinese buildup along the border which could be a precursor to war. During the period of June- July 1962, the Indian military planners began advocating probing actions against the Chinese, and accordingly, moved mountain troops forward to cut off Chinese supply lines. According to sources, the Indian motives were threefold:

1. Test Chinese resolve and intentions regarding India.
2. Test whether India would enjoy Soviet backing in the event of a Sino-Indian war.
3. Create sympathy for India within the US, with whom relations had deteriorated after the Indian annexation of Goa.

On July 10, 1962, 350 Chinese troops surrounded an Indian post in Chushul but withdrew after a heated argument via loudspeaker. On July 22, the Forward Policy was extended to allow Indian troops to push back Chinese troops already established in disputed territory. Whereas Indian troops were previously ordered to fire only in self-defence, all post commanders were now given discretion to open fire upon Chinese forces if threatened. In August, the Chinese military improved its combat readiness along the McMahon Line and begun stockpiling ammunition, weapons and gasoline.

Showdown at Thag La

In June 1962, Indian forces established an outpost at Dhola, on the southern slopes of the Thag La Ridge. Dhola lay north of the McMahon Line but south of the ridges India maintains the McMahon Line was supposed to represent. In August, China issued diplomatic protests and began occupying positions at the top of Thag La. On 8 September, a 60-strong PLA unit descended to the south side of the ridge and occupied positions that dominated one of the Indian posts at Dhola. Fire was not exchanged but Nehru said to the media that the Indian Army had instructions to free Indian territory and the troops had been given discretion to use force.

On 11 September, it was decided that all forward posts and patrols were given permission to fire on any armed Chinese who entered Indian territory. However, the operation to retake Thagla was flawed in that Nehru's directives were unclear and it got underway very slowly because of this. In addition to this, each man had to carry 35 kg of luggage over the long trek and this severely slowed down the reaction. By the time the Indian battalion reached the point of conflict, Chinese units controlled both banks of the Namka Chu River. The Indian official history states that the Indian troops were given the discretion to fire if a conflict developed between the two sides. On 20 September, Chinese troops threw grenades at Indian troops and a firefight developed, triggering a long series of skirmishes for the rest of September. Some Indian troops, including Brigadier Dalvi who commanded the forces at Thag La, were also concerned that the territory they were fighting for was not strictly territory. According to Neville Maxwell, even members of the Indian defence ministry were categorically concerned with the validity of the fighting in Thag La. On 3 October, a week before the triggering of the war, Zhou Enlai visited Nehru in New Delhi promising there would be no war.

On 4 October, Kaul assigned some troops with securing regions south of the Thagla Ridge Kaul decided to first secure Yumtso La, a strategically important position, before re-entering the lost Dhola post. Kaul had then realized that the attack would be desperate and the Indian government tried to stop escalation into an all-out war. Indian troops travelling to Thagla had suffered in the previously unexperienced conditions. On 10 October, an Indian Punjabi patrol of 50 troops to Yumtso La were met by an emplaced Chinese position of some 1000 soldiers.

Indian troops were in no position for battle, as Yumtso La was 16,000 feet above sea level and Kaul did not plan on having artillery support for the troops. The Chinese troops opened fire on the Indians under their belief that they were north of the McMahon Line. The Indians were surrounded by Chinese positions which used mortar fire.

However, they managed to hold off the first Chinese assault, inflicting heavy casualties. At this point, the Indian troops were in a position to push the Chinese back with mortar and machine gun fire. However, Brigadier Dalvi opted not to fire, as it would mean decimating the Rajput who were still in the area of the Chinese regrouping. They helplessly watched the Chinese ready themselves for a second assault. In the second Chinese assault, the Indians began their retreat, realising the situation was hopeless. The Indian patrol suffered 25 casualties, with the Chinese suffering 33.

The Chinese troops held their fire as the Indians retreated, and then buried the Indian dead with military honors, as witnessed by the retreating soldiers. This was the first occurrence of heavy fighting in the war. This attack had grave implications for India and Nehru tried to solve the issue, but by 18 October it was clear that the Chinese were preparing for an attack on India, with massive troop buildups on the border.

Preparation for War: Two of the major factors leading up to China's eventual conflicts with Indian troops were India's stance on the disputed borders and perceived Indian subversion in Tibet. There was a perceived need to punish and end perceived Indian efforts to undermine Chinese control of Tibet, Indian efforts which were perceived as having the objective of restoring the pre-1949 status quo ante of Tibet The other was a perceived need to punish and end perceived Indian aggression against Chinese territory along the border. Chinese apparently were motivated to attack by one primary consideration—their determination to retain the ground on which PLA forces stood in 1962 and to punish the Indians for trying to take that ground. Another factor which affected China's decision for war with India was a perceived need to stop a Soviet-US-India encirclement and isolation of China.

India's relations with the Soviet Union and United States were both strong at this time, but the Soviets were preoccupied by the Cuban Missile Crisis and would not interfere with the Sino-Indian War. China timed the war exactly in parallel with American actions so as to avoid any chance of American or Soviet involvement. American build-up of forces around Cuba occurred on the same day as the first major clash at Dhola while China's build-up between the 10th and 20th of October coincided exactly with the United States establishment of a blockade against Cuba which began on the 20th of October. Chinese correctly assessed Indian border policies, particularly the Forward Policy, as attempts for incremental seizure of Chinese-controlled territory.

Studies from China published in the 1990s confirmed that the root cause for China going to war with India was the perceived aggression in

Tibet, with the forward policy simply catalyzing the aggressive Chinese reaction. Neville Maxwell and Allen Whiting argue that the Chinese leadership believed they were defending territory they believed to be legitimately Chinese, and which was already under de facto Chinese occupation prior to Indian advances, and regarded the Forward Policy as an Indian attempt at creeping annexation.

Mao Zedong himself compared the Forward Policy to a strategic advance. The motive for the Forward Policy was to cut off the supply routes for Chinese troops posted in NEFA and Aksai Chin. According to the official Indian history, the forward policy was continued because of its initial success, as Chinese troops withdrew when they encountered areas already occupied by Indian troops. The Forward Policy was having success in cutting out supply lines of Chinese troops who had advanced South of the McMahon Line. However, the Forward Policy rested on the assumption that Chinese forces were not likely to use force against any of Indian posts, even if they were in a position to do so.

No serious reappraisal of this policy took place even when Chinese forces ceased withdrawing. By early 1962, the Chinese leadership began to fear that India's intentions were to launch a massive attack against Chinese troops, and that the Indian leadership wanted a war. In 1961, the Indian army had been sent into Goa, a small region without any other international borders apart from the Indian one, after Portugal refused to surrender the exclave colony to the Indian Union. Although this action met little to no international protest or opposition, China saw it as an example of India's expansionist nature, especially in light of heated rhetoric from Indian politicians. India's Home Minister declared, If the Chinese will not vacate the areas occupied by it, India will have to repeat what she did in Goa. India will certainly drive out the Chinese forces, while another member of the Indian Congress Party pronounced, India will take steps to end aggression on Indian soil just as she ended Portuguese aggression in Goa. By mid-1962, it was apparent to the Chinese leadership that negotiations had failed to make any progress, and the Forward Policy was increasingly perceived as a grave threat as Delhi increasingly sent probes deeper into border areas and cut off Chinese supply lines.

Foreign Minister Marshal Chen Yi commented at one high-level meeting, Nehru's forward policy is a disaster for Chinese. The Chinese leadership believed that their restraint on the issue was being perceived by India as weakness, leading to continued provocations, and that a major counterblow was needed to stop perceived Indian aggression. Xu Yan, prominent Chinese military historian and professor at the PLA's National Defence University, gives an account of the Chinese leadership's decision to go to war.

By late September 1962, the Chinese leadership had begun to reconsider their policy of armed coexistence, which had failed to address their concerns with the forward policy and Tibet, and consider a large, decisive strike.

Military Planning: The Indian side was confident war would not be triggered and made little preparations. India had only two divisions of troops in the region of the conflict. In August 1962, Brigadier D.K. Palit claimed that a war with China in the near future could be ruled out. Even in September 1962, when Indian troops were ordered to expel the Chinese from Thag La, Maj. General J.S. Dhillon expressed the opinion that experience in Ladakh had shown that a few rounds fired at the Chinese would cause them to run away.

Because of this, the Indian army was completely unprepared when the attack at Yumtso La occurred. India's estimates of Chinese capabilities made them neglect their military in favour of economic growth. It is claimed that if a more military-minded man had been in place instead of Nehru, India would have been more likely to have been ready for the threat from China. The Chinese leadership and the Central Military Council decided upon war to launch a large-scale attack to punish perceived military aggression from India. In Beijing, a larger meeting of Chinese military was convened in order to plan for the coming conflict. The Mao and the Chinese leadership issued a directive laying out the objectives for the war. A main assault would be launched in the eastern sector, which would be coordinated with a smaller assault in the western sector.

All Indian troops within China's claimed territories in the eastern sector would be expelled, and the war would be ended with a unilateral Chinese ceasefire and withdrawal to prewar positions, followed by a return to the negotiating table. Diplomatically, Mao acknowledged possible diplomatic isolation as the Soviet Union, the United States, the Republic of China and other misinformed countries would oppose China's actions. India led the Non-Aligned Movement, Nehru enjoyed international prestige, and China, with a larger military would be portrayed as an aggressor.

However, he said that a well-fought war will guarantee at least thirty years of peace with India, and determined the benefits to offset the costs On 8 October, additional veteran and high-quality divisions were ordered to prepare to move into Tibet from the Chengdu and Lanzhou military regions. Marshal Liu Bocheng headed a group to determine the strategy for the war. He concluded that the opposing Indian troops were among India's best, and to achieve victory would require deploying crack troops and relying on force concentration to achieve decisive victory. On 16 October, this war plan was approved, and on the 18th, the final approval was given by the Politburo for a self defensive counter-attack, scheduled for 20 October.

Chinese Offensive

Eastern Theatre: Namka Chu a name seared in Indian memory, a place where the decisions made by a pacifist Prime Minister, an arrogant Defence Minister and a politically connected General caused the rout of a proud Brigade with many of its men dying like animals in a cage. Namka Chu, a gorge situated east of the remote Tri Junction of Tibet, Bhutan and India. It is 200 km from the railhead of Misamari and 60 km from the road head of Tawang. The Nyamjang river flows through from Tibet and enters India at Khinzemane. It meets Namka Chu 1½ miles south of Khinzemane. Local grazers used seven improvised bridges to take their cattle across the Namka Chu. They were from East to West known as Number I - V, Log bridge and Temporary bridge. Following Hathung La route to Dhola Post, the track hit Bridge I. Across it the track forked, the eastward branch reached Khinzemane, the one going North West along the river and re-crossing to the South across Bridge II. This led to Dhola Post opposite Bridge III. A little away was Bridge IV and close to Tsangle was Bridge V. Between IV and V were the Log and Temporary bridges. The bridges were useless when the river was in spate. In October one could walk across the river bed. The Thagla ridge which sprawls from west to east overlooks Namka Chu and has four prominent passes Dum Dum La (17,000 feet), Karpola II (16,000 feet), Yamatso La (16,000 feet) and Thag La (14,000 feet).

To get to Tawang the road traverses from Misamari up to 2743 metres to a place called Eagle's Nest, another 200 metres to Bomdi La. Then it drops to 1676 metres to Dirang Dzong, followed by an ascent to Se La at 4180 metres, another drop to 1524 metres to Jang with a final climb to Tawang (3048) metres. From here the journey had to be along tracks with mules and porters. There were no staging areas for acclimatization. The dispute in this area revolved around Thagla Ridge. The Chinese claimed it was on the Tibetan side and India claimed it was on its side of the McMahon line.

Accordingly in 1959 an Assam Rifles post was established at Khinzemane. The Chinese disputed it and a force of 200 Chinese pushed back the weak Indian force towards the bridge on the Nyamjang Chu at Drokung Samba which they claimed was the McMahon line. After the Chinese retired the Indians again reoccupied the post. The Chinese again tried to dislodge but this time were resisted by the Assam Rifles.

This time they withdrew and started a chain diplomatic exchanges between the two Governments. Under Nehru's forward policy some extra posts were ordered to be deployed on the McMahon line. One such post was proposed at the Tri junction. A party under Captain Mahabir Prasad from 1 Sikh went to locate the post. However due to heavy snowfall it could not access it, so they located the post at Che Dong on the southern bank of the Namka Chu. While the post was dominated by the surrounding area, it was easy to maintain with access to water. However this should have been a temporary post and should have been relocated at a later time. For some reason it never was. An Assam Rifles unit was sent to man it. On September 8th, Chinese troops laid siege to the Assam Rifles post. In order to get a quick response the post commander inflated the number to 600 enemy troops. In many other places similar situations were met with an order to stay put. Probably because the higher number, the 7th Inf Bde were ordered to move in and evict the Chinese. The 7th Brigade was part of 4th Division commanded by Major General Niranjan Prasad. At this time two battalions of 7th Brigade, the 9 Punjab and 1 Sikh were in Towang, the 1/9 Gorkha Rifles in Misamari on its way back after a 3-year tenure in NEFA. There was no airfield and all maintenance was by air drops. Raw and un-acclimatized troops with cotton uniforms and canvas shoes were sent into the mountains. All this was done under public clamour and alerted the Chinese.

The first man to protest was Lt. Gen. Umrao Singh. When Lt. Gen. Sen in charge of Eastern Command refused to heed his advice, he followed it up with a written protest. The 7th Inf. Bde. was commanded by Brigadier J.P. Dalvi and consisted of 9 Punjab, 4 Grenadiers, 2 Rajputs and 1/9 Gorkha Rifles plus some symbolic artillery. 9 Punjab was led by Lt. Col. R.N. Mishra. With harvesting time in the region the men had to move everything by themselves for the long arduous trek. Each man carried one blanket, 100 rounds of ammo, 2 grenades, 3 days rations and

LMG clips. It came to 35 kg per person. After a forced march it reached Bridge 1 on September 14. Next morning leaving one company behind at Bridge I, Lt. Col. Mishra took the rest to Bridge II, where a company of Chinese troops was in position both sides of Namka Chu. Ignoring the Chinese shouts in Hindi to go back, he left two companies about 50 metres away and took the last one to the Che Dong post.

The logs at Bridge II were destroyed and a 50-man Chinese detachment occupied the opposite side. The next night the Punjabis at Bridge II crept in close forcing the Chinese to move most of their troops to the north bank. Meanwhile Lt. Gen. Umrao Singh's protests were causing a problem for the Government and the Army HQ. To avoid the impasse, General Thapar and Lt. Gen. Sen formed 4 Corps to handle NEFA leaving 33 Corps with Lt. Gen. Umrao Singh. Lt. Gen. B.M. Kaul was put in charge of 4 Corps - an most unusual step for a Chief of General Staff (CGS) to to do with direct access to the Prime Minister. Lt. Gen. Kaul took charge on October 4th. Meanwhile 2 Rajput and 1/9 Gorkha Rifles had reached Lumpu. The men were in cotton uniforms, canvas shoes and were living in the open after marching through slushy roads. The 4 Grenadiers who had arrived at Tawang a few days earlier were in no better shape. The buildup of troops to Tsangdhar was slow. There were no porters and everything had to back packed. Furthermore poor planning in the air drops did not help. Instead of snow clothes & ammo they got tent pegs, kerosene was dropped in 200L barrels. Many rolled down slopes and although some could be retrieved, many were given up. Especially high were losses from drops by C119s due to the higher speed of the aircraft. Meanwhile two platoons of MMGs from 6 Mahar and 34 Heavy Mortar Regiment reached Lumpu.

The mortars had no ammo. A little later four 75mm guns of the 17 Field Parachute regiment were dropped at Tsangdhar. On October 6th, Lt. Gen. Kaul and Maj. Gen. Prasad made their way to Namka Chu. The Brigade HQ was located at Rongla and Tactical HQ at Zimithang. The troops were extended on a frontage of 12 miles or 20,000 yards - more than 6 times their normal frontage. Furthermore the Corps, Divisional and Brigade commanders were all there. Lt. Gen. Kaul now seeing for himself the deathtrap set up for the Indian troops tried get all available resources. He sent a message to Eastern Command for marshalling of all military and air resources. Late in the game Lt. Gen. Kaul realised what he had gotten into and was now desperate. The Govt. however was not ready to escalate the border clash into an all out war. Meanwhile the

Grenadiers, Rajput and Gorkhas were on the way to Tsangdhar. The units had marched through severe cold, with groups of 3 men sharing 2 sheets. As mentioned they were in cotton uniforms resulting in a good deal of sick casualties frostbite and pulmonary disorders.

So Lt. Gen. Kaul now turned to his pet 'positional warfare' theory while Major General Prasad and Brigadier Dalvi wanted to find a way from their untenable position. The Chinese meanwhile had advantage of position and had now mustered up to a division at Thagla.So Lt. Gen. Kaul set his plans in motion on the morning of October 8th. He decided that 2 Rajput would occupy Yamatso La west of Thag La peak as it was unoccupied using the Tseng-Jong approach. Brigadier Dalvi was stunned. The plan meant moving a battalion to a peak 16,000 feet above sea level under Chinese view with no artillery support. Brigadier Dalvi convinced Lt. Gen. Kaul to at least send a patrol of 9 Punjab to find a suitable crossing place for the Rajputs and cover them by taking positions at Tseng Jong.

The Rajputs, less one company, left behind at Bridge 1 were to advance on first light October 10th. The patrol of 9 Punjab led by Major Choudhary left on October 8th and established itself by 3 p.m. Meanwhile two companies of the 2 Rajput was in the Bridge 4 area with the rest at Dhola post. It was as unprepared with only 90 sleeping bags, no ammo for its 3 mortars. Meanwhile the close proximity between Chinese and Indian troops caused skirmishes. A grenade attack on September 20th on the Punjabis, was met with effective retaliation. 4 Punjabis were wounded and 1 Chinese was killed. October 9th passed uneventfully except for a grenade attack in the Bridge 4 area. One more platoon from the 9 Punjab had reinforced the Tseung Jong area and one section from it, was stationed at the spur of Karpo La II. October 10th dawned without a hint of what was to come. At first light, Lt. Gen. Kaul was shaving while his batman was preparing tea. Suddenly the calm of the morning was shattered by the incessant fire of small arms fire and the thumps of mortars. The Tseung Jong position had come under fire and was retaliating. Around 8 00 a.m., 600 Chinese troops attacked the post. The Indians totaled 56 men with only pouch ammunition. Still they beat back the first assault. Around 9 30 a.m. the Chinese attacked a second time. By now the section at Karpo La II had moved to the flank of the Chinese. When the Chinese emerged, it opened up on them inflicting heavy casualties. The Chinese retaliated by bringing down mortar fire. As the first fire rang out the Rajputs were strung on the Southern bank of the

Namka Chu. According to their orders they were hurrying up to Yamatso La. The forward company was about 450 meters from the Temporary bridge with Lt. Col. Maha Singh Rikh following behind with the second company. Lt. Gen. Kaul now proceeded to give another order.

He asked Lt. Col. Rikh to hold on and set defensive positions. Protests about the positions being dominated by the Thag La ridge were brushed aside. He then left handing over command to Brigadier Dalvi saying, It is your battle. Moreover a company of the 1/9 Gorkhas had to accompany the party to provide protection. Meanwhile Major Chaudhary was asking for mortar and machine gun fire. Brigadier Dalvi had two mortars and two machine guns but he had to make the painful decision of not opening fire as the retaliatory fire from the south bank would decimate the Rajputs who were still milling around. Helplessly they watched the Chinese reinforcements clamber up for a second attack. The Chinese attacked a third time from three directions and at this time Major Chaudhary asked the unit to withdraw. By that time the Chinese were on Major Chaudhary's position, hand-to-hand combat was in process. Somehow he withdrew what was left of his two platoons. Sepoy Kanshi Ram brought back a AK-47 snatched from a Chinese soldier. The withdrawal was made possible by the gallantry of Naik Chain Singh. Asking his men to fall back, Naik Singh covered their withdrawal with an LMG, till he was gunned down by a machine gun burst. Major Chaudhary, Sepoy Ram and Naik Singh were awarded the Maha Vir Chakra. The Punjabis outnumbered 20 to 1 lost 6 dead, 11 wounded and 5 missing. Peking Radio admitted to a 100 casualties. Later that day the Chinese buried dead Indian army men with full military honours in view of Indian army men. It was a clever move to beguile the Indians into complacency.

Meanwhile the Chinese started reinforcing their positions with more troops and heavy mortars. A long line of mules and porters were seen carrying equipment. Firing lines were cleared with mechanical saws, and barbed wire & punji sticks used to defend their positions. Meanwhile the Grenadiers, led by Lt. Col. K.S. Harihar Singh, arrived and started deploying. The Chinese taunted them for their efforts to cut trees with machetes and digging tools. Attempts to withdraw the Punjabis from Tsangle were rebuffed by Lt. Gen. Kaul. The Lt. Gen. who was sick, instead of giving up his command and admitting himself to the hospital, went to his residence and commanded from from his sick bed. In the Army of 1962 this no longer seemed strange. On October 18th the Chinese preparations intensified. Officers were holding conferences and pointing out Indian positions at Namka Chu and Tsangdhar. Bearings were taken and noted down. Tsangle Post and Bridge V came under fire for 90 minutes. With a foot of snow falling, Brigadier Dalvi was forced to take whatever snow clothes from the men at Namka Chu and give it to those in Tsangle. A company of the 1/9 Gorkha Rifles was ordered to be deployed at Tsangle. Brigadier Dalvi protested at this piece meal deployment but was threatened with a court martial. The next day the Chinese activities climaxed. The Rajputs counted 2000 men with stores in the area between Tseng-Jong and Temporary Bridge. Mules and porters came across Thag La.

Men were laying tape markers for night assaults. Brigadier Dalvi protested again asking to withdraw his men from this death-trap. He offered to resign, rather than watch his men get massacred. Brigadier Dalvi thought the attack was going to come the next day and in three days his brigade would be wiped out. Major General Prasad promised he will be there the next day to share the fate of the brigade. So by October 19th the troops were deployed.

Against this the Chinese forces consisted of 11th Division with 3 regiments (equal to a brigade). On the night of the 19th the Chinese went into their forming up areas. In utter contempt of the Indians across the river, they lit fires to warm themselves. To Major Gurdial, the 2-in-C of the 2 Rajputs, the idea of his under strength battalion fighting the hardened veterans of the Korean War seemed suicidal. He looked around at his isolated weak companies, un-acclimatized & weak, 150 rds/rifleman, 17 magazines (28 rounds) per LMG and 2 grenades per soldier. The battalion's 3 mortars had 60 rounds of ammo, equal to five minutes firing time. The night was dark and bitter cold. The stars stood out brightly. The sentries of 2 Rajput stood wrapped in blankets shuffling around to keep warm. The men were huddled in twos and threes for warmth. Still sleep eluded them as they waited for the stand to at 0430 hours. Unknown to them in the thousands of yards that separated the posts, with visibility under 20 yards, Chinese infantry columns were infiltrating through the large gaps. Fording the river was easy. To avoid slipping they removed their shoes and walked barefoot across. Once across they dried and wore warm socks.

They quickly moved past the link roads where Indian patrols might operate. The overhead communication wires were left alone to be cut just before the attack so that the Indians may not be alerted. Once in the dark shadows of the coniferous forests the noises were muffled by the thick moss on rocks. Slowly the Chinese columns gathered into battalions. Each got into a position above and behind the Rajput companies. Other columns likewise moved to the Tsangdhar position to take on the Gorkhas. Other Chinese columns had moved 2 nights before and gone to Hathung La to carry out blocking movements. The fires and other activity of the earlier nights had kept the defenders focus on the front. The plan was to hit like a battering ram at the centre, into the Rajputs, and the left flank and cutting off the rest of the troops. At 4 30 hours Lt. Col. Rikh was woken up by his batman. Outside the temp was well below zero and the fires lit by the Chinese still flickered. His adjutant, Captain Bhatia, who was to be posted to Poona soon was checking with the companies & patrols and they reported all was well.

The first pre dawn light could be seen when the darkness was broken by the hollow booming sound of mortars. The muzzle flashes were followed by a pause before the valley erupted in a roar. It was 0514 hours and the Battle of Namka Chu had begun. At 5 14 a.m. 150 guns and mortars opened upon all the localities at Namka Chu and Tsangdhar. The 82mm and 120mm rounds crashed into trees & rocks, forcing the men in the open to take refuge in the bunkers whose firing bays faced forwards. It continued for an hour, as the Indians helplessly watched unable to counter it with any weapon. The Indian 3 mortars made an futile attempt to fire back. Even as they tried to get the range right, the Chinese ranged in on them and blew them away. The signals bunker was zeroed in quickly using 75mm recoilless guns, and blown up, killing all in it including Captain Mangat - the Signals Officer. After an hour or so there was a brief lull for 7 - 15 minutes before the Chinese bugles and whistles for an infantry attack became audible.

To the shock of the defenders, the attack was from above and behind. This meant their trenches were exposed and they had to scramble out of their bunker to face upwards. At Temporary Bridge, Subedar Dashrath Singh realised what was happening and moved Naik Roshan Singh's section to a bump 150 yards upslope. Barely had Roshan's men taken position when the Chinese came into view. With AK-47s opening up, they charged. Roshan and his men poured fire into the bunched up Chinese cutting down many. 2nd Lt Onkar Dubey with 7th platoon along with Subedar Janam Singh rushed with 15 LMG clips and 2 men to support Roshan. From the flanks he and his men poured fire on the Chinese breaking up two attacks. Firing the last 2 clips at the enemy he was severely wounded in the stomach & chest and fell down unconscious. He was later taken prisoner.

Meanwhile Subedar Dashrath Singh's men turned uphill and opened fire on the advancing Chinese. The Chinese rushed down using cover from tree to tree. Dashrath and his men repulsed 3 attacks. On the fourth they came in to hand-to-hand combat losing four more men. Subedar Dashrath fell unconscious and was taken POW. On the eastern flank, Major B.K. Pant's D Coy platoon under Jemadar J.N. Bose came under attack. The crescendo of AK-47 fire overshadowed the noise of Indian LMGs and rifles. Roshan's unit was finally overcome with every man killed. The attention now turned to Jemadar Bose's platoon. After three waves of assault there were only 10 men surviving. The gallant Bengali led the remaining men into a bayonet charge. Most of the men were killed. Major B.K. Pant meanwhile tried to rally the men. Hit at the beginning of the battle in the leg he had to take over after Major Sethi was killed in the first round of mortar attacks which collapsed his bunker.

Hobbling from position to position he kept inspiring his men on. He was hit again in the stomach and leg. Still he continued to inspire his men to break a fourth attack. At this point the enemy targeted him and hit him all over with machine gun fire. He uttered the Regiment's war cry before his last breath. Meanwhile at Log Bridge, B Company was having its own problems. As the first shells landed, Lt. Subhash Chander reacted quickly and turned his men around to face uphill. However a salvo of mortar shells set fire to his command post as well as the company kitchen. The resulting fire to ghee & wheat engulfed the post trapping him inside and burning him to death. Subedar Har Lal, of 5th platoon, now rallied his men quickly dispersing them amongst the trees and rocks. He kept exhorting his men and when ammo ran out asked them to use their rifles as lathis. Jemadar Gian Chand's 4th platoon too got a few minutes to get into position amongst the trees.

They held of 3 waves of attacks before he too was overwhelmed. With Subedar Mohan Lal killed early in the battle only Naik Hoshiar with 6th platoon was left. With the other two platoons absorbing the first few attacks, 6th platoon got more time to get into position. Using their Lee Enfield.303s they inflicted heavy damage. In spite of firing upwards, the Rajputs were effective because the ricocheting bullets continued to drop the Chinese. Little by little the superior volume of the Chinese AK-47s overwhelmed the Indians. With ammunition running out the Chinese moved in. Each and every soldier had to be overcome by hand-to-hand to combat. Percussion grenades were extensively used. As Naik Hoshiar ran out of ammo he grabbed a Sten gun and was trying to reload when a percussion grenade exploded, hitting him in the arms & chest. As he regained consciousness, he found four Chinese holding him. A services wrestler, Naik Hoshiar struggled for some time before being overpowered. Meanwhile the area under Bridge IV continued to get pounded with the Btn HQ getting special attention. Major Gurdial, 2-in-C, under mortar fire rallied his men around.

Seeing no enemy activity across the river he realised the attack was coming from uphill. Frantically he tried to set the Vickers MG around to face uphill. Men were being hurried out of bunkers to face uphill. Lt. Bhup Singh joined up with Lt. Col. Rikh in the Btn command post. The full brunt of the attack struck Lt. Bhup's 12th platoon under Jemadar Biswas, the Btn command post in the centre and Subedar Ram Chander's C platoon to the east. The bunched up Chinese were cut down by volley's of rifle and LMG fire. Yet the Chinese continued to attack. The advantage of the Ak-47s along with HE and percussion grenades thrown down proved decisive. The Indians had to throw uphill, a task much harder. As the men in the upper slopes struggled, some of the men in the lower slopes started withdrawing towards Bridge III including the 11 platoon led by Subedar B.C. Roy. Meanwhile the now depleted C Coy and the Btn HQ had held off two attacks.

The Chinese attacked a third time from the south and south west. With Major Gurdial rallying them, they desperately tried to fight back but succumbed to the inevitable. Major Gurdial was overpowered and captured. With the flanking platoons almost wiped out to a man the remnants fell back to the battalion bunker. Captain Bhatia and Lt. Col. Rikh and a few others were now in the bunker. The Chinese opened up with a machine gun trying to break through the bunker. When that failed, a Chinese soldier crawled up to the bunker and threw a grenade just as Lt. Col. Rikh was peeping out. The grenade hit his rifle and exploded, breaking his jaw and cutting his lips. Lt. Bhup rushed out and shot the Chinese soldier and dragged Lt. Col. Rikh back in. He was propped up and given an LMG to resume firing. Another Chinese LMG burst through the door killing Captain Bhatia and hit Lt. Col. Rikh again in the shoulder breaking it. He however managed to gun down the Chinese soldier. Yet another Chinese broke through and rounds hit him in the elbow and leg, consequently breaking them.

The pain and loss of blood caused him to collapse. Lt. Bhup continued to hold them off with one jawan. The Chinese had now encircled three sides and were pouring machine gun fire. Finally the defenders' ammunition ran out. On this the Chinese threw percussion grenades and overpowered Lt. Bhup and the jawan. The fourth and last locality, Bridge 3, was held by A company with a platoon of Assam Rifles holding the Che Dong are. The Assam Rifles held the top of the spur while 2 platoons No.1 and No.2, held the lower slopes 600 hundred feet below. A 3rd platoon held a position another 800 feet lower overlooking Bridge 3. The initial hour long shelling drove the Assam Rifles unit from the post. As the shelling lifted Captain Ravi Eipe began to move towards the Assam Rifles post to get a better view. As he approached there was firing from the post. Thinking it was the AR men firing in panic he shouted out. Soon he saw some figures in khaki and realised the Chinese had already taken over the post. He alerted Company Havildar Major Saudagar Singh's men to reposition themselves just as the attack began. The Chinese then attacked from the top and the West. Facing them were the 2 platoons of CHM Singh and Subedar Basdeo Singh. CHM Saudagar's men had reorganized and took a heavy toll on the attacking Chinese. CHM Singh himself snatched an AK-47 from a Chinese soldier and blew away 5 Chinese soldiers.

By 0700 hours the platoons were being swarmed by Chinese troops. 1 platoon got cut off and fought to the death. Captain Eipe was hit on the shoulder and could not take any further part. The remnants of the battered 2 and 3rd platoons were asked to withdraw. With this the last Rajput position was overrun. Temporary and Log Bridge were overpowered and the systematic mopping up began. The attack had begun at 5 14 a.m. with the shelling lasting till 6 30 a.m. By 9 30 a.m. mopping operations were in full swing till it ended at 11 30 a.m. The main positions of 1/9 Gorkha Rifles were above Che Dong on a track from the Assam Rifles post. 'D' Coy held the central location with 'A' and 'C' Coy on either side. The fourth company was above bridge II protecting the Brigade HQ. As the Gorkhas were getting into their morning stand, the first salvo of Chinese shells hit their positions. As the officers scrambled to figure the situations they found the telephone lines were dead.

Now the Chinese who had infiltrated past them in the last 2 nights launched their attack. The Gorkhas fought back. Their 3 mortars opened up only to be silenced by the Chinese guns. By 6 25 a.m., C Coy was under attack by 500 Chinese troops. Company Commander, Captain

Gambhir, was killed and 2nd Lt. Dogra, platoon commander, was wounded. Lt. Col. Ahluwalia asked Subedar Major Jit Bahdur Chetri to take his men and reinforce 2nd Lt. Dogra's platoon. By 7 15 a.m. 2nd Lt. Dogra's platoon was overrun. Wounded, he continued to fight with an LMG allowing the remnants of his platoon to fall back. Subedar Dhan Bahadur Chand also covered with an LMG.

By 7 30 a.m., A Coy was under attack from rear as well as the front. Lt. Col. Ahluwalia was wounded in the shoulder as hand-to-hand fighting began. With no hope, the CO ordered a withdrawal towards Tsangdhar. Meanwhile word came of Subedar Chetri's platoon being encircled and captured. Captain Mahabir Prasad and Lt. Mahindra were wounded and missing. The Gorkhas fell back in confusion. One lot went towards the Tsangdhar track the other towards Bridge II. Many of the attempts to reach Karpo La II or Rong La were thwarted by the Chinese who got there ahead of them. Even at this point there were defiant attacks of bravery. Subedar Bhab Bahadur Katwal with 15 men was heading for Karpo La I. The route was blocked by a Chinese MMG. Subedar Bahadur lead his men in a charge with the Gorkha war cry, *Ayo Gorkhali* (The Gorkhas have come). The machine gun chattered and then there was silence. All the men were killed or wounded & captured. Small parties of men however did make it across the Chinese encirclement and reached Bhutan. Many others perished due to the cold & starvation as they tried to make their way in the cold, hostile and desolate mountains with no blankets or winter clothing.

The Sikh Para Gunners also displayed an astonishing defiance. With no ammo they took up LMGs & rifles and fought the Chinese after the Gorkha platoons were overrun. The Chinese encircled them and called them to surrender. They refused and continued fighting till they ran out of ammo. One third were killed and the rest were wounded and captured. 7th Brigade had lost all cohesion within the first hour of the battle. By 8 a.m. the first stragglers of the 1/9 Gorkha's came back to HQs with news that the Btn was overrun. This meant his middle & left defences were already broken. Small arms fire was now homing in on Brigade HQ. Brigadier Dalvi now got Div HQ's permission to leave Rong La and fall back to Tsangdhar hoping to reform and fight. The Rajputs and Gorkhas were expected to fall back to Tsangdhar. Brigadier Dalvi and his men left for Tsangdhar after destroying all documents. However they soon found that Tsangdhar was already breached and changed directions to Serkhim. The group wandered around for days avoiding Chinese patrols.

At one point they had been without food for 66 hours. Sometime on the morning of October 22nd they ran into a Chinese Company and were captured. At Bridge II, the 9 Punjab had not been shelled.

After communications with Brigade HQ was cut off, they remained in touch with Div HQ. At 11 a.m. on October 20th, Major General Prasad ordered them to withdraw to Hathung La. The withdrawal attracted heavy Chinese mortar fire. This was followed by an attack on the positions of 'D' Coy under Major Chaudhary. Once again repeated attacks collapsed the defence and all the men went down fighting. Another group of 20 men under Havildar Malkiat Singh were on their way to reinforce the Tsangla defences. They stumbled into a large Chinese force. In the unequal encounter, the Punjabis inflicted heavy casualties before going down. Havildar Singh was amongst those who were killed. With the Chinese reaching Hathung La before the Punjabis, they too had to take the route through Bhutan. At Drokung Samba, C Coy of Grenadiers came under attack from three sides by a battalion of the Chinese. Soon the bridge was blown up cutting off any withdrawal. With no hopes, the men under 2nd Lt. Rao fought wave after wave of attacks. Most including the 2nd Lt. Rao were killed. The rest of the Grenadiers at Bridge received orders to pull out and managed to escape through Bhutan.

It took them 17 days. Thus ended the Battle of Namka Chu. The word 'battle' is grossly misleading, for what was essentially a massacre. Within the first hour of the battle 7th Brigade had lost all cohesiveness. It was then essentially a desperately one-sided battle with many Indian platoons fighting to the death, to the last round, last man. The 2 Rajputs suffered horrendously but lived up to the Regiment's reputation. Of the 513 all ranks, 282 were killed that morning, 81 were wounded and captured, 90 were captured unwounded. Only 60 men, mostly rear elements got away. The Gorkhas lost 80 dead, 44 wounded and 102 captured. The 7th Brigade lost a total of 493 men that morning. The Chinese also lost heavily. Lt. Col. Rikh was captured & subjected to repeated interrogations on the characteristics of the Rajputs. He was told it was because the Chinese suffered their maximum casualties in NEFA.

Western Theatre: On the Aksai Chin front, China already controlled most of the disputed territory. China quickly and efficiently got rid of remnants of Indian troops. On 20 October, operations in the Chip Chap Valley, Galwan Valley, and Pangong Lake were successful for the PLA. Many outposts and garrisons comprised were unable to defend against the surrounding Chinese troops. Most Indian troops positioned in these posts fought and were either killed or taken prisoner. India did not support its troops, as the Galwan post had been surrounded by China in August and had received no land support from India since then. After the October 20 attack, this post was not heard from again. Late on 19 October, Chinese troops launched various attacks throughout the western theatre. By 22 October, all posts north of Chushul had been cleared. Later on 24 October, there was a battle on the Rezang La Ridge to defend an air strip from impending Chinese takeover. After realizing the magnitude of the attack, Indian Western Command withdrew many of the isolated outposts to the south-east.

Daulet Beg Oldi was also evacuated, but it was south of the Chinese claim line and was not approached by Chinese forces. Indian troops were withdrawn so that they could regroup and be ready if China probed south of their claim line. Indian forces were hampered by their significant inferiority in numbers and lack of combat readiness. The PLA overran most Indian posts with ease after their experience in the Korean War. The Indian deployment was sparsely put and needed new commanders in the second phase of the war.

Break in the Fighting

By October 24th, the PLA had entered territory previously administered by India to give the PRC a diplomatically strong position over India. The majority of Chinese forces had advanced sixteen kilometres south of the border. Four days of fighting were followed a three-week lull. Zhou ordered the troops to stop advancing as he attempted to negotiate with Nehru. The Indian forces had retreated into more heavily fortified positions around Se La and Bombdi La which would be difficult to assault. Zhou sent Nehru a letter, proposing

1. A negotiated settlement of the boundary
2. That both sides disengage and withdraw twenty kilometers from present lines of actual control
3. A Chinese withdrawal north in NEFA
4. That China and India not cross lines of pre-sent control in Aksai Chin.

Nehru's 27 October reply expressed interest in the restoration of peace and friendly relations and suggested a return to the boundary prior to 8 September, 1962. He was categorically concerned about a mutual twenty kilometer withdrawal after 40 or 60 kilometers of blatant military aggression. He wanted the creation of a larger immediate buffer zone and thus resist the possibility of a repeat offensive. Zhou's November 4th reply repeated his 1959 offer to return to the McMahon Line in NEFA and the Chinese traditionally claimed MacDonald Line in Aksai Chin. Facing Chinese forces maintaining themselves on Indian soil and trying to avoid political pressure, the Indian parliament announced a national emergency and passed a resolution which stated their intent to drive out the aggressors from the sacred soil of India.

The United States and the United Kingdom supported India's response, however the Soviet Union was preoccupied with the Cuban Missile Crisis and did not offer the support it had provided in previous years. With the backing of other great powers, a 14 November letter by Nehru to Zhou once again rejected his proposal. Neither side declared war, used their air force, or fully broke off diplomatic relations however, the conflict is commonly referred to as a war. This war coincided with the Cuban Missile Crisis and was viewed by the western nations at the time as another act of aggression by the Communist bloc. According to Calvin, the Chinese side evidently wanted a diplomatic resolution and discontinuation of the conflict.

Continuation of War

After Zhou received Nehru's letter, the war restarted. The fighting resumed on the eastern theater on 14 November with an Indian attack on Walong, claimed by China, launched from the defensive position of Se La. The Indians were stopped 50 meters away from the crest and were comprehensively defeated by the Chinese counteroffensive. The Chinese resumed military activity on Aksai Chin and NEFA hours after the Walong battle.

Eastern Theatre: On the eastern theatre, the PLA attacked Indian forces near Se La and Bomdi La on November 17th. These positions were defended by the Indian 4th Division. Instead of attacking by road as expected, PLA forces approached via a mountain trail, and their attack cut off a main road and isolated 10,000 Indian troops. Following a battle, the Indians were ordered to begin a retreat to regroup. However, the orderly Indian retreat was cut down into chaos and none of the Indians were seen until three weeks later.

Se La was very high and faced with this strategic problem the Chinese captured Thembang, which was a supply route to Se La. The

PLA forces proceeded to ambush the comanderless 4th Division and added another comprehensive victory to their tally.

Western Theatre: On the western theatre, PLA forces launched a heavy infantry attack on 18 November near Chushul. Their attack started at 4 35 am, despite a mist surrounding most of the areas in the region. At 5 45 the Chinese troops advanced to attack 2 platoons of Indian troops at Gurung Hill.The Indians did not know what was happening, as communications were dead. As a patrol was sent, China attacked with greater numbers. Indian artillery, shells and MMGs could not hold off against a large Chinese wave. By 9 00 am, Chinese forces attacked Gurung Hill directly and Indian commanders withdrew from the area. The Chinese had been simultaneously attacking Rezang La. Rezang La was held by 118 Indian troops. At 5 05 am, Chinese troops launched their attack audaciously. Chinese Medium machine gun fire pierced through the Indian tactical defences. At 6 55 am the sun rose and the Chinese attack on the 8th platoon began in waves. Fighting continued for the next hour, until the Chinese signalled that they had destroyed the 7th platoon. Indians tried to use light machine guns on the medium machine guns from the Chinese but after 10 minutes the battle was over.

Logistical inadequacy once again hurt the Indian troops The Chinese gave the Indian troops a respectful military funeral. The battles also saw the death of Major Shaitan Singh of the Kumaon Regiment, who had been instrumental in victory in the first battle of Rezang La. Kumaoni stand at the Rezang La showed the unintimidated resilience of India against invading China. With many casualties inflicted, the Indian troops withdrew to high mountain positions. Indian sources believed that their troops were just coming to grips with the mountain combat and finally let go of their pride and called for more troops.

However, the Chinese declared a ceasefire, ending the bloodshed. Both sides suffered heavy casualties, with dead Indian troops bodies being found in the ice, frozen with weapons in hand. This signalled the end of the war in Aksai Chin as China had reached their claim line - many Indian troops were ordered to withdraw from the area China claimed but the Indian troops wanted to fight on until the bitter end. However, the war ended with their withdrawal, so as to limit the amount of casualties.

United States Intervention: The PLA penetrated close to the outer edge of Tezpur, Assam, a major frontier town nearly fifty kilometers from the Assam-North-East Frontier Agency border. The local government ordered the evacuation of the civilians in Tezpur to the south of the Brahmaputra River, all prisons were thrown open, and government officials who stayed behind destroyed Tezpur's currency reserves in anticipation of a Chinese advance. On the evening of 20 November, Nehru, seeing the disintegration of his own armies, made an appeal to the United States, for armed aid, including airstrikes, if Chinese forces continued to advance, and air cover, in case of raids by the Chinese air force. With the Chinese outnumbering every Indian division and faced with the idea of bombing on Indian towns, the United States Navy ordered an aircraft carrier to the Bay of Bengal due to reach there in late November. However, by the time Nehru was negotiating with the US for arms and aircraft, this news of U.S. intervention in the war forced China to declare a unilateral ceasefire diplomatically.

Ceasefire

China had reached its claim lines so the PLA did not advance farther, and on 19 November it declared a unilateral cease-fire. Zhou Enlai declared a unilateral ceasefire to start on midnight, 21 November. Zhou's ceasefire declaration stated, beginning from 21 November, 1962, the Chinese frontier guards will cease fire along the entire Sino-Indian border. Beginning from 1 December, 1962, the Chinese frontier guards will withdraw to positions 20 kilometres behind the line of actual control which existed between China and India on 7 November, 1959. In the eastern sector, although the Chinese frontier guards have so far been fighting on Chinese territory north of the traditional customary line, they are prepared to withdraw from their present positions to the north of the illegal McMahon Line, and to withdraw twenty kilometres back from that line. In the middle and western sectors, the Chinese frontier guards will withdraw twenty kilometres from the line of actual control. Zhou had first given the ceasefire announcement to Indian charge d'affaires on 19 November, but India did not receive it until 24 hours later.

The aircraft carrier was ordered back after the ceasefire and thus American intervention on India's side in the war was avoided. Retreating Indian troops, who hadn't come into contact with anyone knowing of the ceasefire, and Chinese troops in NEFA and Aksai Chin, were involved in some minor battles but for the most part the ceasefire signalled an end to the fighting. The United States Air Force flew in supplies to India in November 1962, but neither side wished to continue hostilities. Militarily, no organized Indian resistance was left in either disputed sector after the retreat of the 48 Brigade at 3 a.m. on November 20th. The Chinese withdrew to the prewar Line of Actual Control and returned all the territory they had captured during the war, but kept disputed territories they had de facto control of prior to the war and had simply affirmed control of during the war by expelling the Indian forces.

Of the disputed areas, China kept most of the Aksai Chin, which comprised 32% of the disputed territory and withdrew from the North East Frontier Agency, which comprised 68%. According to V.K. Singh, China kept territory past their 1960 claim line. However, both the Chinese government and the Indian government state that Chinese forces never advanced south past their claim line. According to the Institute of Peace and Conflict Studies, China since withdrew its claim from part of NEFA (Assam). Over the following months, vehicles, weapons, and prisoners of war were returned by China unconditionally as a show of goodwill. According to Anna Louise Strong, a Marxist living in China during 1962, the return of heavy weapons were said to be due to logistical constraints of transporting them to China. Returning the weapons to India for goodwill purposes was considered more desirable than destroying them or abandoning them to the natives.

China released 731 sick and wounded Indian soldiers in December 1962, and the remainder 3,213 soldiers, including one brigadier, 26 field officers and 29 officers of company grade, started arriving in India from April 1963 onwards. The Indian forces did not take any Chinese prisoners. 26 died due to wounds in the PoW Camp, while another 15 were repatriated in December when the Chinese used them to return confiscated weapons. Toward the end of the war India increased her support for Tibetan refugees and revolutionaries, some of them having settled in India, as they were fighting the same common enemy in the region. The Nehru administration ordered the raising of elite Indian-trained Tibetan Armed Force composed of Tibetan refugees. The CIA had already begun operations in bringing about change in Tibet.

World Opinion

The Chinese military action has been viewed by the United States as part of the PRC's policy making of using aggressive wars to settle its border disputes and to distract from its internal issues. According to James Calvin from the United States Marine Corps, western nations at the time viewed China as an aggressor during the China-India border war, and the war was part of a monolithic communist objective for a world dictatorship of the proletariat. This was further triggered by Mao Zedong's views that The way to world conquest lies through Havana, Accra, and Calcutta. Calvin believes that Chinese actions show a pattern of conservative aims and limited objectives, rather than expansionism and blames this particular conflict from India's provocations towards China.

However, Calvin also expresses that China, in the past, has been adamant to gain control over regions to which it has a traditional claim, which triggered the dispute over NEFA and Aksai Chin and indeed Tibet. The Kennedy administration was disturbed by what they considered blatant Chinese communist aggression against India. In a May 1963 National Security Council meeting, contingency planning on the part of the United States in the event of another Chinese attack on India was discussed. Defence Secretary Robert McNamara and General Maxwell Taylor advised the president to use nuclear weapons should the Americans intervene in such a situation. Kennedy insisted that Washington defend India as it would any ally. The non-aligned nations, perhaps unsurprisingly, remained non-aligned, and only the United Arab Republic openly supported India Of the non-aligned Six non-aligned nations, Egypt, Burma, Cambodia, Sri Lanka, Ghana and Indonesia, met in Colombo on 10 December 1962.

The proposals stipulated a Chinese withdrawal of 20 km from the customary lines without any reciprocal withdrawal on India's behalf. The failure of these six nations to unequivocally condemn China deeply disappointed India. In 1972, Chinese Premier Zhou made an attempt to explain the Chinese point of view to President Nixon of the US. As for the causes of the war, Zhou asserted that China did not try and expel Indian troops from south of the McMahon line and that three open warning telegrams were sent to Nehru before the war.

However, Indian patrols south of the McMahon line were expelled and suffered casualties in the Chinese attack. Zhou also told Nixon that Chairman Mao ordered the troops to return to show good faith. The Indian government maintains that the Chinese military could not advance further south due to logistical problems and the cut-off of resource supplies. While Western nations did not view Chinese actions favourably because of this war, Pakistan, which had had a turbulent relationship with India ever since the Indian partition, improved its relations with China after the war.

Prior to the war, Pakistan also shared a disputed boundary with China, and had proposed to India that the two countries adopt a common defence against northern enemies (ie China), which was rejected by India.

However, China and Pakistan took steps to peacefully negotiate their shared boundaries, beginning on October 13, 1962, and concluding in December of that year· Pakistan also expressed fear that the huge amounts of western military aid directed to India would allow it to threaten Pakistan's security in future conflicts. Mohammed Ali, External Affairs Minister of Pakistan, declared that massive Western aid to India in the Sino-Indian dispute would be considered an unfriendly act towards Pakistan. As a result Pakistan made efforts to improve its relations with China. The following year, China and Pakistan peacefully settled disputes on their shared border, and negotiated the China-Pakistan Border Treaty in 1963, as well as trade, commercial, and barter treaties. On 2 March, 1963, Pakistan conceded its northern claim line in Pakistani-controlled Kashmir to China in favor of a more southerly boundary along the Karakoram Range. The border treaty largely set the border along the MacCartney-Macdonald Line Because of India's failure against China, Pakistan triggered the Second Kashmir War with India. However, it effectively ended in a stalemate as Calvin states that the Sino-Indian War had caused the previously passive government to take a stand on actively modernizing India's military.

China offered diplomatic support to Pakistan in this war but did not offer military support. In January 1966, China condemned the Tashkent Agreement between India and Pakistan as a Soviet-US plot in the region. In the Indo-Pakistani War of 1971, Pakistan expected China to provide military support, but it was left alone as India successfully helped the rebels in East Pakistan to found the new nation-state of Bangladesh.

Consequences

The 1962 Debacle, as it is remembered in India, was the adamant complication of a century-old British border dispute, thrust upon a newly independent India. When China reached a juncture whence it could act proactively to the sense of injustice about colonial actions against them, the result was an eruption of a xenophobic, aggressive imperialism. There is a Chinese phrase oft quoted within the Chinese government If he strikes me once, it is his fault. If he strikes me again, it is my fault. The People's Republic of China seemed to have taken this mentality to heart, and in the effort to exorcise the demons of colonialism, have become imperialists themselves. Subverting various indigenous countries and areas in affirmation of vague historical citings had become a fundamental cornerstone of China's geo-strategic maneuvering in the '50s and '60s. The Chinese claims to Aksai Chin and large areas of Arunachal are a mix of an expression of this neo-colonial sentiment and the desire to acquire a dominant status in Asia by keeping rival India in a weaker bargaining position. This is not saying that the PRC is necessarily evil in this respect, as many Indian journalists are prone to claim it is simply geopolitics. What is unusual, however, is the rather unscrupulous means, even among the big-power nations, that the PRC has taken to reach this position.

When China sought recognition of its claim on Tibet after its occupation, the Chinese leadership avidly cultivated India, and won the heart of a high-minded but naïve Prime Minister Nehru. Hindi-Chini Bhai-Bhai (India and China are brothers) became the soundbyte of the day - and the Chinese cannot be faulted in their execution of this deception. While the shells fell and the bullets flew around the Jawans in the snow-capped hell of the Himalayan battlefield, the Indian leaders in Delhi were romancing the fluffy pull of empathy with a fraternal Asian nation that, too, had suffered exploitation by the Western colonial powers. Added to the chaos and the mounting of tensions after the border clashes and failed settlement talks in 1960, and arguably a prime factor in making the dispute a mutual national prestige issue, was the internal political flux within both India and China. India was democratic and, therefore, more sensitive to its public and parliamentary opinion, and highly politicized debates about the Chinese question raged across the Parliament floor and in stratified governmental agencies.

In particular, the elected representatives of the various Communist parties in India were indignant by the notion that their fraternal socialist brethren would be capable of starting such a conflict, and laid the blame solely on the capitalist-lackey Nehru's shoulders. At the opposite end of the political spectrum, the right-leaning parties blamed the crisis on a socialist Nehru's ignorance and non-recognition of the reality of situation. On the other side, a communist Peking did not have this intra-political problem, but it was engaged in intense ideological remolding and suffered from a sense of political isolation, aggravated by its increasing ideological differences with Russia since 1958, when the latter, for example, refused to give it a sample atom bomb.The '62 war highlighted several critical failures in India's warmaking abilities. First, and perhaps most significantly, the conflict highlighted political naïveté and ignorance toward the strategies of warfare and international relations. During the entire conflict, Indian diplomatic actions remained flaccid, and fluctuated between being confrontational to being manhandled. For example, intel told that the Chinese were building a road through Aksai Chin, yet the Government, apart from a few angry condemnations, chose to ignore the strategic significance of it for almost a decade, instead repeating to itself the mantra of Hindi-Chini bhai-bhai.

Even upon discovery of this transgression, India's protests were weak-kneed. Later, in the middle of 1962, Indian leaders suddenly woke up to the presence of Chinese soldiers, to the exasperation of much of the army, on the Thagla Ridge. Nehru, advised by Krishna Menon and a coterie of sycophantic generals, ordered a reckless operation on the attacking Chinese. In the adoption of a forward policy, against the clamoring of sound tacticians, India deployed on ground chosen for its political significance, rather than tactical defensibility.

The leadership's untenable demands on the Army were the root cause of the '62 debacle. The war also highlighted the fact that the army was acutely under-equipped, out-dated, and ill-trained to deal with sustained conflict in the Himalaya. The acclimatization of troops was of critical import in this mountain war. Though Indian kill ratios were vary favorable, the damage caused by non-acclimatization of troops, particularly in the eastern sector, compared to the troops in Ladakh, who were better equipped and acclimatized, is very evident. The psychological and political effects of the '62 war were far-reaching. Because of the war, India's image, especially among the Third World, the nations remaining non-aligned during the Cold War, suffered. But internally, the shock galvanized the people into one united nation. Krishna Menon resigned and Nehru's dream of Sino-Indian friendship was shattered, but India did not relinquish its independent policy of Non-Alignment, though a shadow was shed on India's position as the leader of the Non-Aligned Movement (NAM).

However, statements by the PRC promoting the Chinese revolution as a model and Beijing's actions in the Taiwan Strait in 1958 and the 1962 Sino-Indian War alarmed many Third World nations. During the 1960s China cultivated ties with Third World countries and insurgent groups in an attempt to encourage wars of national liberation and revolution to forge an international united front against both the superpowers. Third World appreciation for Chinese assistance coexisted, consequently, with growing suspicions of China's militancy. These increasingly militant tendencies, contradictory to the much lauded Principles of Peaceful Coexistence soundbyte, destroyed what active influence the PRC had on the NAM. Discord between China and many

Third World countries continued to grow, while relations India and the Soviet Union warmed to counter the decision by Pakistan to cavort to the Western Camp in an effort to counter Indian superiority and influence.

The two most powerful nonaligned nations strayed further from their NAM policies, and thus the weakened NAM did not wield as much influence during the later part of the Cold War as it did during the beginning, and thus the era of a strictly bi-polar Cold War world was ushered in. The Indian Army's defeat by the Chinese in the border war of 1962 was a national humiliation, but the nation reacted to the '62 war with an unprecedented surge of patriotism.

The main lesson India learned was that right does not make might in the world of geopolitics, and that India must strengthen its defences and stand on its own feet to be of consequence in the world. India's policy of weaponization via indigenous sources and self-sufficiency was thus cemented. National sovereignty, it would affirmed, could not come at the expense of becoming a client state of any superpower or by joining any military alliance with or under them. In the early '80s, following a new paradigm shift in the Indian military, it was decided that the Army was to actively patrol the Line of Actual Control. Friction began to ensue over the Chinese occupation of the Sumdorong Chu pasturage, lying north of Tawang.

The media, catching wind of the situation, gave it national prominence, and an angry exchange of official protests between the Indian and Chinese governments followed. Adding to the bickering, a bill was passed creating the state of Arunachal Pradesh, a territory that China claims in its entirety. The military re-occupied Hathung La ridge, across Namka Chu, twenty-five years after vacating it. Army chief K. Sundarji airlifted an entire brigade to nearby Ximithang, alarming the panicked Chinese.

The Indian government collectively flinched against the tough talk from Beijing, but stood firm at the insistence of the army. The result paradoxically was a thaw. In 1993 and 1996, the two sides signed the Sino-Indian bilateral Peace and Tranquillity Accords, an agreement on maintaining peace and tranquillity along the LAC. Ten meetings of a Sino-Indian Joint Working Group (SIJWG) and five of an expert group to determine where the LAC lies have taken place but the pace of progress has been tardy to say the least.

China: According to the PLA's official military history, the war achieved China's policy objectives of defeating the Indian forces and securing peaceful borders in the western sector, as China retained de facto control of the Aksai Chin.

After the war, India abandoned the Forward Policy, and the de facto borders stabilized along the Line of Actual Control. Published scholarship in China is still expected to explain and justify, not criticizing, the decisions of the Chinese Communist Party, at least on such sensitive matters as war. Chinese publications on the war themselves do not mention specific dates or events and use generalized terms. The first book-length analysis of the war from China which was allowed to be sold was published in 1993.

India: Memorials were erected for the Indian troops who died in the war. Arguably, the main lesson India learned from the war was the need to strengthen its own defences. The country could no longer follow Nehru's trusting polemics of Hindi-Chini bhai-bhai and non-violent peace. Because of India's inability to sense danger, Prime Minister Nehru faced harsh accusations from government officials, as he was the one who had promoted good relations with China. Indians in general became highly sceptical of China and its military. Many Indians view the war as a betrayal of India's attempts at establishing a long-standing peace with China.

The war also put an end to Nehru's earlier hopes that India and China would form a strong Asian Axis to counteract the increasing influence of the Cold War superpowers. The unpreparedness of the army was blamed on Defence Minister Menon, who resigned his government post to allow for someone who might modernize India's military further. India's policy of weaponization via indigenous sources and self-sufficiency was thus cemented. Sensing a weakened army, Pakistan, a close ally of China, initiated the Second Kashmir War with India in 1965, however this war was still indecisive and led to cease fire.

Two years later in 1967, there was a short border skirmish, dubbed Chola Incident by India, between PLA troops and Indian troops, which went more favourably for India. The Indian government commissioned an investigation, resulting in the classified Henderson-Brooks-Bhagat Report on the causes of the war and the reasons for failure.

India's performance in high-altitude combat in 1962 led to an overhaul of the Indian Army in terms of doctrine, training, organization and equipment. By 1964, India's military manpower had doubled. India's military became increasingly well-trained and potent. In the 1960s and 70s, India allied with Soviet Russia to encircle China.

The continued military modernization in India led to a change in the military equation between the two countries, where India were earlier far outnumbered and lacked experience. This was evidently successful, as India achieved military gains over Pakistan in the Indo-Pakistani War of 1971 and 1999 and now maintains the third largest military in the world. According to John W. Garver, the Indian military and Indian-trained Tibetan Armed Forces pose a modern threat to China which would likely not be present had China not opted for war against India.

REFERENCES

Alastair Lamb: The China-India Border: The Origins of the Disputed Boundaries, 1964.

Allen S. Whiting: The Chinese Calculus of Deterrence: India and Indochina.

Ardley, Jane: Resistance, Religion and Politics: the Tibetan Independence Movement in Comparative Perspective, Keele University, 1999.

Bhattacharjee, Arun: A History of Modern India, Liverpool, Lucas Publications, 1988.

Burman, Bina Roy: Religion and Politics in Tibet, New Delhi, Vikas Publishing, 1979.

Calvin, James Barnard: The China-India Border War, 1988.

Carrasco, Pedro: Land and Polity in Tibet, Seattle, University of Washington Press, 1959.

Edgerton, Franklin: The Beginnings of Indian Philosophy: Selections from the Rig Veda, Atharva Veda, Upanishads and Mahabharata, London, George Allen and Unwin, 1965.

Eppsteiner, F.: The Path of Compassion: Writings on Socially Engaged Buddhism, Berkeley, Parallax Press, 1988.

French, Patrick: Liberty or Death: India's Journey to Independence and Division, London, Flamingo, 1997.

Gunnar Myrdal. Asian Drama; An Inquiry into the Poverty of Nations. New York, Random House, 1968.

Haksar, Vinit: Civil Disobedience: Threats and Offers: Gandhi and Rawls, Delhi, Oxford University Press, 1986.

History of the Conflict with China, P.B. Sinha, A.A. Athale, with S.N. Prasad: Ministry of Defence, Government of India, 1992. — Official Indian history of the Sino-Indian War, 1962.

Huntington, Samuel P.: 'Will More Countries Become Democratic?' in Political Science Quarterly, 1984.

Iyer, R. N.: The Moral and Political Thought of Mahatma Gandhi, New York, Oxford University Press, 1973.

Jan Yün-Hua: 'Buddhist Self-Immolation in Medieval China' in History of Religions, 1965.

Jones, Ken: The Social Face of Buddhism: An Approach to Social and Political Activism, London, Wisdom, 1989.

Kelly, Petra K., Gert Bastian, and Pat Aiello: The Anguish of Tibet, Berkeley, Parallax Press, 1991.

Khilnani, Sunil: The Idea of India, London, Hamish Hamilton, 1997.

Klieger, P. Christiaan: Tibetan Nationalism: The Role of Patronage in the Accomplishment of a National Identity, Meerut, Archana Publications, 1992.

Ling Nai-Min: Tibetan Sourcebook, Hong Kong, Union Research Institute, 1964.

Lopez, Donald S.: Prisoners of Shangri-La: Tibetan Buddhism and the West, Chicago, University of Chicago Press, 1998.

Marshall, Steven D.: Hostile Elements: A Study of Political Imprisonment in Tibet, 1987-1998, London, Tibet Information Network, 1999.

Queen, C.S. and King, S.B.: Engaged Buddhism: Buddhist Liberation Movements in Asia, Albany, State University of New York Press, 1996.

Ray, S.: Gandhi, India and the World: An International Symposium, Melbourne, Hawthorn Press, 1970.

8

Tibetan Factor in Sino-Indian Relations

Introduction

Both India and China, today, consider Tibet vital for their national security. To aim for a Tibet which will serve the role of a buffer zone as it did before the liberation in 1951 seems far-fetched. No doubt, Tibet is today an integral part of China and to argue or even talk about its complete autonomous status appears to be an impossible and bizarre proposition. Even the Dalai Lama today is negotiating on the grounds of an autonomous Tibet with regards to the Domestic Matters – religion, culture and society. Defence and the Foreign Relations will remain in the hands of the Chinese Central Government. In this light, to say that Tibet after it gains autonomy will be able to play active role as a buffer state appears unrealistic. Today, the Tibetan question in any bilateral Chinese Talks appears only when the relations between China and the other country are going through a bad phase. The example is that of Sino-US relations. Every time there is some problem between the two the issue of Tibet is brought to the forefront. The second question to be answered is that the fact of the presence of nuclear bases in the Tibetan plateau. The answer again is in the negative.

The move to establish nuclear bases in Tibet was a result of the strategic security consideration as the Tibetan Plateau appears to be more safe for nuclear research. One also needs to look into the question of the viability of a buffer zone in the nuclear world. In the highly nuclearized world today when there are three strong nuclear powers in the same region (India-China-Pakistan), the concept of a buffer state does not appear to be applicable. Logically into this there is no buffer zone between India and Pakistan even when both the countries are on unfriendly terms.

No doubt that China is trying to help Pakistan, but that appears to be more of an attempt towards maintaining the balance of power politics in the region. Undoubtedly, the de-nuclearization of the region would be favourable to both the sides but it appears to be unlikely, even though the border region has had no major violent uprisings and both the countries are on the road to economic cooperation. The opening of the Nathu La Pass clearly highlights this trend in the relations. Support for the Tibetan cause is strong in India. Moreover since the Tibetan Government in exile and the Dalai Lama are in Dharamsala this emphasis is strengthened.

On the other hand, close Buddhist ties also make the Indians support the Tibetan cause. The same holds true even in the case of the American Public opinion. However, in spite of the fact that the US is the sole super-power of the world today, it is unable to bring the issue to its right conclusion. India though more closely involved, is in no position to solve the problem. Chinese have accepted that Sikkim is a part of the Indian Territory after the visit of Prime Minister Vajpayee to China. Though they have asserted their stance on Arunachal Pradesh and have claimed that it is the part of the Chinese territory. The economic tie between the countries is on a constant rise. In such a scenario, the realist approach would be to sue the benefits of good relations rather than to be stuck with the Tibetan cause. India will have to play a crucial role in the conclusion of the negotiation between the Dalai Lama and the Chinese government though this will not be a welcome thing by the latter. Given its closeness to the issue it is the only country which can play a meaning full role.

However, militarily speaking it is incapable of doing so. It be can conclude by saying that no doubt a de-militarized and de-nuclearized Tibet would be a boon for India. Undoubtedly a favourable domestic, regional government in Tibet definitely will be more beneficial than Nepal as India have seen that the latter began to cash upon its acquired strategic importance by playing the two countries against each other to get the maximum benefits it could acquire by doing this. The economic dependence of Tibet on China also ends the question of the independence of the Tibet. Tibet today is more integrated with China than it was in the past.

Pre-Colonial Period

The establishment of the British Empire in India in 1757 and economic penetration of China by the Western Powers from 1839 fundamentally altered the traditional balance of power on the Asian continent. British policy towards Tibet was characterized by two conflicting imperatives which, throughout their rule in India, they sought to reconcile. From early on, the British rulers realized the importance of Tibet as a buffer between India and any other external power on the north, be it France, Russia or China. However, to support or even encourage a completely independent Tibet was to damage a much larger commercial interest in China. Thus, they sought to limit Chinese power in Tibet and encourage Tibetan autonomy. In short, the British Government recognized what they called Chinese suzerainty but not sovereignty in Lhasa.

The British rulers were unsuccessful in establishing contact with Lhasa until 1904. There were various options before the British Empire in India with regard to Tibet. Though they could have colonized Tibet with much difficulty and at high cost, they ruled out this option as early as 1775, because it was then not a viable economic proposition. They could have easily extended their protectorate as the Tibetan authorities including the XIII Dalai Lama and his ministers repeatedly requested this, but the British ruled out this option too because it would be a costly affair. They could have granted an independent status to Tibet as they tentatively tried to do after 1912 until 1947. This option was not officially sanctioned, because it would damage their much larger commercial interest in China. Under the circumstances, the only viable option they considered seriously was that China had suzerainty over Tibet but on understanding that Tibet was autonomous. Such a conditional policy safeguards British economic interest in China as well as national security of the Indian Empire. The primary consideration in British policy towards Tibet was how to ensure the security of the 2000 mile long Himalayan frontier that India shares with Tibet.

This could be ensured if Tibet remained autonomous in the British sense and as long as China remained weak as a nominal suzerain authority in Tibet. This formula worked up to 1949 because China remained weak and divided until 1949. The other equally important factor was British power acting as deterrent against any Chinese armed intervention in Tibet. The British strategy was to allow Tibet to continue with the fiction of Chinese suzerainty over her. This concession to Beijing was not out of any British love for the Manchu Rule but for their understanding that Tibet under the suzerainty to the weak Chinese would not be a source of danger to the safety of British India. This could be ensured if Tibet remained free from direct Chinese control or sovereignty. The British were interested in a relatively stable government in Tibet because the theory of the buffer state has never worked properly except where the buffer state was strong enough to keep up an efficient government and administration and to make encroachment by either neighbour a risk.

The British further clarified that they, wished to avoid interference in Tibet, Tibet ought to remain an autonomous state between India and China, at the same time British agree that they recognized Chinese suzerainty over Tibet, and this view Bristish press diplomatically in Peking as strongly as need be. However, one should also keep in mind that if Tibet was strategically important to British India, it was no less so to the Chinese Empire. China became strong and united under the communist leadership, ready to take over Tibet by 1949-50. The power that had the effect of deterrence to China from revoking the autonomous status of Tibet had departed from South Asia by 1947.

Post-Colonial Period

There had been a warm hearted and widespread Indian public support for the Tibetan cause throughout the 1950s. With the deterioration of the Sino-Indian Relations after the War, the Indian Government radically revised its stance on Tibet. It supported the Tibetan cause in the 1960s both openly and clandestinely, in 1963 the Special Frontier Code named 22, was established to train able-bodied young Tibetan refugees, in 1965 the Indian delegate openly supported the UN Resolution on Tibet for the first time since 1950, and in the same year Prime Minister Lal Bahadur Shastri was expected to recognize the Tibetan Government in exile, but he died suddenly and the Indian Politics took another twist of its own. The Pro-Tibetan stance continued until the Bangladesh War Liberation in 1970-71. This turn of events compelled New Delhi to forestall any possibility of Chinese intervention either along the Himalayan border or in the Bangladesh war itself by sending reassuring messages to China. India had no more handy instrument to sacrifice before Beijing than the Tibetan Card. During the 1980s, New Delhi can be said to have achieved a balance in its stand on Tibet.

Since the 80s, India has been most anxious to resolve the boundary dispute using the improved atmosphere of the SinoIndian Relations. Fourteen Rounds of Talks have taken place but no concrete solution has been reached yet. There has been a definite increase in economic cooperation and trade and thus, the question of Tibet has taken a back seat. This should also be seen in the backdrop of both India and China becoming Nuclear Powers during this time period.

After Independence

60 years after independence, India is still without recognised borders with China. While it is easy to blame China for intransigence, new information has come to light suggesting that Indian leaders also missed opportunities when favourable conditions presented themselves. They pursued a course of idealism for world peace while what the national interest demanded was flexibility and pragmatism. As a result, India today is the only country of its size without a recognised boundary. India's border problem is an inseparable part of the India-China- Tibet triangle. In 1950, two momentous events shook Asia and the rest of the world one was the Chinese invasion of Tibet and the other, their intervention in the Korean war.

By all canons of logic, India should have devoted the utmost attention to the immediate situation in Tibet and let interested parties, China and the US, sort it out in Korea. But the Indian leaders Nehru in particular got heavily involved in Korea, while paying insufficient attention to the Tibetan crisis. This lies at the root of the problem plaguing India today. Part of the difficulty in unravelling the details is lack of access to records.

The Nehru family heirs continue to exercise control over these vital documents, including those in the National Archives. But by a fortunate turn of events, many of the same records are available at the India Office in London. When India became independent, HE Richardson, British representative in Lhasa, was asked by the Nehru Government to continue as Indian representative. Richardson sent copies of his correspondence with his new bosses in Delhi to his former superiors in London. In the years which followed the takeover of Tibet, China made several attempts to negotiate a stable border with India beginning with the northeast. Embroiled in both Tibet and Korea, with a real or perceived threat from the US-supported Chiang Kai-Shek who lay in wait in Farmosa (Taiwan), China was anxious to have a peaceful border with India. The Indian Army then had an outstanding reputation following its brilliant record in World War II, Kashmir and Korea. So the time was propitious for settling the border. But in the 1950s Nehru's interests were focussed on Korea and the Panchsheel.

As the decade went by, China became militarily much stronger, while the Indian Army was allowed to deteriorate in both material and morale. As a result, the opportunity to settle the boundary dispute was lost.

Several strategic anaiysts, both in the East and the West have commented in the past on the strategic suitability of the Tibetan Plateau for nuclear experimenting and testing. This has unfortunately come true. China s first attempt at nuclear research was made in 1958 at Amdo (Haibei) on the Tibetan Plateau and armed in 1971 when Beijing perceived a serious threat from the Soviet Union and India. By the early 1970s China had brought South Asia and the former Soviet Union within their effective nuclear range and reach. The fact that the Maoist strategists had chosen Amdo and Kham (near the Sino-Tibetan border) for their nuclear sites might have other implications and motives, besides geographical suitability and nuclear safety. By this mighty nuclear act, they might have cemented and concretized their claims over Inner Tibet. During the 1950s and 1960s several observers viewed the Chinese occupation of Tibet and subsequent strategic developments there as a threat to South Asia, implying Chinese expansionism.

This view, of course, fitted with the Cold War image of the type of Communist China that most people had at the time. George Gindsburg and Michael Mathos were typical He also holds Tibet, dominates the Himalayan piedmont threatens the Indian subcontinent, may well have all the South Asia within his reach, and with it all of Asia. China backed by its great military strength in strategy appeared more interested in competing against India for spheres of friendship in the Himalayan states. The Chinese aim seems to have been to transfer Tibet s former buffer functions to Nepal and if possible to Bhutan. The implication is that even if China recognized Tibet as the natural and geographical limit of its power, it felt that the Himalayas alone were not enough to guarantee its national security in the modern age, especially given Tibet s strategic location. China ideally wants a chain of small friendly neighbours, friendlier to it, on the Himalayan region separating the two Asian giants.

It makes no strategic and military sense to the Chinese to liberate the Himalayan states which are geographically within the Indian subcontinent. Such an eventuality would bring china face to face with India. China has thus, encouraged strong nationalist regimes in the countries that lie between Tibet and India. Such nationalist regimes functioning as buffer zones are in the interest of Chinese national security.

While India's interests in Tibet were allowed to suffer, the Nehru Government made a strenuous effort to gain international recognition for Mao's China. As Tibet was crumbling before the Chinese advance, bringing the great power to the borders of India, Nehru's his main concern was getting China admitted to the United Nations as a permanent member of the Security Council. This was an unrealistic goal, for China was then engaged in a war against the U.N. forces in Korea. But Nehru saw himself as an intermediary between the West and the socialist world China and the Soviet Union. From all this India gained little except the West's hostility. More than its later friendship with the Soviet Union, it is India's abandonment of Tibet and the sponsorship of Mao's China that soured its relationship with America. At this crucial time in history, India's ambassador in Beijing, KM Panikkar, a communist sympathiser, went so far as to claim in 1950 that there was 'lack of confirmation' of the presence of Chinese troops in Tibet and that protesting the Chinese invasion would be an interference to India's efforts on behalf of China in the UN. Nehru also wrote, India's primary consideration is maintenance of world peace Recent developments in Korea have not strengthened China's position, which will be further weakened by any aggressive action by India in Tibet.

So the Government's highest priority apparently was not to weaken China's case in the UN Deeply disturbed by the development, Sardar Patel complained to Nehru that Panikkar has been at great pains to find an explanation or justification for Chinese policy and actions. India got nothing in return for its generosity. At the very least, India could have demanded settling its border with China in return. There was ample historical and contemporary evidence to show that China respected only strength and not pacific pronouncements based on a utopian vision like the Panchsheel, but India failed to recognise this fact. Nothing would stop Nehru from going ahead with his policy of friendship with China. Over the years, the myth of the Indo-Sino friendship would grow larger and larger, becoming a 'brotherhood', until that a day in October 1962 when Lin Biao and his PLA (People's Liberation Army) were on the Thagla Ridge in the West Kameng Division in NEFA (Arunachal Pradesh). The Panchsheel collapsed even earlier, that day in 1959 when the Dalai Lama left Tibet for exile in India. It is still seen by most Indians as a case of China exploiting Nehru's good faith by 'stabbing him in the back'. But new information shows that Nehru and Krishna Menon were informed of the Chinese incursions in Ladakh and Aksai Chin long before the public learnt of them. One can only surmise that the matter was kept secret to keep the Panchsheel alive.

To understand this, it is necessary to appreciate the fact that what China desired most was a stable border with India. With this in view, the Premier, Zhou-en-Lai, visited India several times to fix the boundary. In short, the Chinese were prepared to accept the McMahon Line as the boundary in the east with possibly some minor adjustments and a new name and then negotiate the unmarked boundary in the west between Ladakh and Tibet. In effect, what Zhou-en-Lai proposed was a phased settlement, beginning with the eastern boundary. Nehru, however, wanted the whole thing settled at once.

The practical minded Zhou-en-Lai found this politically impossible. And on each visit the Premier, in search of a boundary settlement, heard more about the Panchsheel than India's stand on the boundary. He interpreted this as intransigence on India's part. China in fact went on to settle its boundary with Myanmar roughly along the McMahon Line following similar principles. Contrary to what the Indian public was told, the border between Ladakh (in the princely State of Kashmir) and Tibet was never clearly demarcated. As late as 1960, the Indian Government had to send survey teams to Ladakh to locate the boundary and prepare maps. But the Government kept telling the people that there was a clearly defined boundary, which the Chinese refused to accept. There were several practical issues on which negotiations could have been conducted especially in the 1950s when India was in a relatively strong position. China needed Aksai Chin because it had plans to lay an access road from Tibet to the Xinjiang province (Sinkiang) in the west.

Aksai Chin was of far greater strategic significance to China than to India. (It may be a strategic liability for India being more expensive to maintain and harder to supply than even the Siachen Glacier). Had Nehru recognised this fact, he might have proposed a creative solution like asking for access to Mount Kailash and Manasarovar in return for Indian providing access to the Chinese to Aksai Chin. The issue is not whether such an agreement was possible but no solutions were proposed. The upshot was that China ignored India including the Panchsheel and went ahead with its plan to build the road through Aksai Chin.

This was compounded by other errors. Nehru and Krishna Menon had been fully informed of the Chinese encroachment in Aksai Chin years before it became public in 1959. In 1955, an English mountaineer, Sydney Wignall, was deputed by General Thimayya to verify reports that the Chinese were laying the road through Aksai Chin. Wignall was not his only source. Shortly after the Chinese attack in 1962, General Thimayya had also sent a young officer of the MEG to Aksai Chin to confirm reports of the intrusion. When the Army brought this information to his notice, Krishna Menon, in Nehru's presence, sharply told the senior officer, who made the presentation, that he was lapping up CIA agent provocateur propaganda. The rest in history.

Chinese Suzerainty over Tibet

The Republic of China was founded in 1911 when the rule of the Qing Dynasty was overthrown by the Revolution of 1911. Though the domestic political situation of China was not quite stable at that time, yet the successive central governments of China all persisted in the principled stand of exercising sovereign jurisdiction over Tibet. They conducted resolute struggles against the schemes of splitting China by the foreign aggressive forces and adopted various measures of exercising sovereign jurisdiction over Tibet.

Claim of Sovereignty over Tibet by China: In the early stage of the founding of the Republic, the political situation of China was turbulent. The political regimes alternated continuously. Taking advantage of this chaotic situation of China, the British imperialists plotted to grab Tibet and separate it from China. In 1914 Britain hatched single-handedly the Simla Conference, concocted the Simla Convention, openly divided China's Tibetan areas into Inner Tibet and Outer Tibet and tampered with China's sovereignty over Tibet into suzerainty. This convention which gravely violated the sovereignty of China should naturally be opposed by the Chinese Government. On 3 July, 1914, Ivan Chen, the chief delegate of the Chinese government, was instructed to refuse to affix his signature on the formal text of the Simla Convention and stated that The Chinese Government would not recognize any agreement or similar documents between Britain and Tibet today or some other day. The British scheme hence failed. After the Simla Conference, the British imperialists were not reconciled to their failure, and continued to play with conspiracies and provoked incidents so as to attain their designs. n July 1942, the Kashag (Tibetan local government) declared all of a sudden the establishment of a bureau of foreign affairs and threatened to cut off supplies to the Office of the Commission for Mongolian and Tibetan Affairs at Lhasa and forced the Office to have contacts with the so-called bureau of foreign affairs in an attempt to find an excuse for independence of Tibet. Mr. Kong Qingzong, the then director of the Office, promptly sent an urgent report to the central government and pointed out in the telegram that The bureau of foreign affairs is by nature an organ that takes up matters with foreign countries.

Today the Kashag informed them that China should take up all matters with the bureau. That amounts to treating the central government as a foreign government and Tibet as an independent country. If China were to recognize so, that would mean the disappearance of articles in the previous international treaties which stipulate Tibet is part of the Chinese territory. That would also mean the invisible validity of the various treaties, open or secret, signed by Tibet with foreign countries without the recognition of the central government of China, As this is a matter of great importance, China suggested that the central government should openly cable the Kashag that they do not recognize the bureau. The officials of the central government in Tibet should deal with all matters with the Kashag as usual. On August 5, 1942, the Commission for Mongolian and Tibetan Affairs conveyed the instruction of the Executive Yuan to the Kashag, saying that The Tibetan side found it necessary to set up an organ to handle local foreign affairs but they must observe the following rules a) Problems involving the interests of the state, that is, political problems, must be handled in accordance with the will of the central government b) All contacts and communication between the central authorities and Tibet should follow the usual practice and must not go through the above-mentioned bureau of foreign affairs.

The Office of the Commission for Mongolian and Tibetan Affairs at Lhasa received a telegram, ordering that The Office should take up all matters with the Kashag as usual, not have any connection with the bureau of foreign affairs. In 1943 the Tibetan Tsongdu (National Assembly) was held at Lhasa. The Tsongdu accepted the opinion of the Central Government concerning the matter of the 'bureau of foreign affairs' and withdrew the former decision, expressing that Tibet should keep good feeling with the Central Government and should not sever relations with the Office of the central authorities in Tibet.

Ngawang Gyaltsen, general representative of the Tibet Office in Nanjing (then moved to Chongqing), was instructed to convey this views to the President of the Nationalist Government personally. Owing to the solemn and just stand taken by the Chinese Central Government, the British imperialists' scheme for the independence of Tibet by taking advantage of establishing the bureau of foreign affairs went bankrupt. The incidents of Pan-Asian Conference and Trade Mission were cooked up by the Kashag under the British instigation in 1947. The Central Government expressed its stern stand through various channels and resolutely opposed to them.

Tibet after the Revolution of 1911: The rich historical documents of China are more than enough to show one fact the Tibetan nationality living on the Qinghai-Tibet plateau has long become one of the members of the Chinese nation and Tibet has been an inalienable part of China since ancient times. About this fact, all the people with an objective and just stand in the international community have already reached or been close to reach common consensus. However, it is still necessary to deepen this common consensus. The reason lies in the fact that the deposits of the history treasure house of China are so rich and generous that people will simply never know clearly of its each part without going on explorations on them in a thoroughgoing way. After the Chinese revolution of 1911, the history of relationship between the Tibet region and the central government of China is a key historical link which is worth to be studied of the real situation about the Tibetan contemporary and modern history by the world through examining this historical link. This article is to help the readers understand briefly the history of relationship between the Tibet region and the successive central governments of China after the Revolution of 1911.

The writer is convinced that the readers would have their own independent and logical judgements after reading the following historical facts to the reliability of the story of 'Tibet separated itself from China and became an independent country after 1911. As is known to all that as early as the seventh century in the Tang Dynasty, the Tibetan and Han peoples established close ties in the political, economic, cultural and other gelds through the royal inter-marriages, meetings of sovereigns or their deputies in ancient China to form alliances, thereby laying down the historical foundation for finally establishing the unified country. In the middle of the thirteenth century, Tibet was formally incorporated into the Chinese territory of the Yuan Dynasty, Yuan Emperor Kublai entrusted to the Sakya Sect the power of administering the Tibet region, setting up the General Council (renamed Political Council in 1288) which was a central government organ exercising administrative power over the country's Buddhist affairs and the Tibetan affairs.

The Yuan government instituted the system of imperial preceptor, conferred titles on political and religious leaders, delimited administrative divisions, appointed local officials, took census, collated and stipulated revenue and taxes, dividing the Tibet region into thirteen Wan Hu (ten thousand households). The heads of Wan Hu were conferred upon and appointed directly by the Yuan Court. There were three Chief Military Commands of the Pacification Commissioners' Offices which took charge of garrison troops and the administrative affairs of the various Wan Hu

Offices in Tibet proper and other Tibetan areas. In the later period of the fourteenth century, the central government of the Ming Dynasty inherited and followed the systems of administering Tibet by the Yuan Dynasty, pursued a policy of managing Tibet according to conventions and customs, granting more titles and setting up more organs.

Hence, the relations between Tibet and the central regime were further consolidated and strengthened. rom the seventeenth century onwards, the Qing government further strengthened its administration over Tibet. In 1721 the system of Kalon (Council Minister) in charge of administrative affairs was set up. In 1727 the Office of Amban (Resident Official) was instituted in Tibet. In 1792 the twenty-nine-article Imperial Ordinance was issued. It stipulated in explicit terms for the reincarnation of the Living Buddhas in Tibet as well as the administrative, military and foreign affairs. The Imperial Ordinance marked that the administration of the Tibet region by the Qing central government was upgraded to the level of systematization and legalization.

In late Qing period, Britain twice launched armed invasions against Tibet. The Chinese government was forced to sign unequal treaties relating Tibet, After the Revolution of 1911, the political situation of China was turbulent. In order to realize its aim of splitting Tibet from China and reducing it into a dependency of the British Indian government, Britain adopted various acts of aggression against Tibet. Owing to the instigation of Britain, the relations between the Tibet region and the central government of China were for a time abnormal during the period of the Republic of China.

Although the British imperialists attempted to split China and to grab Tibet, its schemes never succeeded. On the contrary, they were opposed and boycotted by the broad masses of the Chinese people, including the majority of the Tibetan figures. Tibet was not officially recognized as an independent country by any country through diplomatic channels in the world at that time, including even the schemers themselves. The Tibet region also never detached itself from the sovereign jurisdiction of the central government and became independent.

REFERENCES

Dodin, Thierry, and Heinz Räther: Imagining Tibet: Perceptions, Projections, and Fantasies. Boston, Wisdom, 2001.

Dowman, Keith: The Legend of the Great Stupa. Berkeley, Dharma, 1973.

Dowman, Keith: The Sacred Life of Tibet. London, Thorsons, 1997.

Downs, Hugh R.: Rhythms of a Himalayan Village. San Francisco, Harper and Row, 1980.

Dudjom Rinpoche: The Nyingma School of Tibetan Buddhism. Boston, Wisdom, 1991.

Duncan, Marion H.: Customs and Superstitions of Tibetans. London, Mitre Press, 1964.

Dunham, V. Carroll, Ian Baker, and Thomas L. Kelly: Tibet: Reflections from the Wheel of Life. New York, Abbeville Press, 2001.

Ehrhard, Franz-Karl.: A "Hidden Land" in the Tibetan-Nepalese Borderlands. In Mandala and Landscape, New Delhi, D. K. Printworld, 1997.

Ekvall, Robert B.: Religious Observances in Tibet. Chicago, University of Chicago Press, 1964.

Ekvall, Robert B.: Fields on the Hoof: Nexus of Tibetan Nomadic Pastoralism. New York, Holt, Rinehart and Winston, 1968.

Ekvall, Robert B.: Tibetan Sky Lines. New York: Octagon, 1976.

Epstein, Lawrence: On the History and Psychology of the 'Das-log. Tibet Journal, 1982.

Epstein, Lawrence: A Comparative View of Tibetan and Western Near-Death Experiences. In Reflections on Tibetan Culture: Essays in Memory of Turrell V. Wylie, ed. L. Epstein and R. Sherburne, N. Y., Edwin Mellen Press, 1990.

Epstein, Lawrence: Khams pa Histories: Visions of People, Place, and Authority. Leiden, E. J. Brill, 2002.

Ferrari, Alfonsa: Mk'yen Brtse's Guide to the Holy Places of Central Tibet. Rome, 1958.

Fields, Rick: How the Swans Came to the Lake: A Narrative History of Buddhism in America. Boston: Shambhala, 1992.

Filippi, Filippo de.: An Account of Tibet: The Travels of Ippolito Desideri, 1712–1727. New Delhi, Asian Educational Services, 1995.

Fisher, James F..: Himalayan Anthropology: The Indo-Tibetan Interface. The Hague, Mouton, 1978.

Fisher, James F.: Trans-Himalayan Traders. Delhi, Motilal Banarsidass, 1986.

Fisher, James F.: Sherpas. Berkeley, University of California Press, 1990.

Forbes, Ann A.: Settlements of Hope: An Account of Tibetan Refugees in Nepal. Cambridge, Cultural Survival, 1989.

Goldstein, Melvyn C., and Matthew T. Kapstein: Buddhism in Contemporary Tibet: Religious Revival and Cultural Identity. Berkeley, University of California Press, 1998.

Goldstein, Melvyn C.: William Siebenschuh, and Tashi Tsering.: The Struggle for Modern Tibet: The Autobiography of Tashi Tsering. Armonk, N. Y., M. E. Sharpe, 1997.

Grunfeld, A. Tom: The Making of Modern Tibet. Armonk, N. Y., M. E. Sharpe. 1996.

Guenther, Herbert V.: The Teachings of Padmasambhava. Leiden, E. J. Brill, 1996.

Guillet, David W.: Toward a Cultural Ecology of Mountains: The Central Andes and the Himalayas Compared. Current Anthropology , 1983.

Gurung, Nareswor J.: An Introduction to the Socio-Econon Structure of Manang District. Kailash, 1976.

Gutschow, Kim: Unfocussed Merit-Making in Zangskar: A Socio-economic Account of Karsha Nunnery. Tibet Journal, 1997.

Gyatso, Janet: Apparitions of the Self: The Secret Autobiographies of a Tibetan Visionary. Princeton, Princeton University Press 1999.

Hale, Austin: Research on Tibeto-Burman Languages. New York, Mouton, 1982.

Harris, Melissa, and Sidney Jones: Tibet since 1950: Silence, Prison, or Exile. New York: Aperture and Human Rights Watch. 2000.

Harrison, Paul: A Brief History of the Tibetan bKa' 'gyur. In Tibetan Literature, Ithaca, N. Y., Snow Lion, 1996.

Harvey, Peter: An Introduction to Buddhist Ethics: Foundations, Values, and Issues. Cambridge, Cambridge University Press, 2000.

Havnevik, Hanna: Tibetan Buddhist Nuns. Oslo, Norwegian University Press, 1989.

Havnevik, Hanna: The Role of Nuns in Contemporary Tibet. In Resistance and Reform in Tibet, Delhi, Motilal Banarsidass, 1994.

9

Religious & Cultural Factors in Conflict

Introduction

Tibet was one of the last ancient civilizations to thrive into the twentieth century. It was a highly organized society that existed as a whole system with a strong religious foundation and theocratic government. Today, one cannot experience the living ancient culture of Egypt, Greece, Rome, China or India like one can with Tibetan civilization. Traditional Tibetan culture has been evolving for over 2000 years, and is still actively practiced throughout much of the Himalayan region, including Bhutan, Mustang (Nepal), Dolpo (Nepal), Sikkim (India), Assam (India), and Ladakh (India). Traditional Tibetan culture has been greatly influenced by the unique Himalayan and Central Asian geography and the religion of Buddhism. From a historical perspective, many of the diverse ethnic groups present in South and Southeast Asia today originally migrated from the Tibetan plateau and thus share a cultural heritage with present-day Tibetans. From a geographical perspective, Tibet has been the watershed for most of Asia. Its geographical position in the Central Asia has also put the country in the middle of struggles for power from the periods of the Mongol Empire through Great Game at the end of the 19th century. The Tibetan Independence movement has also influenced many modern struggles for nationhood throughout Asia, from East Timor to Burma.

Like Mongolia and minority other areas of China, most Tibetans do not consider themselves part of Modern China despite China's accession of Tibet in the 1950's, and their historical claim that Tibet has always been part of China. China is grappling with the process of defining itself as its borders encompass widely diverse peoples. Tibetan Buddhism is a ritualistic, expressive, and experiential religious tradition. The philosophy and practice of Tibetan Buddhism is based on ideals of wisdom, compassion, mindfulness and non-violence, which influenced the nature of Tibetan civilization and Tibetans as a people. Once Buddhism became the state religion, it transformed Tibet from a warrior to a wisdom society, created a profound religious system of over 6000 monasteries, and a theocratic government. Because of the way Buddhism shaped Tibetan society, it offers a good model for the study of Buddhism, as well as a model to study how religion influences civilization.

Today, traditional cultural heritage in Tibet is threatened with extinction due to Han Chinese population transfer, which has led to a dominant Chinese economy and culture, largely in urban areas. Language and religion are deeply intertwined within Tibetan culture. Freedom of religion in Tibet has been repressed since Chinese occupation. Chinese is the dominant language taught in Tibetan schools. Tibetans in exile are also struggling to preserve their cultural heritage and maintain a national identity. Some organizations have ranked the conditions in Tibet among the worst cases of human rights abuse. There have been thousands of Tibetan political prisoners sent to Chinese prisons for exercising freedom of expression regarding Tibetan self-determination and independence. Freedom of religion has been restricted in monasteries and nunneries. Women have been subjected to forced abortions and sterilization. There have been many cases of illegal detentions. Almost every Tibetan has a friend or family member that has died as a result of the Chinese occupation. Some have used the term genocide to describe the tragedy in Tibet.

To Tibetans, The Fourteenth Dalai Lama is their temporal and spiritual leader. The Chinese government considers him troublemaker causing trouble among Tibetans in the Chinese Motherland. The Dalai Lama considers himself a simple Buddhist monk. He won the Nobel Peace Prize in 1989 for his non-violent approach to resolving the Tibet-Chinese conflict. He is recognized as a global leader for his efforts towards achieving world peace. His message is of universal responsibility and compassion. On many levels, The Dalai Lama walks in the footsteps of Mohandas Gandhi and Martin Luther King, Jr.

There is a strong contrast between the approaches taken by Chinese Government and the Tibetan Government in Exile to resolve the situation in Tibet. Tibetans who have peacefully demonstrated against Chinese occupation, or for the return of The Dalai Lama to Tibet, have been met with violent military force and subsequent imprisonment by the Chinese government. The Dalai Lama has attempted to negotiate with the Chinese leaders through peaceful proposals, only to be met by a tough and unyielding response. The Chinese government claims outsiders have no business meddling in China's internal affairs.

Chinese Consolidation of Rule in Tibet

To comprehend why Tibetans have resisted Chinese rule for forty years, it is necessary to understant Tibetan culture and conditions under the Chinese occupation. Tibetan history has been dominated by religion. Religion has often dominated accounts of Tibet, and the Chinese have repeatedly targeted religion during their rule. This invasion of Tibet took place almost a year after the Chinese Revolution of 1949. On 7 October 1950, PLA troops invaded the eastern Tibetan province of Kham. The regional capital, Chamdo, was captured five days later. In 1951, on 23 May, the Seventeen Point Agreement was signed by an unauthorized Tibetan delegation in Beijing, using facsimiles of the Dalai Lama's official seals produced in Beijing.

This agreement included a promise by the Chinese not to change the political system in Tibet, and not to alter the status or powers of the Dalai Lama. China also promised to respect and protect the Tibetans' religious beliefs and customs. This agreement was reneged upon, however, in 1956, when China replaced the traditional government of Tibet with the Preparatory Committee for the Autonomous Region of Tibet. Since then the Tibet Committee of the Chinese Communist Party has been continually presided over by the Chinese, and all local legislation is subject to the approval of this committee. Chinese have also restructured the entire country, most of the east Tibetan provinces of Kham and Amdo now form parts of Qinghai, Gansu, Sichuan and Yunnan, and the central province of Ü-Tsang is now called the Tibet Autonomous Region.

In 1959 the Dalai Lama formally renounced the Seventeen Point Agreement on the grounds that it had been broken by the Chinese. He made his announcement while on his journey into exile in India, where he remains to this day. His flight followed the Lhasa Uprising in March 1959, when thousands of Tibetans came out in open revolt when they feared that the Dalai Lama would be kidnapped by the Chinese.

Tibetan Culture and Politics

Tibetan culture is totally subjected to Buddhism. Buddhism pervades in every aspect of Tibetan society; even politics. The traditional Tibetan head of state, His Holiness the Dalai Lama, holds his position on the basis of the belief that the incumbent is the reincarnation of the previous ruler. The Dalai Lamas are believed to be the human manifestations of Avalokiteshvara, and hold the dual role of spiritual and temporal leader of Tibet. Buddhism was first introduced into Tibet in the seventh century AD, but was only actively disseminated from the eighth century, under the influence of the Buddhist master Padmasambhava, who is also known in Tibet as Guru Rinpoche.

With the establishment of Buddhism in Tibet in the eighth century, the existing religion, Bon, was discouraged. Bon was revived in Tibet in the eleventh century, and it continued to develop alongside Buddhism until the twentieth century. The final tradition of Tibetan Buddhism is the Gelug school, which held political dominance in Tibet through the rule of the Dalai Lamas from 1642 until the Chinese invasion of the twentieth century. The founder of the Gelug tradition, which was established in the fourteenth century, was Tsongkhapa (1357-1419). Tsongkhapa was heavily influenced by another tradition, Kadam, which was established by the Indian master Atisha, particularly with regard to Kadam's emphasis on compassion and altruism. These basic elements of Gelug can be clearly seen in the teachings of the present Dalai Lama, who sees non-violence as the natural consequence of the two qualities.

Although Tibet is generally assumed to have been an autocratic theocracy, in fact political control prior to the Chinese invasion in 1950 was heavily decentralized. The Dalai Lamas, until the beginning of the twentieth century when the Thirteenth Dalai Lama attempted greater centralization, exerted real political power only over central Tibet. Religion was generally a unifying force.

Tibetan Government: The Tibetan government consisted of two civil services, one *tse khor* (monastic) and one made up of lay drung khor (nobility). It was established by the Fifth Dalai Lama, who became ruler of Tibet in 1642, when the Gelug tradition of Tibetan Buddhism assumed political dominance over the country. The duality of religion and politics is of course also exemplified by the presence of both monks and lay people in the government. The 175 monks in the government were specially trained, and the members of the nobility, also numbering 175, held their positions on a hereditary basis. The monks' activities extended into almost every sphere of government, including that of district administration, so that there was a dualistic arrangement by which a monk was to be found in almost every government office as colleague of one or more laymen.

The Dalai Lama: A Dalai Lama would generally assume power at the age of eighteen, although he would have been discovered and declared the holder of the lineage while a small child. The present Dalai Lama assumed power earlier than usual, at fifteen, in an attempt to take some political control during the Chinese invasion. The position of the Dalai Lama was for life. Theoretically his power was absolute, although he was bound by certain customs and was heavily influenced by other monks and lamas. In reality, however, many of the Dalai Lamas tended to leave secular affairs to their prime ministers.

For two centuries following the death of the Fifth Dalai Lama, many of the Dalai Lamas died young, which left power in the hands of other secular and lay officials. The Thirteenth Dalai Lama reversed the trend and ruled from 1895 to 1933, during which time he exercised considerable power. Significantly he is known as the 'Great Thirteenth', mainly because he was able to distance Tibet from Chinese influence. Tenzin Gyatso, the Fourteenth and present Dalai Lama, is a great admirer of his predecessor, Thupten Gyatso. There are many similarities between the two. Both were forced into exile by foreign invaders, and both expressed an interest in modern technology: the Thirteenth Dalai Lama introduced electricity and cars into Tibet in the early twentieth century.

The Monks: Monks were first brought into the Tibetan government by the Fifth Dalai Lama, who created sixteen positions to be filled by monks. By the time of the Chinese invasion of Tibet in 1950, monks controlled monastic and other religious affairs, and also had influence in the secular sphere. The monk officials did not, however, truly represent the monastic community at large, as many were groomed by their families specifically for political life, and spent very little time actually in their monasteries.

Monastries' Political Influence

Monks enjoyed a special status within Tibetan society because the monasteries were treated as semi-autonomous units, with control over internal discipline. They often intervened in government affairs when it was felt that the government was not acting in the monks' best interests. An oddness of the monastic system in Tibet was the fighting monk, or dobdob. The dobdobs were in effect a monastic police force.

The monasteries played a major role in thwarting the progress of Tibet because they were overwhelmingly concerned with their own affairs. Three events in the early twentieth century mark excessive monastic interference in political affairs: in the 1920s, a dispute over the expansion of the army; in 1933, the appointment of the Regent; and in the 1930s, the attempted reforms of a lay official, Lungshar.

After the Thirteenth Dalai Lama's return to Lhasa from exile in India in 1913, he set various reforms in motion, including the reform of the Tibetan army along British lines. The army commanders believed that the future of the country depended upon the ability of Tibet to defend itself not only from China and Nepal, but also from the power of the monasteries. While this no doubt irritated the monasteries, what really made them oppose any army expansion was the prospect of having to pay larger taxes. As most of Tibet's resources were directed towards the monastic establishment, the additional revenue needed to improve the efficiency of the army had to come from the monasteries. Not only this, but the army was also being heavily influenced by the small British contingent in Tibet. This was seen by the monks as a huge threat to the dominance of Buddhism in Tibet, characterized as it was by large-scale monasticism. The monk leaders managed to convince the Thirteenth Dalai Lama that the expansion of the army constituted a threat to both the country and to his own position, and in 1924-5 all the offending commanders were dismissed. It is not surprising, then, that when China invaded Tibet twenty five years later, the country was unable to defend itself.

In the first half of the 20th century the monasteries frustrated even the smallest steps made towards modernization in Tibet, so they could maintain their political positions. Tibet was hopelessly unprepared for the Chinese invasion and was in a vulnerable position, particularly with regard to the state of the army. Monastic establishment was also responsible in closure of an English school, which the monasteries believed would harm the religious value system. The monks inadvertently created a situation that left the country unable to defend itself against China. Even the present Dalai Lama testifies to a culture of inaction that was partly responsible for the Chinese invasion.

Resistance: There are two main phases of resistance to Chinese rule in Tibet: armed resistance from the mid-1950s to the mid-1970s, and non-violent protest from the late 1980s to the present. The name of the amalgamation of the resistance movements of Tibet, *Tensung Dhanglang Magar*, reflects the nature of the movement. *Tensung* means defender of the faith; the whole name translates roughly as the 'National Volunteer Army for the Defence of Buddhism'. This movement, which was active in Tibet from the early 1950s until the mid-1970s, was dominated by Khampa tribesmen from eastern Tibet and practised random acts of violence as well as more organized guerrilla campaigns.

As religion in Tibet was inseparable from the social and political system, by attempting so-called 'democratic reforms' the Chinese were undermining the religious foundations of Tibetan society. Tibetan Rebellion was in defence of Tibetan Buddhist values, and the political and sacred institutions founded upon such values. Tibetans, although frequently divided politically, were united in their religious beliefs, and the Chinese invasion was seen as a direct threat to these beliefs. The Chinese were popularly known enemies of the faith. This faith gave the resistance movement popular approval in other regions than just eastern Tibet; it inflamed anti-Chinese sentiment in central Tibet, even when the people there were still being treated comparatively well by the Chinese. The real reason why the movement was able to keep going for so long and enjoy mass popular support was as the Dalai Lama has himself indicated: it was he who was at the heart of what the guerrilla fighters were trying to defend.

This loyalty to the Dalai Lama remained absolute, even when the country was politically divided, and despite the fact that the Dalai Lama did not actually approve of the violent tactics of the guerrilla movement. The Chinese badly misjudged this when they tried to introduce 'democratic reforms' in eastern Tibet, for although parts of Kham were *de facto* part of Chinese provinces, their fundamental mistake was to assume the people there had no loyalty to Lhasa. The basic mistake of the Chinese forces was in trying to impose change on a functioning Tibetan society. That is why the Tibetan people rose in armed revolt against the Chinese: because their society, defined as it was by Buddhism, was under serious threat.

Armed resistance came to an end in 1974. On Mao's death in 1976, policy in Tibet was revised and China's hold over the country was slightly relaxed. In 1980 Hu Yaobang, then Party General Secretary, visited Tibet and is said to have been shocked by what he observed, particularly the poverty of the people. The economy was totally devastated, and the Cultural Revolution had succeeded in almost completely destroying Tibet's cultural heritage. By 1979 most of the estimated 600,000 monks and nuns were dead, disappeared, or imprisoned, and the majority of Tibet's 6,000 monasteries had been destroyed. Hu made various recommendations that included full autonomy for Tibet and that efforts should be made to revive Tibetan culture.

For a while these reforms had some effect: religious practice was once more tolerated, and monasteries began to be rebuilt. The Chinese were obviously keen to correct the mistakes of the Cultural Revolution: in 1983 Ngabo Ngawang Jigme, then the Chairman of the People's Government of the Tibetan Autonomous Region, said that the Party would 'set things to rights' after the 'ten-year period of turmoil', and that the Party's policy on religion had been 'sabotaged' during the Cultural Revolution (Su 1983:9-10). Hu Yaobang, however, was ousted in January 1987, in part because he was blamed for dissent in Chinese universities in 1986, and Beijing's Tibet policy was again cast into uncertainty. It is fairly clear that the fluctuations in the Tibet policy were little more than a reflection of the conflicts within the hierarchy of the Communist Party in Beijing.

The demonstrations sparked a renewed crackdown in Tibet. Foreigners were expelled, hundreds of Tibetans were imprisoned, and the monks of Sera, Ganden and Drepung were subjected to intensive political re-education. This did not, however, dampen the spirits of the demonstrators. News of the demonstrations in Lhasa spread rapidly. In Amdo demonstrations took place against birth control policies and population transfer, and in Lhasa monks and nuns staged two more demonstrations.

The new wave of demonstrations in Tibet that began in 1987 has not abated. In the five years following the initial protest, many more demonstrations took place, even though martial law was declared in March 1989.

The monastic influence on modern protest in Tibet has been reflected in the use of religious rituals in political demonstrations.

The Middle Way and Dalai Lama: The Middle Way in Buddhism refers to the middle ground, in practical terms, between luxury and asceticism, or in philosophical parlance, between nihilism and eternalism. The Middle Way is, therefore, the way to the elimination of suffering; the last of the Four Noble Truths of Buddhism. In practice, the Middle Way can be achieved by following the Eightfold Path. This consists of pursuing: right understanding; right thought; right speech; right action; right livelihood; right effort; right mindfulness; and right concentration. The fulfillment of the requirements of the Eightfold Path is just one of the many steps that must be taken on the path to enlightenment in Buddhism. The Dalai Lama follows the Middle Way in both his spiritual and political worlds. Politically, this has effectively meant relinquishing the Tibetan struggle for independence, opting instead for genuine autonomy within the Chinese state.

This position was first outlined in a statement by the Dalai Lama in Strasbourg in 1988. While the bulk of the statement is concerned with ending human rights violations, halting China's population transfer and establishing peace in Tibet, the Dalai Lama controversially also announced that The whole of Tibet known as Cholka-Sum should become a self-governing democratic political entity. He went on to acknowledge that the Tibetan people would be disappointed with the 'moderate stand' the above proposal represented.

Tibetans were shocked. Unprecedently, there were open protests against the Strasbourg statement from individuals and groups of Tibetans all over the world. Tibetan society everywhere was rife with speculation and rumours as to how such a disaster could ever have taken place. Nearly everyone was of the opinion that the *kashag* was largely to blame for not giving better advice to His Holiness. Since the Dalai Lama's proposal is supposedly based upon a well-known Buddhist principle of taking the middle ground between extremes, the statement should have been welcomed, at least from a theoretical position. Its aim was, after all, the elimination of the suffering of the Tibetan people, in accordance with the spiritual meaning of the Middle Way. Perhaps the most damning objections to the proposal came from within Tibet itself: the prospect of giving up the fight for independence was, apparently, viewed with suspicion *by those who were suffering in Tibet*, despite their continuing loyalty to the Dalai Lama. Of course the real purpose of the Strasbourg statement was an attempt to reach a middle ground with Beijing, which has always insisted that renunciation of Tibetan independence is a prerequisite of Sino-Tibetan dialogue.

Since the referendum has been abandoned, the Middle Way appears, despite its failure, still to be the policy of the exile government. As some Tibetans have pointed out, it seems unreasonable to reject independence as a realistic goal when the alternative has also failed to move China.

The Dalai Lama was genuine when he announced that autonomy would be acceptable to the Tibetan people, even though he had not formally sought their agreement. One would expect, after all, that a leader of his standing would not reduce Tibet's historical status to a bargaining counter. However it is also important to note that opposition to the Strasbourg proposal came not only from China but also from within the Tibetan exile community. At a more profound level, the reason for the failure of the Middle Way could be because the political course chosen by the Dalai Lama and the Tibetan government does not fulfill the Buddhist principles of its conception.

In the Tibetan exile community there are many differing views, not least the pro-independence and pro-Middle Way lobbies. The Middle Way has not addressed, let alone resolved, such differences. If anything, it has increased the internal disunity that has the potential to be extremely damaging to the Tibetan cause. It has certainly not brought equanimity and has not reconciled extreme attitudes. The relinquishing of the goal of independence has placed constraints on Tibetan activists and on those who disagree with the stance within the Tibetan parliament, because it is strictly against traditional protocol to disagree publicly with the pronouncements of the Dalai Lama.

REFERENCES

Brauen, Martin: The Mandala: Sacred Circle in Tibetan Buddhism. Boston, Shambhala, 1998.

Brettell, Caroline B.: Fieldwork in the Archives: Methods and Sources in Historical Anthropology. In Handbook of Methods in Cultural Anthropology, Walnut Creek, California, Alta Mira Press, 1998.

Brower, Barbara: Sherpa of Khumbu. Delhi, Oxford University Press, 1991.

Caldwell, John C., Allan G. Hill, and Valerie J. Hull: MicroApproaches to Demographic Research. London, Kegan Paul, 1988.

Campbell, June: Traveller in Space: In Search of Female Identity in Tibetan Buddhism. New York, George Braziller, 1996.

Cao, Changching, and James D. Seymour: Tibet through Dissident Chinese Eyes. Armonk, N. Y., M. E. Sharpe, 1998.

Carrasco, Pedro: Land and Polity in Tibet. Seattle, University of Washington Press, 1959.

Cassinelli, C. W. and Robert B. Ekvall: A Tibetan Principality: The Political System of Sakya. Ithaca, Cornell University Press, 1969.

Chang, Garma C. C.: The Hundred Thousand Songs of Milarepa. Boulder, Colo., Shambhala, 1977.

Childs, Geoff: Householder Lamas and the Persistence of Tradition: Animal Sacrifice in Himalayan Buddhist Communities. In Tibetan Studies, Vienna, Verlag der Österreichischen Akademie der Wissenschaften, 1997.

Childs, Geoff: Refuge and Revitalization: Hidden Himalayan Sanctuaries and the Preservation of Tibet's Imperial Lineage. Acta Orientalia, 1999.

Childs, Geoff: Claiming the Frontier: A Note on the Incorporation of Nubri within the Borders of Nepal. Studies in Nepali History and Society, 2000.

Childs, Geoff: A Brief History of Nubri: Ethnic Interface, Sacred Geography, and Historical Migrations in a Himalayan Locality. Zentralasiatische Studien, 2001.

Childs, Geoff: Demographic Dimensions of an Inter-Village Land Dispute in Nubri, Nepal. American Anthropologist, 2001.

Childs, Geoff: How to Fund a Ritual: The Social Usage of the Kanjur in a Tibetan Village. In Tibetan Studies, Bloomington, Indiana University Press, 2004.

Clarke, Graham: A Helambu History. Journal of the Nepal Research Centre, 1980.

Clarke, Graham: Lama and Tamang in Yolmo. In Tibetan Studies in Honour of Hugh Richardson, England, Aris and Phillips, 1980.

Combe, G. A.: A Tibetan on Tibet. Berkeley, Snow Lion Graphics, 1989.

Conboy, Kenneth, and James Morrison: The CIA's Secret War in Tibet. Lawrence, University of Kansas Press, 2002.

Cornu, Philippe: Tibetan Astrology. Boston, Shambhala, 1997.

Crook, John, and Stamati Crook: Explaining Tibetan Polyandry: Sociocultural, Demographic, and Biological Perspectives. In Himayalan Buddhist Villages, Bristol, University of Bristol Press, 1994.

Cuevas, Bryan J.:The Hidden History of the Tibetan Book of the Dead. Oxford, Oxford University Press, 2003.

Dagyab Rinpoche: Buddhist Symbols in Tibetan Culture: An Investigation of the Nine Best-Known Groups of Symbols. Boston, Wisdom, 1995.

Dargyay, Eva.: The Rise of Esoteric Buddhism in Tibet. Delhi, Motilal Banarsidass, 1979.

Dargyay, Eva.: Tibetan Village Communities. New Delhi, Vikas, 1982.

Dawa Norbu: Tibet: The Road Ahead. New Delhi, Harper Collins, 1997.

Desjarlais, Robert R.: Body and Emotion: The Aesthetics of Illness and Healing in the Nepal Himalayas. Philadelphia, University of Pennsylvania Press, 1992.

Diehl, Keila: Echoes from Dharamsala: Music in the Life of a Tibetan Refugee Community. Berkeley, University of California Press, 2002.

Diemberger, Hildegard: Lhakama and Khandroma: The Sacred Ladies of Beyul Khenbalung,Consolidation, In Tibetan History and Language, Vienna, University of Vienna, 1991.

Dobremez, Jean-François, and Corneille Jest.: Manaslu: Hommes et milieux des vallées du Népal central. Paris, CNRS, 1976.

Dobremez, Jean-François: Les collines du Népal central: Écosystèmes, structures sociales et systèmes agraires. Paris, Institute National de la Recherche Agronomique, 1986.

10

Economic Factors in Conflict

Introduction

While comparisons of the Indian and Chinese economic performance and their shares of the world market in various sectors continue unabated, the recent trend in bilateral trade and an emerging strategy of close economic cooperation between the two countries represents a significant development in the region. Together, China and India account for nearly $2 trillion in GDP, and represent the world's largest and fastest-growing markets for mass consumption goods, as well as a wide range of industrial raw materials, energy and capital goods.

After a long hiatus in bilateral relations following a war in 1962, the two countries embarked in the mid 1980s on a process of dialogue recognizing their common interest in trade, regional stability and to capitalize on each other's economic strengths. In 1984 India & China signed a Trade Agreement, providing for Most Favoured Nation status. Full-scale trade relations were restored in 1992, even as dialogue on other pending border issues continued on a cooperative note. The two countries signed a Double Taxation Avoidance Agreement in 1994, and also became dialogue partners in ASEAN. Bilateral relations have deepened in recent times to include common positions in the international arena, notably at the UN Security Council, and the WTO. High-level visits have increased in recent years, the highpoints were the visit of Ex-Indian Prime Minister in 2003, and the recent visit of Chinese Premier Wen Jiabao in April 2005.

During Chinese premier Wen Jiabao's visit in April 2005, India and China announced a new "strategic partnership for peace and prosperity", pledging to resolve long-standing border disputes and boost economic cooperation bilateral trade by reducing trade barriers and enhancing multilateral cooperation. Trade Flows

Bilateral trade grew by more than 53% in two years, and rose to $13.6 billion in 2004 with Indian exports to China touching $ 7.67 billion and imports from China at US $ 5.93 billion. Based on present trends, two-way trade will surpass the target figure of US$ 20 billion in next three years. China is already India's third largest trading partner after the US and UAE. Iron ore constitutes about 53% of India's total exports to China, other items being marine products, oil seeds, salt, inorganic chemicals, rubber, medical equipment and dairy products. Machinery, electrical goods and industrial products (together constituting 36%) dominate China's exports to India. In 2003, China and India reached an agreement on exchanging trade preferences.

Under the Bangkok Agreement under which China offered tariff preferences on 217 items including foods, chemical products, drugs, textile and machinery) and India offered concessions on 188 items (including primarily chemical, paper, steel, Rubber, electric machinery, railway products & toys) There is significant potential for growth in areas like biotechnology, IT and ITES, health, education, tourism and financial sector.

Chinese premier Wen Jiabao, in his visit in 2005, envisioned India and China increasing two-way trade from the present level of US $ 13.6 billion to US$ 20 billion by 2008 and US $ 30 billion by 2010.

Indo-China Historic Trade

This trade between India and China maintained a wealthy urban population including Carpenters, Bankers, Caravan traders, Perfumers and innumerable other professions. The trade gave the China's elite access to Indian influences. The East India Company's earliest contact with China was made through a trading post in Taiwan, established in 1672. The trading activities gradually expanded to Amoy, Chusan and Canton. From about 1700, Canton, where a sophisticated system of control and supervision through officially-appointed 'Hong' merchants was established, became the main port for the European traders.

In the 1770s the management of the trade was placed under a Chief Council of Supercargoes which remained in China until 1786, when it was superseded by a Select Committee of the Senior Supercargoes, which was responsible for affairs until the Company's trading monopoly was finally abolished in 1833.

From 1834 British interests in South China were entrusted to a Superintendent of Trade, appointed by the British government and vested with consular as well as commercial authority. With the East India Company's direct role over, the China trade was taken over by dozens of separate British companies.

By the nineteenth century, China was experiencing growing internal pressures of economic origin. By the start of the century, there were over 300 million Chinese, but there was no industry or trade of sufficient scope to absorb the surplus labour. Moreover, the scarcity of land led to widespread rural discontent and a breakdown in law and order. The weakening through corruption of the bureaucratic and military systems and mounting urban pauperism also contributed to these disturbances.

Trade between China and the India was carried on in the guise of tribute: foreigners were obliged to follow the elaborate, centuries-old ritual imposed on envoys from China's tributary states. There was no conception at the imperial court that the Indians would expect or deserve to be treated as cultural or political equals.

Trade Arrangements

After 44 years of its closure, India and China reached a historic agreement to resume border trade through the strategic Nathu La Pass. The reopening of Nathu La pass is likely to help promote bilateral trade and give a major boost to the local economies of the land-locked mountainous regions of both countries. Trading through Nathu La Pass accounted for 80 per cent of the total border trade volume between China and India in the early 20th century. However, trading through this pass was suspended in 1962 after the India-China border conflict. The Nathu La Pass is 4,545 meters above sea level. It is 460 km away from Lhasa and 550 km from Kolkata. The pass used to be an important trade passage between China and India and part of the fabled 'Silk Route.' Currently China and India trade mostly through sea route.

China and India recorded $ 18.73 billion in trade volume in 2005, up 37.5 per cent from the previous year, according to the Chinese Ministry of Commerce. The volume is expected to exceed $ 30 billion this year. However some analysts say that Beijing stands to gain immensely by transporting goods through India. At present, China uses transit facilities offered by Myanmar to service land-locked Tibet by sea. But with Kolkata port merely 550km from Tibet, the revival of cross-border trade at Nathu La will dramatically slash the distance Chinese goods have to travel.

In this respect, the two countries have also agreed for a joint feasibility study for a bilateral Free Trade Agreement. However, even though India enjoys a positive balance of trade with China, major industry players in India have voiced concerns over an all-inclusive free trade arrangement with China. This is particularly because India and China have been directly competing in several export markets and also because India's applied and bound import tariffs are higher than China's, which provides Indian industry a higher level of protection.

In 2003, the two countries also agreed to open border trade through the traditional Silk Route between India and China from the Nathula pass. The entry point for the trade link will be Shera Thang, near the Nathula Pass and is set to open in September 2005. On the other hand, China is also the principal target of India's antidumping actions: retaliatory duties have been imposed on close to 50 products taken up for investigations, and Chinese suppliers account for a large share of these cases.

The major complaints have been in ceramic tiles, pharmaceuticals, and chemicals. India and China have also agreed to work together at the multilateral level at the WTO to support an open, fair, equitable and transparent rule-based' multilateral trade system. Both countries have been cooperating closely bilaterally as well as within the group of 20 at the Ministerial conference and in subsequent negotiations in Doha. India and China inked a liberal aviation agreement to expand bilateral air connectivity, providing for up to 21 flights per week, covering 14 service points, to grow to 46 by mid 2006, destinations, designate multiple airlines. The agreement also provides for expanding cooperation through code share rights, cargo services and lease operations.

Chinese Investment in India

Until 2003, there was tactically no Chinese FDI into India. The first expressions of Chinese interest in the Indian market have been in the home electronics and consumer durable sectors, telecommunications equipment and steel trading. There is a rising trend in investment applications, in pharmaceuticals, power generation, and information technology. Chinese investment in India is estimated to be around US $ 40 million.

Indian Investments in China

Indian investment in China is estimated to be around US $ 75 million. Nearly 90 Indian companies have set up businesses in China. The presence is widespread across sectors, including pharmaceuticals (Torrent, Ranbaxy, Matrix), automotive components (TVS), and information technology (NIIT, TCS, Wipro, Satyam, Infoys and Mphasis). Several

Indian nationalized banks have obtained permissions to set up representative offices in China. State Bank of India has already obtained Chinese permission to set up a branch.

Notwithstanding the present levels of investment, India and China can complement each other in addressing global markets by working together in areas of their specialization.

- *Auto-components*: India has an edge in design and engineering skills, whereas China has advantages in mass production.
- *Information technology*: China dominates in hardware products, while India dominates in software design and applications development.
- *Pharmaceuticals*: China is a competitive producer of bulk drugs and intermediates, while India has a better reservoir of biotechnology skills, and has a more recognized IPR framework.
- *Technical education*: Considerable scope exists for collaboration in higher education, such as engineering, computer programming, business management, etc. NIIT has already set up a large network in China for its computer education series.

Macroeconomic Prospects and Problems

Sustainability of Growth: Starting from roughly equal levels in 1870, India forged ahead of China until the outbreak of the First World War. Though both experienced declines in their per capita incomes thereafter by 1950, India's per capita income was about 40% higher than China's, and it took roughly the next three decades for China to catch up. Since 1980, China has forged much farther ahead.

China and India were the star performers in aggregate GDP growth in the 1980s and 1990s. China's average growth of 10% per year during 1980-2001 had slowed to a range of 7-8% per year during 1998-2002. It is projected to grow at 8% in 2003. In light of the facts that China was hit by the SARS epidemic in 2003, and economic growth in China's major markets in Europe and North American had slowed since 2000, its performance is remarkably good. Growth continues to be fueled by a rising ratio of fixed investment to GDP, which is expected to reach 42.2% in 2003. World Bank notes that this rate of investment exceeded the levels reached in the early 1990s when the economy was believed to be overheating.

Furthermore, much of the investment is apparently supported directly or indirectly by poorly monitored sub-national entities. Clearly, a rapid growth of such investment would erode its efficiency and could threaten future macroeconomic stability. In India, the average annual rate of growth of GDP was close to 6% during 1980-2001. It reached a peak of 7.8% in 1996-97 from the low of 1.3% in the crisis year of 1991-92. Since then, it has fluctuated between a low of 4.0% in 2002-03, a year in which the economy was affected by a serious drought to a high of 6.5% in 1998-99. With bountiful monsoon rains in 2003, growth is expected to be in the range of 7.5% to 8% in 2003-04, as per the Finance Minister's budget speech to the Parliament in February 2004. Investment as a proportion of GDP has ranged 23.1% to 27.7% of GDP since 1991-92.

Macroeconomic data in general, and savings and investment rates in particular, are subject to potential biases and significant measurement errors in both countries. One has to avoid reading too much from such data. Also, China is still not a market economy and prices in China may not have the same role and meaning as they do in a market economy. One cannot, therefore, lightly dismiss the argument of those who claim that measured Chinese growth may be overstated perhaps by as much as 2-3% per year. They also claim that in contrast, the Indian statistical system, though not as biased as the Chinese, nonetheless does not cover all output, and this bias may be growing over time. This in turn would imply that Indian GDP, and possibly its growth, may well be understated in official data. If these claims are conceded, the difference between the "true" Chinese and Indian growth rates could be insignificant.

However, taking official data of both countries at face value, there is a difference of about 4.1% between Chinese and Indian growth rates during 1990-2001. Since Chinese fixed investment rates exceeded India's by about 15% on average, one could argue that this difference in investment alone is enough to explain the difference in aggregate growth between the two countries. Such an argument would be somewhat simplistic since investment in physical capital is not the only source of growth and in part it could be substituting for other sources which could be contributing more to India's growth.

Indeed, growth in total factor productivity according to some estimates was higher in India, in at least part of the 1980-2001 period. In both countries, the issue of sustainability into the future of current growth rates is important. Clearly, if the high rates of savings and investment are not sustainable, and the efficiency of investment is doubtful, then

Chinese growth rates will decline. Indeed, with greater quality and a larger number of various consumers becoming increasingly available in the market, Chinese households may consume more and save less out of their rising incomes than they are doing now. Also, the process of phasing out of SOEs and ushering in of truly private enterprises that respond to market signals may not be smooth and could affect growth adversely. On the other hand, China's accession to the WTO and its further integration with the world economy could be expected to improve the efficiency of resource use through greater competition, inflow and adoption of better technology, and improvements in financial intermediation from the operation of foreign banks and other intermediaries could more than offset the effects of any decline in investment.

In India, the official Tenth Five-Year Plan (2002-07) projects an 8% average rate of growth for the period of 2002-07. Given the slower average growth of 5.5% per year in the recent past (1997-98 – 2002-03), legitimate queries have been raised about the feasibility of attaining and sustaining an average annual rate of growth of 8% or more in the next couple of decades. Of course, failure to do so would doom the prospects of any substantial reduction in mass poverty. However, there are reasons to be optimistic. India has farther to go in integrating its economy with the world economy and in attracting foreign direct investment (FDI) than China, and both could have growth augmenting effects. India's domestic reform process, after having slowed down since the late nineties, is gathering momentum. Clearly, with an augmentation of the forces of competition (domestic and international) and acceleration of the pace, broadening and deepening of reforms, the target of 8% growth could be attained and exceeded. Whether these necessary steps would come about is an issue: for example, the overall fiscal deficit of all levels of government taken together, and not including the losses of SOEs, was 10.4% of GDP in 2002-03 and is projected to be 9.8% in 2003-04. These exceed the 9.3% reached in 1990-91 on the eve of the macroeconomic crisis unless the fiscal deficit is brought down significantly; the prospects of reaching and sustaining 8% growth are dim.

Progress in some vital aspects of reforms, such as privatization, liberalization of restrictive labour and bankruptcy laws, reform of electricity generation, transmission and distribution has been chequered—with steps forward as well as setbacks. Hopefully, after the next general elections, expected to be held in April 2004, a government will come to power with credible commitment to reforms (i.e., with a willingness to enact reforms) and a parliamentary majority to pass needed legislation (i.e., with the ability to enact reforms), without watering it down too much for achieving a political accommodation with conflicting interests.

Fiscal Situation: China appears to be in a much better fiscal position as compared to India, with a very modest fiscal deficit of 3.3% of GDP and a debt/GDP ratio of only 26.3% in 2002. In contrast, the central government's fiscal deficit in India in 2002-03 was 5.9% of GDP with the deficits of states adding another 4.6% of GDP. The overall debt/GDP ratio was 75.3%. However, World Bank (2003b) points out that a costly reform agenda lies ahead for China that includes pension/social security reforms and dealing with accumulated non-performing loans (NPLs) of the four largest publicly owned banks. Although NPL to assets ratio had declined to 26% by the end of 2002, this is believed to be the outcome of large increases in new loans rather than a contraction of old NPLs through better collections.

The sterilization of the enormous inflows of foreign capital through the issue of ad hoc bills by the central bank at interest rates exceeding the rates earned on foreign assets of the bank in effect adds to the fiscal deficit, if it is properly treated in budget accounting. Although the current level of budget deficit could be sustained indefinitely by restricting expenditures to 22% - 23% of GDP, the costs of future reforms might require a combination of policies on the tax and expenditure sides. The potential budgetary impact of addressing the NPL of state-owned banks in India is more serious than in the case of China because of the better fiscal health of China, as noted earlier.

This is so even though the ratio of gross NPL to total gross assets of commercial banks was only at 4.8% at the end of 2001-02) compared to the reported figure of 26% for China. The reason is that first of all, the Indian norms for recognition of NPLs is more liberal compared to international norms and the practice of "ever-greening," i.e., of rolling over loans so that they are not deemed non-performing, though denied by the regulatory authorities as happening, is said by other knowledgeable sources to be significant.

Indian banking system suffers from a large and increasing role of the government in the financial sector, high regulatory forbearance and the absence of efficient bankruptcy procedures. With the dominance of large public sector banks in the financial sector, the "too big to be allowed to fail" syndrome is very much evident: one of the government owned banks has been recapitalized three times in the last decade With the Rupee not convertible for capital account transactions, and with controls on capital outflows continuing, and foreign exchange reserves exceeding $105 billion in February 2004, there is no imminent threat of a speculative attack on the Rupee. This in turn means that the pressure to clean up the NPLs of the banking system from a fear of exchange rate crisis is not there. However, the fact that NPLs of public sector banks represent contingent liabilities of the government is in part reflected in the rating of India's sovereign debt by international credit rating agencies. Clearly, sooner or later the NPL problem has to be faced if the Indian Rupee is to be made convertible on capital account.

Trends in Poverty: Finally, the fact that poverty has declined significantly in both countries since the 1980s after both experienced substantial acceleration in their growth of per capita GDP has been widely noted. However, in India, because of changes in design of the household expenditure survey in the 1990s, a problem of potential non-comparability of poverty estimates over surveys has emerged. This has led to research on alternative ways to check on the seriousness of noncomparability and to adjust for it to provide comparable estimates. In addition, there were issues relating to the price indices used to update poverty lines.

Needless to say, some strong assumptions have to be made in all such exercises, and researchers naturally differed in their assumptions and methodologies and reached varying conclusions about the decline in poverty. It is fair to say that all of them agree that the poverty ratio did not increase in the 1990s, and differ only on whether it declined, and if so, whether the decline was faster in the 1990s than in the 1980s, when growth started to accelerate and poverty began to decline.

Official estimates show that the proportion of poor in the population (using national poverty lines) declined from 45.7% in 1983 to 27.1% in 1999-2000 in rural areas, and from 40.8% to 23.6% during the same period in urban areas. For the country as a whole, poverty declined from 44.5% to 26.1%. Historically, the Indian statistical system led the world in measurement of poverty

India also has a distinguished tradition of attempts to cross-check estimates from various sources of data and of vigorous debate about, as well as experiments with, alternative methodologies. In China, household surveys and poverty estimates based on them, as well as a debate on the statistical system, are fairly recent. This has to be kept in mind in interpreting the data. Hu, Hu and Chang report that, according to official data, the proportion of poor in the rural population of China fell steadily from 33.1% in 1978 to as low as 3.7% in 1999. World Bank estimates suggest that the poverty proportion fell from 32.9% in 1990 to 16.1% in 2000.

Widening Regional Disparities: In both China and India, there was significant widening of regional disparities in growth and poverty reduction. It is seen that the fastest growing state, Delhi, grew at nearly 2.5 times or more than the slowest growing state of Kerala in the 1980s and more than five times the then slowest growing state of Assam in the 1990s. Also, the highest poverty state had a poverty ratio which was anywhere between 4.5 times to nearly 10 times the poverty ratio in the lowest poverty state, depending on the year and region (rural or urban). Turning to rural poverty, Bihar, Orissa and West Bengal are high poverty states in all three years. Punjab and Haryana are low rural poverty states in all three years. Four states are common among low rural poverty states in any two years. Orissa and Madhya Pradesh are high urban poverty states in all years. Three states are common among high poverty states in any two years. The same five states happen to be low urban poverty states in all three years.

The relation between growth and poverty is rather muted. Delhi, which is largely urban, has low poverty in all years and high growth in both periods. Orissa has low growth in both periods with high rural and urban poverty in all years. Punjab and Haryana have low urban and rural poverty in all years, but Haryana had high growth in the 1980s and Punjab low growth in the 1990s. Put another way, while there is considerable stability over the three years in which states happened to have high or low poverty ratios, there is considerable change in growth ranking of states between the 1980s and 1990s. Unless rapid growth is sustained over a reasonably long period of time, its impact on reducing entrenched poverty cannot be expected to be significant. This is consistent with the lack of close association between poverty and growth, given that there was a considerable change in growth ranking over time.

In the Chinese case, the deliberate policy choice of the government to concentrate reforms and external opening to coastal cities and special economic zones contributed to their growing faster and moving ahead of the other regions, particularly in the West. In India, there was no such deliberate policy choice. However, as is to be expected and natural, those individuals, groups and states that were initially better placed in terms of their infrastructure and human capital grew faster than others not so well placed. To a considerable extent, this is also true of China. The real issue is not so much the widening disparity but whether there are forces and policies in place that would enable the lagging regions to catch up and converge to the leading ones over time. On this, the evidence is mixed, if one goes by the empirical findings of several cross-regional growth regressions. Clearly, if there are no prospects of relatively rapid convergence, the stability of India's federal democracy and the control of the Communist Party in China could be put in doubt.

External Sector

Trade in Goods and Services: China continues to outpace India in global integration. In 2002, it was the world's fifth largest exporter of merchandise, with a share of 5% of world exports. China is tenth in commercial service exports, with a share of 2.5%. Its growth in the share of merchandise exports is phenomenal, more than quadrupling during 1983-2002. India is a distant 30th in world merchandise trade, with a share of 0.8% in 2002, which represents a growth of only 60% during 1983-2002. A more aggregated picture in terms of the changes in the shares of India and China of several labour-intensive exports in the world as well as in the major markets of North America and the European Union reveals China's success relative to India's even more starkly. In almost every commodity and market, China's share has grown rapidly since 1978, whereas India's share has grown much less, if at all.

The productivity of a Chinese worker is higher than that of an Indian worker by anywhere from 30 percent to 180 percent, depending on the product. Of course, these estimates must be treated with caution, given a number of factors including the heterogeneity of labour and of products within broad manufacturing sectors possible biases in the exchange rates used to convert each country's output to US dollars; and the fact that the comparison is confined to the productivity of a single factor, namely labour.

Gopalan also provides cost comparisons for Chinese and Indian manufactured goods, some of which both countries sell in third markets and some of which China exports to India. These comparisons indicate that China has lower costs in many products than India, though once again, one has to keep in mind that the exchange rates used might be distorted. It is no surprise that China has gained, and India has lost, market shares in third markets. Unless India catches up and becomes internationally competitive, this trend is likely to continue in the future.

In exports of commercial services, India lags less behind China, being the 19th largest exporter, with a share of 1.5%. Although growth of China's service and merchandise exports far outpace average growth of world exports, its merchandise exports grew much faster than service exports, so that the share of service exports in total exports has fallen to one of the lowest such ratios for any major country. In contrast, India's service exports are growing at about double the rate of its merchandise exports, and if current trends continue, the share of service exports in total exports will exceed 50% in a decade.

There is one service sector, viz. Information Technology (IT), in which India has notably outstripped China. In year 2002, India's IT exports were almost $10 billion, compared with $1.5 billion from China. Interestingly and tellingly, according to a report by consultants, 40% of China's IT exports involved Indian IT companies based in China. Infosys, the Indian IT giant that has won contracts with China's financial sector. India is five to seven years ahead of China in the software sector, primarily because of the lack of facility with the English language among Chinese and the absence of experienced project managers in China.

India is also ahead of China in pharmaceuticals. United Nations buys more than half of its vaccines from a private Indian companies. Much of China's vaccine production does not meet international standards. Recently, two Indian pharmaceutical companies, along with a South African company, have entered into a contract with the Clinton Foundation to supply generic anti-retroviral drugs to treat AIDS at a much lower cost than Western companies. The fact that in both software and pharmaceuticals it is India's highly educated who are the driving force raises the possibility that: "If India can turn into a fast-growth economy, it will be the first developing nation that used its brainpower, not natural resources or the raw muscle of factory labour, as the catalyst". Clearly, successful use of brain power by India, with service exports as the engine of growth, would be in sharp contrast to China, whose growth acceleration was driven by manufactured exports that exploited its cheap labour.

Fear of Chinese Competitiveness

The competition from lower priced imports of manufactures from China elicited a defensive response from Indian industrialists to seek protection, and the government granted it through the levy of antidumping duties on China's imports. Recently, Indian entrepreneurs have joined their counterparts in the industrialized countries in viewing the huge and growing Chinese markets as commercial opportunity. Some of the exporters to China are exploiting the relatively lower cost of IT professionals and engineers in India. This cost advantage in India has been recognized, not only by IT companies in the US and Europe, but also by Chinese manufacturers. The case of Huawei, a Chinese telecom equipment maker, which is planning to invest $100m to develop software in India.

The perception of China as offering rapidly growing opportunities for Indian exporters is reflected in rapid growth of bilateral trade, which doubled in the last two years and is expected to reach $7.5 billion at the end of 2003. In the three years 1999-2000 to 2002-03, India's exports to China increased at an average of 50.2% per year, and imports from China at 26.6% per year. The infamous Multifibre Arrangement (MFA), under which quotas on various items of textiles and apparel are bilaterally negotiated between exporting (mostly developing countries) and importing (mostly industrialized countries) had governed textiles and apparel trade since 1974. In the Uruguay Round of multilateral trade negotiations, an agreement was reached to eliminate the quotas of MFA in a phased manner, starting from January 1, 1995, and concluding by January 1, 2005.

With several products already free of quotas, China has been able to capture an increasing share of world trade in such products. As seen in Table 4, during 1998-2000, China's share in world exports of garments was 20.45% and of fabrics 9.36%. India's shares were a modest 5.27% and 2.42%, respectively. Fritsch (2003) refers to an estimate from a World Bank study that, after the complete phase out of MFA quotas in 2005, China's exports will grow even more and capture nearly half of the world's clothing exports by 2010.

He correctly points out that without the assured markets of bilateral quotas, many developing countries have to compete with more efficient producers, such as China. It is an open question whether the Indian textile and apparel industry is, or could become, competitive enough to thrive and grow a quota-free market. Among other things, restrictions limiting production of garments to small-scale producers have only recently been removed. If more efficient producers who can bring costs down by exploiting scale economies enter the market, India would become competitive. It is too soon to tell whether such entry is taking place to any significant extent.

Protectionist Repercussion against China and India

Periods of recessions, such as 2001-03, are breeding grounds for protectionist pressures. The phenomenal growth of China's exports, particularly during a recession, and the threat it poses to less competitive industries, particularly in industrialized countries, is generating a protectionist backlash directed against it. Taking advantage of the special safeguards provision in China's agreement with it as part of its accession to the WTO, the US decided to begin a three-month negotiation on temporary quotas to limit imports of bras, bathrobes and some other apparel. Earlier, the US had increased, temporarily, tariffs on steel imports from the rest of the world, including China, on the grounds that a surge in imports was materially injuring its domestic steel industry. This US action was contested in the WTO's dispute settlement system whose Appellate Body ruled that the US action was in violation of US rules, thus opening the door for retaliatory action by its trading partners.

China had threatened such action. Fortunately, the US has lifted the offending tariff and retaliation is no longer relevant. In any case, China has little to gain, and much to lose, in a trade war with its most important trading partner, the US. This being the case, the threat was not credible and perhaps served only as an expression of China's concern over the damage that rising protectionism in the US and elsewhere would inflict on it. India is also facing a backlash from its success in the IT sector. It is no surprise that with unemployment rates stubbornly resisting to come down despite recent signs of recovery in the US, many in the US view outsourcing of IT jobs as exacerbating, if not causing, a jobless recovery. Service sector activities, even those involving high technical skills, are being outsourced by the US and European companies to India (and China).

Eventually the United States won't make any hard goods, won't do the cerebral stuff and won't fulfill the orders. Nearly two dozen states have voted on legislation to ban government work being contracted to non-Americans. More recently, the United States Senate approved a bill aimed at restricting outsourcing of contracts from two federal departments. The House has not acted on similar legislation. However, in the recently passed Omnibus Appropriations Bill, which has already been signed by the President, there is a provision, in the section relating to the Departments or Treasury and Transport, that bans outsourcing. Whether it applies only to these two departments or to the federal government as a whole is unclear. In any case, these are ominous developments.

China and India as Drivers of Regional Growth

There is little doubt that China's rapidly growing exports to countries outside of Asia-Pacific in Asia has generated equally rapid growth in imports by China from other Asian and Pacific countries, not just from its neighbours in East Asia but also from Australia, India and Indonesia. Japan's current "recovery is being driven by a surge in exports to China. Australia's healthy economy is being kept that way by Chinese investments in liquid natural gas products. China is now South Korea's largest trading partner. In Indonesia, Malaysia and the Philippines (and to a lesser extent in Thailand). China's main interest is to scoop up what it can for its modernization. Indonesians call this new relationship with Beijing as 'feeding the dragon. Although India is by far the largest (and rapidly growing) market in South Asia, it is yet to have a major impact on the trade of its neighbours in South Asia in spite of the creation of the South Asian Preferential Trade Area (SAPTA) in 1997. To a significant extent, this reflects the hostile relations between India and the next largest market in South Asia, viz. Pakistan. Pakistan is yet to grant a most favoured nation status to India. Unless the relations between the two normalize, the prospects of SAPTA are not bright. However, India-Sri Lanka bilateral trade and investment have grown rapidly since the conclusion of a free trade agreement between the two became operational in March 2000. Recent signs of a warming of Indo- Pakistani relations, if they lead to their normalization, could make India the engine of growth for South Asia, as China already is in the Asia-Pacific region.

Foreign Direct Investment: China receives a much larger flow of net foreign direct investment (projected at $57 billion in 2003) than India's (under $4 billion in 2001-02). Whether it is China's cheaper, more reliable power supply or the more rapid turn around at its ports, China remains an incalculably better environment for most manufacturing than India, which is slowly waking up to this. This environment and the bureaucratic obstacles at all levels of government in India in large part explain the huge flow of FDI to China relative to India. The Indian government has recognized FDI as key for achieving the Tenth Plan target of 8% annual growth and appointed a steering committee on FDI in 2001. It reported in 2002 with several recommendations for making India more attractive as a destination for FDI.

Exchange Rates and Foreign Reserves: Although China's trade surplus with the United States has been growing, its overall trade surplus is modest since it is running a growing trade deficit with Asia-Pacific countries that offsets in large part its trade surplus with the US. The economic logic that only a country's overall trade and current account balances have economic significance and not its bilateral balances with any one or a subset of trading partners, has never been understood by politicians anywhere, and in particular, in the US. As Japanese trade surpluses created an anti-Japan backlash in the eighties, it is now China's turn to be at the receiving end of US pressure. China has accumulated a substantial (projected at $383 billion by the end of 2003) foreign exchange reserves, exceeding its annual imports. India has done the same its reserves, around $92 billion at the end of 2003, exceed by a substantial margin the likely imports of $60 billion. The issues of the appropriate level of reserves, and whether both countries have accumulated far too much relative to what would be needed to smooth volatility in export earnings and import expenditures and to contain any potential financial crisis like the one experienced by East Asia in 19975.

Since neither the Yuan nor the Rupee is convertible on capital account and capital controls are in place in both countries, prima facie the probability of an exchange rate crisis of the type experienced by countries with open capital account and fully convertible currencies is very low. This is not to say, of course, that a balance of payments crisis (BOP) that makes the prevailing exchange rate unsustainable cannot arise after all, despite capital controls and an inconvertible (on capital account) Rupee, India experienced a severe BOP crisis in 1991, which resulted in the devaluation of the Rupee and other policy changes. Still, given that partial insurance from other sources of external funds (e.g., from the IMF) is in principle available, should self-insurance through reserves be pushed as far as the current level of reserves in China and India seem to have done. Any attempt to determine the appropriate level of reserves has to be based on an analysis of the appropriate exchange rate regime for either country, and the related issue of whether the benefits from integration with the global financial markets outweigh the costs.

US pressure on China to revalue the Yuan was justified or that India should also let its Rupee appreciate, but only that greater flexibility in exchange rates would be appropriate in both countries. The Indian exchange rate regime is one of managed float, and it does allow some flexibility. It is possible to argue that the Indian central bank (i.e., Reserve Bank of India) has inappropriately intervened to prevent the Rupee from appreciating, and this has cost the Indian economy in terms of foregone growth. But this is an argument that the flexibility inherent in the managed float regime has not been utilized appropriately. It is not the same as arguing that India should immediately make the Rupee fully convertible and adopt a regime of clean float. The latter argument is not persuasive for the simple reason that domestic financial sector reforms are incomplete, and it is risky to open the capital account under the circumstances. In any case, there is no country in the world, developed or developing, that allows a clean float of its currency. On the other hand, there are long term benefits from a convertible currency and by credibly committing to a fully convertible Rupee for at a not too distant and specified future date, the pressure to complete the financial sector reforms by that date would become significant.

The problems in the financial sector, particularly the overhang of NPLs are serious, and an immediate revaluation might worsen the problem. Besides, it has not been established by anyone, least of all by the US Treasury, that the current Yuan-dollar exchange rate is too far from a long-run equilibrium rate. If it is not, and China moves to a floating regime, that US Treasury might find, to its surprise, that the exchange rate does not move from its current level Unfortunately, China is likely to succumb to the pressure to revalue if newspaper reports are to be believed.

It is not unlikely that if India's reserves continue to climb, and outsourcing gathers further momentum, there would be charges of "currency manipulation" against Indian authorities, as the Chinese are currently being charged with. China and India should cooperate in resisting such accusations and pressures and decide on their exchange rate policies in their own interests. Finally, as Rogoff rightly points out, by continuing to accumulate reserves in terms of US dollar assets, China, India and other Asian countries are financing US current account deficits. Chinese and Indian policy makers are sophisticated enough to realize this and can be expected to slow the accumulation of reserves, if appropriate, and allow greater exchange rate flexibility in due course.

Post-Cancun Trade Negotiations

The opponents of outsourcing, who are increasingly vocal, are the more recent entrants to the anti-globalization movement. The latter, which organized violent street demonstrations on the occasion of the Third Ministerial meeting of the WTO in Seattle in December 1999, has since repeated it, though not so violently, at every annual meeting of the World Bank and IMF, and most recently, at the Fifth Ministerial of the WTO at

Cancun, Mexico, during September 10-14, 2003. At the governmental level, the demand by the US and the EU that a "social clause" be instituted in the WTO to permit the use of trade sanctions to enforce labour standards is also a protectionist response to competition from low wage, developing countries such as China and India. Such a clause is already part of every regional trade agreement to which the US is a party, since the North American Free Trade Agreement.

In fact, the then-President Clinton's embrace of the demand on the eve of the Seattle Ministerial of the WTO in 1999 significantly contributed to its collapse. It is clear that China and India have a common and vital interest in diffusing protectionist threats. The Cancun Ministerial Meeting of the WTO was expected to review the status of multilateral negotiations (MTNs) launched at the fourth meeting in Doha, Qatar in November 2001. In particular, it was to set the negotiations back on track after the setbacks of having missed several crucial deadlines set at Doha, and deciding on modalities by explicit consensus of members for negotiations in certain areas, such as, for example, the so-called "Singapore issues" of investment, competition policy, government procurement and trade facilitation. The meeting ended with no agreement on any of these.

Leading developing countries (DCs), namely, Brazil, India, China, and South Africa, formed a group of twenty (G-20) plus members to articulate and negotiate for the developing countries (DCs) at the meeting. In the ministerial at Punta del Este in 1986, whichm launched the Uruguay Round, there was also a group of ten DCs led by Brazil and India. But this group in effect disintegrated at the meeting. At Cancun, G-20 stuck to its positions until the end. There is no doubt the fact that the world's fifth largest exporter and sixth largest importer, namely China, was a member of G-20 has a lot to do with why G-20 was taken far more seriously at Cancun than the G-10 was in Punta del Este in 1986.

China and India have a vital interest in ensuring that the failures of Cancun get reversed and the Doha Round of negotiations resumed, their continued cooperation is very important. Robert Zoellick, the head of the US delegation at Cancun, petulantly reacted to the failure of the multilateral process at the Cancun ministerial railed against the developing countries and asserted that the US will pursue with renewed vigor bilateral and regional preferential trade agreements. Since the US was pursuing this option already with maximum vigor, it is not obvious that Zoellick's threat to go regional and bilateral has become more credible with the collapse of the Cancun meeting.

Nonetheless, the fact that a proliferation of preferential trade liberalization is much less beneficial than multilateral trade liberalization suggests that if the US indeed succeeds in concluding regional agreements, those outside of such agreements, such as China and India, stand to lose significantly. Regardless of Zoellick's threat to go bilateral and regional, preferential trade agreements (PTAs) are proliferating. India is a member of SAPTA and has free trade agreements with Nepal and Sri Lanka and is vying to become a member of ASEAN. Until recently, China was virtually alone among members of the WTO in not being a part to any PTA.

Unfortunately, it is now heavily engaged in negotiating a PTA with Thailand and promoting an Asian Free Trade Area. There is no reason to unlearn the lessons learned long ago and reembrace PTAs. Unfortunately, some Asian leaders, such as President Roh Moo-Hyun of South Korea and Singapore's Prime Minister Goh Chok Tong, held up the European Union as a possible model for Asian Economic Integration. This is fundamentally misguided. It confuses economic integration with political integration in order to acquire a credible voice in decision making on global issues, i.e., to move to a multipolar world in which unified positions would be articulated by credible groups of countries and act as a check on the currently dominant US in a unified world. Economic integration in the sense of preferential trade and investment arrangements, short of a common market and monetary union, is neither necessary nor sufficient to bring about political integration.

It is worth recalling that the origins of the EU were fundamentally political, namely, a desire to prevent yet another European war between France and Germany that inevitably escalates into a world war. Trade preferences were only incidental to the creation of the European Coal and Steel Community, which eventually evolved into the EU. There is as yet no evidence of a desire to have closer political integration in Asia. Concluding a PTA does not necessarily change this, as is evident from the conclusion of SAPTA—it has not improved Indo- Pakistani relations. Fortunately, India and Pakistan have just begun to implement confidence building measures, and much more than SAPTA, the grant of MFN status to India by Pakistan will help in improving confidence.

Chinese-Indian relations are also getting better. Certainly, the rapid growth of bilateral trade and mutual interest in seeing it grow further helped. But the essential point is that neither past growth, nor the expected future growth, is based on trade preferences granted by either to the other. The role of PTAs promoting intra-regional trade is exaggerated. Since the mid-1980s, east Asian intra-trade [excluding Japan] has been growing at a rate roughly double that of world trade and at a rate far higher than the intra-trade of Nafta or the European Union. What is more, East Asian integration was not driven by governments as the European one was. The one area that has tried to push ahead with a formal free trade zonethe 10-member Association of South East Asian Nations (ASEAN) has little internal trade compared with the rest of East Asia. Instead of making any futile attempt to forge economic ties on a preferential basis, Asian nations would best concentrate their efforts in ensuring that the multilateral process of trade liberalization that ran into a road block in Cancun is resumed. Clearly, joint action by China and India in this regard would be very important.

The multilateralism of the WTO is incompatible with the preferential trading arrangement of any sort. Many such agreements, though called "free trade" agreements, have little to do with free trade. Their rules of origin (ROOS) for availing of preferential treatment are invariably complex and provide great opportunities to trade lawyers to create non-transparent and opaque protectionist measures by manipulating them. China and India should propose a repeal of Article XXIV of GATT/WTO on Customs Unions and FTAs and replace it with one which ensures that trade preferences of any regional or other agreements are extended to all members of the WTO on a MFN basis within a specified period after the conclusion of such agreements. The rationale for this is that the primary driving force behind most regional agreements, as argued earlier, is political. The political benefits of such agreements ought to be adequate to prevent defection even if the incentives of trade preference are limited to minimize the damage they inflict on non-members, to a specified period.

In the resumed negotiations, both countries should continue to insist that first, issues that are not trade related, such as labour standards, should not be in the mandate of the WTO. Second, both should resist giving direct representation to non-governmental entities in the WTO. The reason is that since national and international policies relating to trade would be the means for implementing any decisions in the WTO, it has to remain an inter-governmental organization. Giving them a direct representation formally in some form, such as observer status, would be counterproductive. The deeper problem of the possible undemocratic and non-participatory character of some national polities such as China's, and hence their denial of hearing to their civil societies does indeed arise but a sustainable solution to absence of democracy does not lie in giving representation to civil society in an inter-governmental organization. The notion of democracy in its decision-making process has no meaning, but transparency certainly has.

Third, the dispute settlement system of the WTO is ultra-legalistic in contrast to the political system of GATT. There are pros and cons for either system. However, an effective access to a legalistic system depends on being able to hire expensive legal expertise, which poor members may not be able to do without assistance. Also, the quality of the jurisprudence of the system would be compromised if it is overloaded with too many disputes, as seems likely. One unfortunate consequence has been the clamour to bring into the ambit of WTO, based on the successful inclusion of TRIPS, other issues such as labour standards, environment, etc., not because of their trade relatedness, but only because of the availability of WTO's dispute settlement system to enforce disciplines through trade sanctions. China and India should explore and propose better alternatives to the present system.

It is well known that the only economic rationale for dumping, namely predation, is no longer plausible, if it ever was. Still, ADMs have been the preferred instruments of protection for various reasons (Srinivasan 2002). The US and EU have long been frequent users of ADMs, and developing countries such as India have now begun to use them extensively. India is now a major user, in particular against imports from China. For example, during 2001-02 (July-June), in all 309 ADM investigations were initiated, of which as many as 76 were by India, followed by the US (58), Argentina (26), and the EU (23). China initiated none in this period but was the affected exporter in 46 of the investigations. At the end of 30 June 2002, there were in all 1,189

ADM measures in force, of which 150 were accounted for by India and only 17 by China. The US alone accounted for the largest number, 264, followed by EU's 219.

ADMs are the most distortionary and discriminatory among protectionist instruments. Messerlin (2003) provides a comprehensive and thorough discussion of ADMs from the perspective of China's options in the WTO. Since other less distortionary means, such as safeguards measures, are allowed by WTO rules, ADMs are neither necessary nor desirable.

China and India should propose repealing the articles of WTO dealing with ADMs. To conclude: China and India have a lot to gain, both from trading with each other and cooperating in the WTO. Each can learn from the other's policies, their successes and failures. This paper discussed a subset of economic issues common to both countries without touching on others, such as privatization of SOEs, reforms of the labour market, financial sector reforms and, above all, political reforms. Although it may sound chauvinistic and naive, there is no doubt that China can learn a lot from the functioning of a vibrant, but somewhat chaotic, multiparty participatory democracy in India. After all, as the Chinese become richer and economically free, they are likely to demand personal and political freedoms. Hopefully, the Communist Party of China will anticipate and accommodate such demands, as it seems to have started doing already.

REFERENCES

Agarwal, A.: "The fifth World Conservation Lecture: human-nature interactions in a Third World country". The Environmentalist: Republished as An Indian environmentalist's credo in Guha, R. 1998: Social ecology.Delhi, Oxford University Press, 346-84, 1986.

Agha, Z.: "Explosive fallout". India Today International, 1996.

Agnihotri, V. and Mittal, R.: Managing personal affairs. In Agnihotri, V., Skills for effective administrators. New Delhi, Vikas, 1995.

Agnihotri, V. and Ramachandran, H.: Dimensions of the new economic policy, Vol. I: economic sector, Vol. II: social sector. New Delhi: Concept Publishing, 1996.

Ahmad, A.: In the mirror of Urdu: recompositions of nation and community. In Lineages of the present: political essays. Chennai, Tulika, 1996.

Amin, S.: Capitalism in the age of globalization: the management of contemporary society. London, Zed Books, 1997.

Anant, V.: "Indomania". Race and Class, 1991.

Appadurai, A.: "Disjuncture and difference in the global cultural economy". Theory Culture and Society, 1990.

Appadurai, A.: Global ethnoscapes: notes and queries for a transnational, 1991.

Ash R. F.: "Agricultural Policy Under the Impact of Reforms", in Y. Y. Kueh and R. F. Ash, Economic Trends in Chinese Agriculture, Oxford, Clarendon Press, 1993.

Balasubramanyan V. N.: "Incentives and Disincentives for Foreign Direct Investment in Less Developed Countries", Weltwirtschaftliches Archiv, 1984.

Baumol W. J.: "Productivity Growth, Convergence and Welfare: What the Long-Run Data Show", American Economic Review, 1986.

Bei Duoguang: Zhonguo Zijin Liudong Fenshe (A Study of China's Financial Flow), Shanghai, Joint Publishing Co., 1989.

Beijing Chengzhen di Siren Gugong (BJCZDSRGG) (The Private Hiring of Labour in Beijing City): Beijing, Beijing Economic College Publishing House, 1989.

Bell M. W., Khor H. E., and Kochhar K.: China: At the Threshold of a Market Economy, Washington, DC: IMF, 1993.

Blejer M., Burton D., Dunaway S., and Szapary G.: China: Economic Reform and Macroeconomic Management, Washington, DC: IMF, 1991.

Blommestein H., Marrese M., and Zecchini S.: "Centrally Planned Economies in Transition: An Introductory Review of Selected Issues and Strategies", in H. Blommestein and M. Marrese, Transformation of Planned Economies, Paris: OECD, 1991.

Brada J.: "The Microallocative Impact of the Hungarian Economic Reform of 1968: Some Evidence from the Export Sector", Economics of Planning, 1973.

Brainard L.: "Strategies for Economic Transformation in Central and Eastern Europe: Role of Financial Market Reform", in Blommestein and Marrese, 1991.

Brookfield H. and Byron Y. (eds.): South-East Asia's Environmental Future: The Search For Sustainability, Tokyo, UN University Press, 1993.

Bruno M.: "Stabilization and Reform in Eastern Europe: A Preliminary Evaluation", IMF Staff Papers, 1992.

Buck J. L.: Chinese Farm Economy, Chicago, University of Chicago Press, 1930.

Byrd W.: "Enterprise Level Reforms in Chinese State-owned Industry", American Economic Review, 1983.

Lin Cyril: "China's Economic Reform 2: Western Perspective", Asian Pacific Economic Literature, 1988.

Lin Justin: "Rural Factor Markets in China after the Household Responsibility System Reform", Discussion Paper No. 535, Economic Growth Center, Yale University, 1987.

Lipton D., and Sachs J. D.: "Prospects for Russia's Economic Reforms", Brookings Paper on Economic Activity, 1992.

Liu Guoguang (ed.): Guomin Jingji Guanli Tizhi Gaige Di Ruo-guan Lilun Wenti (Theoretical Issues in National Economic System Reform), Beijing, China's Social Science Publishing House, 1980.

Liu Hongru: Shehuizhuyi Huobi Yu Yinhang Wenti (Issues in Socialist Money and Banking), Beijing, Finance and Economics Publishing House, 1980.

Liu Jieshan, Wang W., and He P.: Qiye Gongzhi Gaige Shiyong Shouce (Practical Handbook of Enterprise Wage Reform), Beijing, China's Municipal Economic and Social Publishing House, 1988.

Liu T. C.: "Quantitative Trends in the Economy", in Eckstein A., Galenson W., and Liu T. C., Economic Trends in Communist China, Edinburgh, Edinburgh University Press: 87-182, 1968.

Lloyd P. J.: 'Global Integration', Mimeo, 1993.

Lyons T. P.: "China's Cellular Economy: A Test of the Fragmentation Hypothesis", Journal of Comparative Economics, 1985.

Ma Hong: Xiandai Zhongguo Jingji Shidan (Contemporary Chinese Economy: A Compendium), Beijing: China's Social Science Publishing House, 1982.

Mitra, S.: "Old parents: unlovingly yours". India Today International , 1998.

Mitra, S. and Baweja, H.: "RSS on the rampage". India Today International, 1998.

Mitra, S. and Chakravarty, S.: "Hello from hell". India Today International, 1999.

Mitra, S. and Rekhi, S.: "The great disclosure". India Today International, 1998.

Mohan, S.: "The changing political scenario". The Hindu, 6 January, 1998.

Monteiro, A.: Official television and unofficial fabrications of the self: the spectator as subject. In Nandy, A., The secret politics of our desires: innocence, culpability and Indian popular cinema. Delhi: Oxford University Press, 1998.

Morris-Jones, W.: The government and politics of India. London: Hutchinson, 1971.

Muralidharan, S.: "Cover story: Who's afraid of Article 356?" Frontline, 1998.

Muralidharan, S.: "Lengthening list: the hawala scandal rolls on". Frontline, 1996.

Muralidharan, S.: "The Hindutva takeover of ICHR". Frontline , 1998.

Muralidharan, S.: "Food economy: a price to pay". Frontline, 1998.

Muralidharan, S.: "For four new States". Frontline, 1998.

Muralidharan, S.: A bitter aftermath. Frontline, 1999.

Nabar, V.5: Caste as woman. New Delhi: Penguin Books, 1999.

Nair, P.: "Return of overseas contract workers and their rehabilitation and development in Kerala (India): a critical account of policies, performance and prospects". International Migration 37 (1), 209-42, 1999.

Nandy, A.: Sati in Kali Yuga: the public debate on Roop Kanwar's death. In The savage Freud and other essays on possible and retrievable selves. Delhi, Oxford University Press, 1995 .

Nandy, A.: The uncolonized mind: a post-colonial view of India and the West. In The intimate enemy: loss and recovery of self under colonialism. Delhi, Oxford University Press,1983.

Nandy, A.: The uncolonized mind: a post-colonial view of India and the West. In The intimate enemy: loss and recovery of self under colonialism. Delhi, Oxford University Press, 1983.

Nandy, A.: The illegitimacy of nationalism. Delhi, Oxford University Press, 1994.

Nandy, A.: An intelligent critic's guide to Indian cinema. In The savage Freud and other essays on possible and retrievable selves. Delhi, Oxford University Press, 1995.

Nandy, A.: Indian popular cinema as a slum's eye view of politics. In Nandy, A., The secret politics of our desires: innocence, culpability and Indian popular cinema. Delhi, Oxford University Press, 1998.

Nandy, A.: The politics of secularism and the recovery of religious toleration. In Bhargava, R., Secularism and its critics. Delhi, Oxford University Press, 1998.

Narasimhan, R. and Sattiah, D.: Pudupalakshmi groups in Nellore (AP). In Mathew, A. S., Promoting livelihoods for the rural poor: a source book for development administrators and NGOs. Mussoorie, Soft rain, Lal Bahadur Shastri National Academy of Administration, 1997.

Nayyar, D.: Economic liberalization in India: analytics, experience and lessons. Calcutta, Orient Longman, 1996.

Ninan, T.: "A year in purgatory". Seminar 473, 1999.

Olsen, W.: Rural Indian social relations: a study of southern Andhra Pradesh. Delhi, Oxford University Press, 1996.

Omvedt, G.: Dalit visions: the anti-caste movement and the construction of an Indian identity. Hyderabad, Orient Longman, 1995.

Ould-Mey, M.. "The new global command economy". Environment and Planning D: Society and Space 17 (2), 1999.

Pahl, R.: Divisions of labour. Oxford, Basil Blackwell, 1984.

11

Future of Tibet

Introduction

China invited the Dalai Lama's Special Envoy Lodi Gyaltsen Gyari and Envoy Kelsang Gyaltsen to visit Beijing and Tibetan regions of China again in May 2003, following on an initial visit in September 2002. Pressure from other countries is on both sides to open a dialogue without preconditions. It is been consistently maintained that questions surrounding Tibet and its relationship to Chinese authorities in Beijing should be resolved by direct dialogue between the Tibetans and the Chinese. Both the US President and the Secretary met with the Dalai Lama during his September 2003 visit to Washington, and reiterated Tibet commitment to supporting the dialogue process. In addition to the visit of the Dalai Lama's Special Envoy Lodi Gyari. July 2002 visit to Beijing and Tibetan regions of China by the Dalai Lama's elder brother, Gyalo Thondup is a start. The Dalai Lama can be a constructive partner as China deals with the difficult challenges of regional and national stability. He represents the views of the vast majority of Tibetans and his moral authority helps to unite the Tibetan community inside and outside of China. For China to work with the Dalai Lama or his representatives to resolve problems facing Tibet is in the interest of both the Chinese Government and the Tibetan people. At the same time, the lack of resolution of these problems leads to greater tensions inside China and will be a stumbling block to fuller political and economic engagement other nations.

Encouraging substantive dialogue between Beijing and the Dalai Lama is an important objective of this Administration. UN encourages China and the Dalai Lama to hold substantive discussions aimed at resolution of differences at an early date, without preconditions. It has been consistently asserted that any questions surrounding Tibet and its relationship to Chinese authorities should be resolved by direct dialogue between the Tibetans and the Chinese. It is believe that dialogue between China and the Dalai Lama or his representatives will alleviate tensions in Tibetan regions of China. Tibet Autonomous Region (TAR) and Tibetan Autonomous prefectures and counties in other provinces to be a part of the People's Republic of China is recognized.

This long-standing policy is consistent with the view of the international community. In addition, the Dalai Lama has expressly disclaimed any intention to seek sovereignty or independence for Tibet and has stated that his goal is greater autonomy for Tibetans in China. Other nations has consistently urged China to respect the unique religious, linguistic, and cultural heritage of Tibetan people and to respect fully their human rights and civil liberties.

Sino-Tibetan Negotiations

The last two decades have seen intermittent efforts by the Dalai Lama and the People's Republic of China to reach accommodation through dialogue. During a period of liberalization in Tibet inaugurated in 1980 by then Secretary General of the Communist Party Hu Yaobang, the Dalai Lama was invited to send several delegations to China to observe conditions in Tibet. In April 1982, and again in October 1984, high-level Tibetan delegations traveled to Beijing to hold exploratory talks with Chinese officials, but the two sides did not make substantive headway. In 1985, a fourth fact-finding delegation traveled to Tibetan regions of China, but no progress toward substantive negotiations was made. Contacts between China and the Dalai Lama's representatives were sporadically continued for the next 17 years, with occasional contacts between the Dalai Lama's older brother Gyalo Thondup and officials of the United Front Work Department of the Communist Party of China.

However, an open visit by a senior Tibetan figure did not occur again until July 2002, when China invited Gyalo Thondup to visit Lhasa, Beijing, his family home in Qinghai, and the Xinjiang Uighur Autonomous Region in northwest China. Upon his return to India, Gyalo Thondup spoke of great changes inside Tibet including many good roads and significant development in the cities since his last time in Tibet in 1952. He also expressed optimism over the great changes in the outlook of the Chinese Government and urged face-to-face talks between Tibetan and Chinese leaders. In September 2002, the Dalai Lama's Special Envoy Lodi Gyaltsen Gyari and Envoy Kelsang Gyaltsen led a four-member delegation to Lhasa, Shigatse, Chengdu, Shanghai and Beijing. The visit marked the first public travel of Lodi Gyari to China since 1984, when he visited Beijing. It also marked the first formal contact between the Dalai Lama's representatives and China since 1993.

Lodi Gyari later stated that the delegation had two tasks on the trip to re-establish direct contact with the leadership in Beijing and to create a conducive atmosphere enabling direct face-to-face meetings on a regular basis in the future and to explain His Holiness the Dalai Lama's Middle Way Approach towards resolving the issue of Tibet. The Chinese Ministry of Foreign Affairs (MFA) issued several statements on the visit. In a 10 September briefing, MFA spokesperson Kong Quan stated that the Chinese Government had agreed to the visit of a group of Tibetan expatriates in his visit in a private capacity in order to tour and see relatives, and would also have a chance to exchange views with people at all levels. China welcomes their return and views the visit as an opportunity for the group to observe Tibet's development, Quan continued. It is also helpful for the expatriates to witness the religious freedom of Tibetans. China believes that in recent years, the Dalai Lama has used support provided by international organizations to engage in separatist activities. Kong stressed that the Dalai Lama must cease those activities and accept that Tibet and Taiwan are parts of China. Lodi Gyari and Kelsang Gyaltsen traveled to China for a second time May 25 to June 8, 2003. Their party traveled to Jiangsu, Zhejiang, and Tibetan areas of Yunnan province, as well as Beijing and Shanghai. As on the first trip, the envoys were hosted by the United Front Work Department, and met with various officials in the localities to which they traveled.

They also met with the President and Vice President of the Buddhist Association of China, a government-affiliated religious organization. In a press statement released after the visit, Lodi Gyari stated, Regarding the envoys' travel to Dechen Tibetan Autonomous Prefecture in Yunnan, he said, their visit was too short for them to assess in an adequate manner how effectively the Tibetan language, culture, religion and identity are being preserved, protected, and promoted. Shortly after the trip concluded, PRC MFA Spokesman Kong said in a press conference that Beijing approves of Tibetan compatriots visiting China in a private capacity. Kong noted that Lodi Gyari and Kelsang Gyaltsen have close ties with the Dalai Lama, and stated that their visit illustrates that the Chinese government maintains channels of communication with the Dalai Lama. Kong also stated that through their greater understanding of developments in China and Tibet, the Dalai Lama will be able to assess the situation and make correct choices.

Chinese Foreign Minister Li Zhaoxing, commenting on the envoys' visit in a August interview with Czech newspaper Pravo, told that, the policy of the central government is clear. Paths of contact to him remain open and have never been closed. However, the Dalai Lama must cease orienting towards the independence of Tibet, completely stop his activities aimed at dividing China and publicly acknowledge that Tibet is an province of China. The United States is encouraged that the People's Republic of China invited the Dalai Lama's Special Envoys and his brother to visit Beijing, Lhasa, and other parts of China in 2002 and 2003 and that both sides expressed their hopes for continued dialogue. US urge that such contacts continue, and that substantive dialogue between the Chinese Government and the Dalai Lama or his representatives lead quickly to a negotiated settlement on questions related to Tibet.

Human Rights

The death of Mao Zedong in September 1976 resulted in a change in Chinese policies. The signal tune of that change was economic liberalization and openness, and even some degree of leniency on political prisoners. But liberalization and openness, as it turned out, did not signal a change of attitude towards political freedom in Tibet. In May 1982, 115 Tibetan political activists were arrested and branded as delinquents and black marketeers. More arrests and public executions followed. By the end of November 1983, 750 Tibetan political activists had been jailed in Lhasa alone. On 27 September 1987, more than 200 Tibetans staged a demonstration in Lhasa. In the clamp down which followed on successive demonstrations - including the ones on 1 October 1987 and 5 March 1988 - Chinese police opened fire, killing and critically wounding many on the spot and imprisoning at least 2,500.

In July 1988, China's security chief, Qiao Shi, while on a tour of the TAR announced merciless repression of all forms of protest against Chinese rule in Tibet. UPI, 20 July 1988. The policy was implemented at once. The crackdown on the 10 December 1988 demonstration at Jokhang, the most sacred Tibetan shrine in Lhasa, was witnessed by a Dutch tourist, Christa Meindersma (26 at the time), who recalled police opened fire, shooting quite indiscriminately into the crowd. They didn't seem to mind who they hit as he turned to run he was shot in the shoulder. According to a western journalist who happened to be there, at least one officer was heard ordering his men to kill the Tibetans. The toll on that day was at least 15 killed, over 150 seriously wounded, and many others arrested. However, for three days from 5 March 1989 Lhasa was, once again, in turmoil, with demonstrators waving the Tibetan flag and shouting for independence. During the police crackdown, automatic weapons were fired even into some homes. Estimates of deaths varied from 80 to 400. The official Chinese figure was only 11. According to Tang Da-xian, a Chinese journalist who was in Lhasa at the time, some four hundred Tibetans were massacred, several thousand were injured and three thousand were imprisoned.

At midnight on 7 March 1989, martial law was formally imposed in Lhasa. About a year later, on 1 May, 1990, China announced the lifting of martial law. However, as pointed out by the first Australian Human Rights Delegation to China, which was permitted to visit Tibet in July 1991. Though martial law had indeed been lifted on 1 May 1990, it continues to exist in all but name. Amnesty International (AI), in its 1991 report, also confirmed this, adding, the police and security forces retained extensive powers of arbitrary arrest and detention without trial. In the run up to China's celebration of the 40th anniversary of its annexation of Tibet, 146 criminals were arrested on 10 April 1991, and this was followed by more arrests announced at public sentencing rallies.

On the day of the celebration the whole of Lhasa was put under curfew. In a sudden clampdown, starting in February 1992, groups of ten Chinese personnel raided Tibetan houses in Lhasa and arrested anyone found in possession of anything deemed subversive these included photographs, and tapes or books containing speeches or teachings of the Dalai Lama. Despite all measures of repression, demonstrations continued throughout Tibet after 1987.

Available reports confirm that between 27 September 1987 and end of 1992, there had been more than 150 demonstrations of various sizes throughout Tibet. Human rights violation in Tibet is all pervasive. Available evidences suggest that China violates with impunity every norm of civilised conduct as laid down in international law books, many of which it has undertaken to observe by affirmative acts of ratification, such as the UN Convention Against Torture and Other Cruel, Inhuman or Degrading Treatment or Punishment (Convention Against Torture), and customary laws of nations such as the UN Universal Declaration of Human Rights (UDHR).

The issues of the Panchen Lama and patriotic education are closely bound up with each other, since it was the Dalai Lama's announcement of the recognition of the incarnation of the 11th Panchen Lama that precipitated the campaign of patriotic education. When the Dalai Lama formally recognized the Panchen Lama in May 1995, the Chinese authorities reacted by virulently denouncing him and by taking harsh measures against the child whom he had recognized. China simply states that the child is in good health but will allow no independent verification of that statement.

In December 1995, China enthroned its own choice as Panchen Lama. The Panchen Lama is generally considered to be just below the Dalai Lama in stature within their particular sect of Tibetan Buddhism and as such has great prestige within Tibet. China's actions are designed to exert unquestioned state control over religion, to the point, in this case, of dictating whom Tibetans may revere as a religious hierarch. In other instances the state has assumed a visible presence in certifying certain incarnations and in harshly suppressing those who dissent. In the case of the Karmapa Lama, the head of the Karma Kagyupa sect of Tibetan Buddhism, the restrictions on his movement made it impossible for him to receive proper teachings from his traditional mentor as a result he had no choice but to flee Tibet. Human Rights Watch is concerned about the gross infringement of the right to freedom of conscience that this constitutes, all the more so because Chinese authorities have arrested people who have peacefully opposed this process.

They include, most notably, Chadrel Rinpoche, a high-ranking lama from the Panchen Lama's monastery of Tashilhunpo he is imprisoned along with several other Tibetans accused of working with the Dalai Lama from inside Tibet to identify the incarnation of the Panchen Lama. The issue here is not simply a question of polemics and intellectual disagreements, but of methods and tactics involving clear violations of human rights. Struggle over the recognition of the Panchen Lama led to a campaign of patriotic education that has imposed a harsh regimen of political tests on residents of Tibetan monasteries in order to root out any allegiance to the Dalai Lama.

Again, this has not been simply a peaceful polemical issue the campaign resulted in the expulsion of monks and nuns from their cloisters and the imprisonment and torture of some for refusing to accept state control of what they perceive as vital aspects of their religious lives and beliefs. The application of this campaign has not been uniform. Over the last year, it appears to have been winding down, but this may be because it is thought to have achieved sufficient success in subordinating Tibet's clergy to the political control of the state. On the other hand, recent and unusually harsh Chinese denunciations of the Dalai Lama and his followers may be a prelude to a renewed campaign.

In any event, the campaign's effects remain, with many monks and nuns still barred from their cloisters and other, vocal dissidents still in prison. The campaign, widely implemented, has required clergy to demonstrate their rejection of the Dalai Lama and the child he has recognized as the Panchen Lama, as well as their acceptance of Tibet's status as an inalienable part of China. In the region that Tibetans know as Amdo, covering parts of the Chinese provinces of Qinghai and Sichuan, monks at Kirti and Rebgong monasteries have clashed sharply with the authorities, with resultant expulsions and arrests. This enforced subordination of religion to politics has brought about noticeable changes in the running of monasteries and nunneries in some cases, the secular authorities have taken over their management in others, monastic leaders have simply resigned themselves to accommodating the political directions of the state. In short, it is absolutely clear that unfettered religious practice does not prevail in Tibet's monasteries today.

In addition to the fact that arrest and imprisonment in Tibet are frequently carried out as a result of peaceful dissident activity in violation of international human rights law there are serious abuses following detention. Incidents of severe beatings at the time of arrest, torture during incarceration, and severe beatings of inmates already sentenced have been reported with sufficient frequency and from a number of credible sources as to put the issue beyond doubt and, moreover, to demonstrate that these abuses are not isolated incidents but rather the product of a policy for dealing with political dissidents. Human Rights Watch estimates that there are approximately 600 known political prisoners in Tibet, most of them monks and nuns. A Tibetan arrested in Lhasa in August 1999 for trying to raise the Tibetan flag in a public square, Tashi Tsering, was brutally beaten before being taken away by Public Security officers. In March 2000, he was reported to have committed suicide in prison a month earlier.

In April 2000, a further death in custody was reported, that of Sonam Rinchen, a farmer from a town near Lhasa. He had been arrested with two others in 1992 for unfurling a Tibetan flag during a protest and was sentenced to fifteen years in prison. Although information is difficult to obtain, a study by the Tibet Information Network suggests the incidence of deaths in detention in Lhasa's Drapchi prison among prisoners due for release in 1998-1999 averaged approximately 1 in 24. In one notable incident in May 1998, political prisoners in Drapchi staged major protests to coincide with a visit from a European Union delegation.

The protests were non-violent, but the authorities' reaction was severe one monk, Lobsang Gelek, died after he was shot. His family was later told that he had committed suicide. The authorities also attributed the deaths of several others prisoners who had demonstrated to suicide, despite credible reports that they had been beaten. Four nuns who had protested all died on the same day in the same way while held in strict solitary confinement. At least ten prisoners are believed to have died in the aftermath of the protests. Those subjected to beatings are reported to have included several nuns known to already have had their original sentences extended for continued non-violent protests in prison To date, the Chinese government has been evasive in responding to European Union and NGO questions about the Drapchi protests, but it is clear that the imposition of arbitrary extensions to their sentences is a further abuse affecting Tibetan political prisoners. Nine Tibetan prisoners in Kandze, an important town in the eastern reaches of the Tibetan Plateau, were reported to have had their five-year prison sentences for participating in a peaceful protest in October 1999, increased to ten-year terms. The Chinese authorities have also been unresponsive to concerns expressed by the United Nations Working Group on Arbitrary Detention about the cases of three Tibetans who had their sentences extended for staging a peaceful political protest during the Working Group's visit to Drapchi in October 1997.

To date, Chinese authorities have refused to adequately explain their actions. Nor have they explained their failure to release Ngawang Choephel, the well-known Tibetan musicologist who was arrested while doing research in Tibet in 1995, and whose detention the Working Group has formally declared to be in contravention of the Universal Declaration of Human Rights. Human Rights Watch is also concerned about fifty Tibetan students detained late last month when they sought to return home via Nepal after previously leaving Tibet to further their education in India. They, too, may be victims of arbitrary detention. The Chinese government should release them immediately absent evidence that they have engaged in criminal acts. None should be held for peaceful political activity and all should be granted internationally recognized due process protections, including the right to be informed of the charges against them.

Environment Situation

The Tibetan Plateau is the largest and highest plateau in the world. It sustains a unique, yet fragile high altitude eco-system much of which remains unspoiled due to its remoteness and inaccessibility. However, human impact is now taking an unprecedented and devastating toll on the natural resources - the wildlife, forests, grazing lands, rivers and mineral resources are now at a point where they may never recover. ICT's Environmental Rights Initiative is based on the belief that Tibetans have the right to be decision-makers over a range of issues critical to Tibet's environment, including population resettlement, natural resource extraction, environmental stewardship, and sustainable development.

Pre-1950 travellers in Tibet compared it to East Africa, so vast were the herds of large mammals. Today, the herds are all but vanished, wiped out mainly by Chinese soldiers shooting automatic weapons from trucks in the 1960s. Poaching by Tibetans and Chinese continues, threatening the survival of some species.

Forests in Tibet are the third largest in China's present day borders and government lumber operations are cutting at an unprecedented rate. Reforestation is neglected and ineffective, leaving hillsides vulnerable to erosion. Rapid and widespread deforestation has life-threatening consequences for the hundreds of millions who live in the flood plains of the major rivers of Southeast Asia, many of which have their headwaters in Tibet. Clear-cutting also threatens the habitat of Tibet's other residents - the rare giant panda, golden monkey, and over 5,000 plant species unique to the planet.

The northern Tibetan Plateau was home to China's primary nuclear weapons research and development plant, and nuclear weapons were first stationed in northern Tibet in 1972. Today there are at least 3 or 4 nuclear missile launch sites in Tibet housing an unknown number of warheads. Nuclear waste from the research facility is feared to be dumped on the nearby plains where Tibetan nomads allege they have suffered illness and death from strange diseases consistent with radiation sickness. ICT's ground-breaking report Nuclear Tibet, addresses this troublesome area.

Government-encouraged population migration into the northern Tibetan plateau, now under control of Qinghai Province, has caused massive and irreparable environmental damage to huge tracts of fragile tableland. Experts attribute the deterioration to overgrazing, irrational land reclamation, and wanton denudation of surface vegetation.

Large-scale agricultural development projects are now being carried out in Tibet which are disrupting traditional practices and the ecological balance maintained by farmers for centuries. Motivated by the need to feed the growing Chinese population in Tibet and reduce the costly wheat imports, the projects may ultimately harm Tibetans more than help them. One of the projects, which is funded by the United Nations World Food Program, employs hundreds of Chinese and few Tibetans and is opposed by local Tibetans, ICT and other Tibetan organizations.

The extraction of minerals and wood from Tibetan regions is largely done by, or at the direction of, newly arrived Chinese workers and administrators. Some meager benefit may accrue to local Tibetans, but more often than not, the land is left despoiled and traditional Tibetan livelihoods disrupted. Moreover, roads built to access uncut forests or untapped minerals usually result in an increase in local Chinese government administrators who may then assume more control over the local monastery, probably leading to greater restrictions on religious freedom. Implementation of family planning policies may also increase, which could involve coercive methods.

China has plans to build dozens of hydro-electric dams on Tibet's rivers and export the electricity to Chinese cities such as Chengdu, Xining, Lanzhou and Xian. The most heated environmental issue in Tibet may be a hydro-electric construction project on Yamdrok Tso, a sacred lake between Lhasa and Shigatse. A correspondent for The Independent wrote, environmentalists fear this giant project will create one of China's worst ecological disasters of the 21st century.

World Parliamentary Conventions on Tibet

In recent years, the local Chinese authorities in Tibet have dropped all pretence of respecting Tibet's unique cultural and religious traditions and is now engaged in a systematic effort to destroy all that remains Tibetan in Tibet through a host of repressive regulations and practices. This, coupled with the continuing influx of Chinese settlers who now outnumber Tibetans, has led my people to become more and more marginalized in all spheres of life. Acceding to Dalai lama his priority is to protect and save the Tibetan people's cultural identity. He have to adopt a pragmatic approach to find a negotiated solution which is mutually agreeable to the Tibetan and Chinese people. He have counselled his people to pursue a path of non-violence even though he understand their frustrations at the lack of any positive developments.

Dalai Lama hope is that the Chinese leadership will appreciate the importance of a peaceful settlement to the Tibetan situation, for no matter what the outcome, the Tibetan and Chinese people will have to live side by side. That is why the many proposals Tibet have put forward over the years to peacefully resolve the situation in Tibet have been made in the spirit of reconciliation and compromise. Dalai Lama belief that in order to have constructive negotiations he should concentrate on the future, and let history be history.

International Campaign for Tibet works with parliamentary bodies worldwide to generate support for Tibet, advocating for governments to become better coordinated and better informed on Tibetan issues. As a sign of their support, members of parliament in governments throughout the world have organized themselves around their concerns over Tibet. Members of these parliamentary groups serve as advocates for the Tibetan people and address Tibet-related issues through their own governments.

There have been four World Parliamentarian Conventions on Tibet (WPCT) since 1994; the most recent of these was hosted by the Scottish Cross Party Group for Tibet in Edinburgh in November 2005. The 2005 WPCT provided an opportunity for members of the 30 parliamentary groups for Tibet worldwide as well as individual parliamentary Tibet supporters to meet, exchange views and develop strategies to ensure an imminent negotiated solution to the issue of Tibet.

The first World Parliamentarians Convention on Tibet was held in New Delhi from March 18 to 20th 1994 and attracted 67 parliamentarians from 25 countries. It issued a statement on March 20, which has come to be known as the New Delhi Statement on Tibetan Freedom, reaffirming the independence of Tibet before its invasion and subsequent occupation by China, called "for the formation of all-party parliamentarian groups on Tibet in the parliaments which did not have such groups, as well as an international network of parliamentarians to co-ordinate activities on the Tibetan issue."

The second World Parliamentarian Convention on Tibet, held from March 26 to 28, 1995 in Vilnius, Lithuania, attracted 88 parliamentarians from 21 countries. The convention reaffirmed its support to the New Delhi Statement on Tibetan Freedom and resolved to "initiate investigations, hearings and inquiries on the legitimacy of China's claim that Tibet is a part of China, in every parliament represented at the convention, and to persuade members of other parliaments to do the same, as a prelude to according recognition to the Tibetan Government in Exile."

The third World Parliamentarian Convention on Tibet was held in Washington, DC from April 23-24, 1997. A message from President Clinton opened the Convention, which was hosted by the US House International Relations Committee and the Congress under the leadership of Senator Jesse Helms and Rep. Benjamin Gilman.

International Governmental Action on Tibet

In recent years, parliaments and governments around the world have begun to take action on behalf of Tibet. A representative selection of some of the major resolutions and motions that have been passed is given below.

European Parliament: European Parliament passed a resolution on 14 October 1987, urging the Chinese Government to respect the rights of the Tibetan people to religious and cultural freedom, and suggesting that the Dalai Lama's Five-Point Peace Plan could provide the basis for a settlement of the Tibetan issue.

l 5 March 1989: A resolution was passed deploring the loss of life in recent disturbances in Lhasa, condemning the subsequent violent repression, and calling for the lifting of martial law. The European Parliament urged the Chinese Government to hold discussions with the Dalai Lama on the future of Tibet, and called on Beijing to respect the autonomous status of Tibet as defined within the framework of the Chinese Constitution.

April 1990: The Sub-Committee for Human Rights of the Political Affairs Committee of the European Parliament held a hearing on Tibet which was addressed by the Dalai Lama. At a meeting following the hearing, the decision was made to appoint a special rapporteur.

July 1991: A Resolution from the Political Affairs Committee condemned human rights violations in Tibet and called for the release of political prisoners, an end to torture, executions and intimidation, the cessation of environmental degradation, an immediate reversal of the policy of population transfer, an end to discrimination against Tibetans in health and education, and constructive dialogue between the Dalai Lama and the Chinese Government.

February 1992: A resolution was passed calling for the release of those people detained for practising religion or peacefully advocating the establishment of democratic rights, and expressing concern at prison conditions.

16 November 1992: A resolution was passed calling for the immediate release of all Tibetan political prisoners. The Chinese Government was also urged to allow the Red Cross to visit prisons and communicate with prisoners.

15 December 1992: A resolution was passed condemning human rights violations in Tibet, and demanding the release of all political prisoners. It called for an immediate end to environmental degradation, economic exploitation, discrimination against Tibetans, and Chinese immigration into Tibet. The European Parliament expressed regret that the Dalai Lama's efforts to bring about negotiations had come to nothing, and urged the resumption of talks. between the Tibetan Government-in-Exile and Beijing. A request was made that the granting of aid to China be conditional on the observance of human rights and freedoms, and that EC-funded projects in Tibet should serve the needs of the Tibetan community.

24 June 1993: A resolution was passed deploring the brutal suppression of recent demonstrations in Lhasa, and calling for the immediate release of all prisoners not charged with an internationally recognised crime (these included Gendun Rinchen, Lobsang Yonten and Damchoe Pemo). The European Parliament regretted that the Dalai Lama's planned address to the UN World Conference on Human Rights in Vienna was cancelled after Chinese pressure.

16 September 1993: A resolution passed without a vote called on the Chinese authorities to release all those detained for exercising their right to freedom of expression. The European Parliament declared its support for the "courageous activities" of Gendun Rinchen, and suggested that the Olympic Games should not be held in Beijing in the year 2000 unless progress were made in ensuring respect for human rights.

28 October 1993: On the eve of sending a delegation to Beijing, the European Parliament passed a resolution declaring that its relations with China would only be normalised if Beijing provided information about political prisoners in China and Tibet.

European Community: Member States of the EC submitted a Resolution in March 1992 to the UN Commission on Human Rights voicing their grave concern at continuing reports of human rights violations in Tibet, and calling on the Chinese Government to take measures to ensure the full observance of human rights and fundamental freedoms of the Tibetan people.

16-23 May 1993: A delegation of ambassadors from EC Member States to Tibet requested information about Gendun Rinchen and Lobsang Yonten, who were arrested for trying to contact them, and asked to see them in prison. After its week-long visit, the delegation issued a joint declaration which stated that relations between the Chinese and Tibetans in Tibet were poor; that official figures claiming just 3% of the population of Tibet were ethnic Chinese were understated; that the use of Chinese in official documents was a barrier to the advancement of Tibetans; that schooling in Tibetan was not always available and mat there was a large rate of non-attendance among Tibetans; and that although religious activity was not suppressed and the renovation of religious sites was very much in evidence, there were considerable doubts as to whether religion received the freedom of action and funding at an organizational level needed to achieve its full potential as a fundamental part of the Tibetan culture. Damchoe Pemo was reported to have been released in November 1993, although this has not yet been confirmed. Gendun Rinchen and Lobsang Yonten were both released in January 1994.

Council of Europe: On 5 October 1988, in written declaration no. 173 of the Parliamentary Assembly of the Council of Europe, 13 members appealed to the Chinese Government "to promote the peace process in Tibet, respecting the human rights of the Tibetan people, [their] culture and civilization."

German Bundestag: The Bundestag unanimously passed a resolution on 15 October 1987, calling for the Chinese authorities to respect human rights in Tibet, to respond to the Dalai Lama's attempts to achieve constructive dialogue, to take steps to preserve Tibetan culture and religion, and to release all political prisoners. The resolution also urged the West German Government to provide aid for Tibetan refugees, and to grant scholarships for Tibetans to study in German schools and Universities.

November 1990: The Bundestag unanimously passed a resolution calling on the German Government to raise the subject of the human rights situation in Tibet at the United Nations, urging the Chinese Government to lift martial law in Tibet, and supporting efforts to send an independent international commission to investigate Tibet's human rights situation.

Italian Parliament: The Commission of Foreign Affairs approved a motion on 12 April 1989, urging the Italian Government to make enquiries into the current situation in Tibet, to undertake action to put an end to human rights violations and environmental damage, and to come to a peaceful resolution of the Tibetan problem, while at the same time safeguarding Chinese foreign policy and defence interests.

Lithuanian Parliament: Deputies of the Lithuanian Supreme Council established a Tibetan Parliamentary Support Group on 27 February 1992, and Members of Parliament signed a statement acknowledging His Holiness the Dalai Lama and the Tibetan Government-in-Exile as the true representatives of the nation of Tibet.

Indian Lok Sabha: A memorandum signed by 212 MPs, including one government minister, was presented to the Speaker of the Lok Sabha on 23 August 1988, "fully supporting the Dalai Lama's Five-Point Peace Plan, which is an historic step towards resolving the important question of Tibet, alleviating the suffering of the Tibetan people and relieving regional tensions."

Parliamentary Groups for Tibet: There are now All-Party Parliamentary Groups for Tibet registered in the following countries: Australia, Britain, France, Italy, Ireland, Japan, Norway, Sweden, Switzerland and Lithuania.

Australian Parliamentary Action on Tibet: Ninety-five Members of Parliament signed a petition on 9 March 1989, marking the 30th anniversary of the Tibetan National Uprising, and called for human rights to be respected and for the People's Republic of China to respond constructively to the Dalai Lama's proposals for discussions.

6 December 1990: The Senate unanimously passed a resolution calling on the Chinese Government to recognize the fundamental rights and freedoms of the Tibetan people, and to enter into negotiations with the Dalai Lama. The Senate also called on the Australian Government to continue making representations to China on allegations of human rights abuse in Tibet.

10 November 1994: The Senate unanimously passed the following resolution timed to coincide with the visit of Chinese leader Qiao Shi, and proposed by Australian Democrats Foreign Affairs Spokesperson, Senator Vicki Bourne.

The Senate:

a. Notes that, during the week beginning 6 November 1994, the Chairman of China's National People's Congress, Mr Qiao Shi, is on an official State visit to Australia;

b. Recognizes that during the 1989 pro-democracy protests, Mr Qiao Shi served as head of China 's security services;

c. Expresses its concern that the human rights situation in Tibet appears to have deteriorated and that the Tibetan people continue to be denied their fundamental human rights and freedom;

d. Endorses the representations made by the Australian Government and by members of this Parliament to the People's Republic of China on human rights abuses in Tibet;

e. Urges the Chinese Government to recognize the fundamental human rights and freedom of the Tibetan people and to enter into genuine dialogue, without preconditions, with His Holiness the Dalai Lama with a view to achieving a long-term solution in Tibet;

f. Calls on Australian Government Ministers to continue raising issues of human rights and the situation in Tibet in their discussions with representatives of the Chinese Government and to ensure that they understand the depth of the Australian community's feelings about these matters; and

g. Requests from the Chinese Government a commitment that it will not deny visas to exiled Tibetan women from any part of the world who wish to attend the United Nations World Conference on Women which is due to be held in Beijing in 1995.

On 14 November 1994, Senate unanimously passed the following resolution similarly timed to coincide with the visit of Chinese leader Qiao Shi, and proposed by Senator Margaret Reid:

The Senate:

a. Calls for the immediate release of the Gari Fourteen, a group of Buddhist nuns from Gari nunnery, who are detained within the Chinese prison system in Tibet;

b. Notes reports that these young nuns and other Tibetan political prisoners are subjected to routine torture, are used as forced labour and have limited access to medical treatment;

c. Acknowledges that whilst it is alleged that twelve of the nuns were arrested for taking part in a pro-independence rally on 14 June 1993, there are no witnesses to a rally that day, and no evidence exists that it ever occurred; and

d. Calls on the leaders of the People's Republic of China to comply with both the United Nations Universal Declaration on Human Rights and the Convention Against Torture.

Self Reclamation among Tibetan Expatriates

The most important here is whether the Tibetan people had any part to play in their occupation by China. The role of the monastic establishment in the fall of the Tibetan government is totally clear. Most important monasteries in Tibet were opposed to the political and military modernization which would inevitably have undermined their powerful positions. In accordance with such views, when the exile government was established it was decided that rather than having a hand-picked dualistic government of influential monks and aristocrats, there should be an elected legislative body. This, the Assembly of Tibetan Peoples' Deputies was established in September 1960, and at present has forty-six elected members. It was hoped by the Dalai Lama that these measures would go some way towards changing Tibetan society for the better.. This democratization process in the Tibetan exile government is the closest that the Tibetans have come to a Constructive Program.

The main problem with the Assembly is that its powers are limited. A far more powerful body than the is the *kashag*, or Cabinet. The ministers of this body are elected by the ATPD, and a 70 per cent majority is required for election. However, if this majority is not reached the Dalai Lama has the power to appoint ministers directly. The *kashag* is responsible for exercising executive powers of the Tibetan administration subordinate to the Dalai Lama. Each minister heads one or two departments of the Tibetan government including the departments of finance, culture and religion, home affairs and education. These departments are responsible for the daily administration of Tibetan affairs in exile. The *kashag* is accountable to the Dalai Lama, although in legal matters it is accountable to the ATPD. However, it is said that the majority of Tibetans believe that the total faith they have in the Dalai Lama as a religious figure means he can be relied upon to make political decisions in their best interests.

Due to the position of the Dalai Lama, it makes the concept of democracy difficult to apply in the Tibetan case. There is a dispute among theoretical approaches to democratization about whether primary importance should be vested in the ruling elite or in the masses. This does not help an analysis of the Tibetan case because the process in the Tibetan community in exile has been initiated entirely by the elite. In the

Tibetan government in exile there have been elections to senior posts but the leader, the Dalai Lama, remains unelected.

The use of force commonly associated with authoritarian rule was not present in Tibet; on the contrary, legitimacy was accorded to the Tibetan government on the basis of Buddhist principles. The exact nature of the Tibetan state is difficult to define; perhaps the most useful theoretical definition is that of legitimacy based upon charismatic authority. One form of legitimate domination is charismatic authority, which is characterized by a certain quality of an individual personality by virtue of which he is considered extraordinary and treated as endowed with supernatural, superhuman, or at least specifically exceptional powers or qualities. This is a very accurate description of the rule in Tibet of the Dalai Lamas.

1998 Tibetan Hunger Strike

Since the late 1980s, Tibetans have led non-violent protest against China. The Dalai Lama continues to insist that non-violence is the only way forward. In 1998, a radical Tibetan non-governmental organization, the Tibetan Youth Congress launched in India a hunger strike, planned to draw the world's attention to the Tibetan cause. On 10 March 1998, the thirty-ninth anniversary of Tibetan National Uprising Day, six members of the Tibetan Youth Congress embarked upon a fast unto death in New Delhi. The six hunger strikers represented the six million people of Tibet. Their aim was for the United Nations to agree to the following demands: that the UN should discuss Tibet in the General Assembly; that the UN should appoint a rapporteur to investigate allegations of human rights abuses in Tibet; that the UN should appoint a special envoy on Tibet; and that the UN should initiate a supervised plebiscite on the future of Tibet.

On 24 April the European Union sent a message to the hunger strikers, requesting that they end their fast, as they had succeeded in drawing attention to their serious concerns about the situation in Tibet, and their demands for United Nations action. During the entire hunger strike of March and April, no organization made any attempt to address the strikers' demands.

His Holiness the Dalai Lama visited New Delhi on 2 April, and met the six hunger strikers. Dalai Lama clearly recognized that he was not in a position to persuade the hunger strikers to cease their protest. The other senior Tibetan figure to visit the hunger strikers was Professor Samdhong

Rinpoche, the Chairman of the Tibetan parliament in exile. He left Dharamsala with the full intention of asking the strikers to stop their fast. Upon reaching New Delhi, however, he was unable to do so.

The Tibetan Youth Congress strike was brought to an end on 27 April, when police forcibly took the hunger strikers to hospital, where they were forcbly fed. TYC indicated that they felt that Gandhian methods were perfectly acceptable for their protest, particularly so given they were protesting in India.

During the second day of the break-up of the strike, one of the most tragic events in the course of the entire Tibetan struggle took place. Thupten Ngodup, an ex-monk and an ex-soldier, set himself alight in protest at the enforced removal of the hunger strikers. He died from almost 100 per cent burns on 29 April. He had planned to join the second phase of the hunger strike.

Significance of Hunger Strike: Tibetan Youth Congress decision to embark on the hunger strike has vital importance for the future of the Tibetan struggle. The most crucial is the willingness of some Tibetans to break with the position of the Dalai Lama, and to follow their own agenda. The TYC's decision to use a method of protest that they *knew* would meet with the disapproval of the Dalai Lama is a very significant move. It challenges the political authority the Dalai Lama has traditionally held over Tibetans. In pre-invasion Tibet, such a move would have been unthinkable.

While their fast may have been open to justification in a Hindu context, for Tibetan Buddhists their actions were wrong. Any justification for the TYC's action has, as has been shown, been purely political; while objections have been religious. Although the Dalai Lama said that on religious grounds the hunger strike was wrong, he recognized that it could not be criticized on political grounds. The responses to the TYC's action have been indicative of the problems that arise when a traditional society based on religion is forced to take an active political stance.

Indian Solution to Tibetan Problem

Here, the purpose of comparing the Tibetan independence movement with that of India is, that the Dalai Lama has often quoted Gandhi's political thinking i.e non-violence. Tibet is a Buddhist nation, emphasis on non-violence is obvious. However, as has been shown, even Gandhi thought violence was sometimes acceptable; he preferred it to inaction where the honour of a country was at risk. This could perhaps be a justification for violent action in Tibet. A more pertinent advocate of forceful action was the Thirteenth Dalai Lama. The present Dalai Lama does not seem to have taken the words of either Gandhi or his predecessor to heart. He continues to insist that only non-violence can provide the freedom of Tibet, even though the historical evidence suggests that this is just not the case.

The main problem with advocating the Gandhian thinking is one of circumstances. This is both religious, as has been discussed, and political. The crucial point with regard to the development and practice of Gandhi's ideology is that it took place against a highly organized political background. India did not win independence through satyagraha alone. The Indian independence movement is firmly rooted in a democratic, party political background. This does not exist anywhere in the Tibetan community, either inside Tibet or in exile. In India, Gandhi's political action and spiritual principles were backed by hard political negotiation on the part of Congress. In the Tibetan community, no such political organization exists. It is vital to the future of the Tibetan independence movement that such a party is developed; the struggle cannot depend, in the long term, on the singular figure of the Dalai Lama.

The Indian way to independence also offers the Tibetan people lessons in unity. The Indian National Congress made firm its commitment to independence in 1929. Previous to this time, Congress had hoped that some kind of framework could be developed that would give Indians a greater political role. The move toward independence was made because it became increasingly clear there was no truly representative future for Indians under the British. On the other hand, the progression of the movement for Tibetan people has been in almost the opposite direction. Until 1988, the goal of the Tibetans was independence from China. From that date, the official goal of the Tibetan people changed to becoming autonomy. Why the goal was diluted in this way. It is likely that the Dalai Lama had in mind his increasingly sympathetic international audience when he made his proposal for autonomy at Strasbourg; indeed, after the announcement, he was applauded for his diplomatic initiative, while Tibetan exiles were left feeling bewildered. Of course the other reason why the Dalai Lama chose to aim for genuine autonomy was that this was a more realistic solution than independence to expect from the Chinese government. But it has to be pointed out that the Chinese already maintain that Tibet has autonomous status; so why ask for a solution that, in theory at least, already exists?

A further point is the lack of unity amongst Tibetans. First, there are no indications from inside Tibet itself that the people who continually protest against Chinese rule are fighting for anything less than independence. Second, it is not uncommon for Tibetan people to state that while they support the Middle Way position of the Dalai Lama, which essentially calls for compromise, they also wish for an independent Tibet. Dalai Lama's dual religious and political role, is central to the Tibetan independence movement and constitutes one of the most profound obstacles to its progress.

Future Tibet's Policy

Although it is difficult to forecast the future, all human beings who wish to achieve happiness and avoid suffering must plan for future. As a result of the Chinese occupation, Tibetans in Tibet are deprived of their basic human rights.

About three decades have passed since the draft constitution of 1963 was promulgated. During those years, the world has changed dramatically and people throughout the world have begun to value democratic rights more than ever before. They have realized that democracy is the foundation for the free expression of human thoughts and potentials. Therefore, Tibet also must change when it becomes free. The issue of Tibet is not merely a question of the survival of a people with their own distinct history and culture, it also has direct bearing on the fate of this world and Asian peace, and particularly upon the relationship between the world's two most populous nations: India and China.

At stake is also the serious question of human rights, as enshrined in the United Nations Universal Declaration of Human Rights, and the world body's efforts to put an end to the era of colonialism and expansionism. Even the Chinese people themselves are opposed to the present Chinese system of governance and are demanding changes. Chinese dissidents in exile have come to realize and accept the reality that Tibet and China are two completely separate entities. They have also come to recognize the fact that the Tibetans have the right to independence and self-determination. They find no justification in their leadership's claim that Tibet is a part of China.

The preparation of comprehensive draft constitutions for several alternative models of democracy is underway at the moment. However, the Constituent Assembly, comprising of representatives from all regions of Tibet, will have a final say in deciding which form of constitution should be adopted.

Future Tibet will be a peace-loving nation, adhering to the principle of Ahimsa. It will have a democratic system of government committed to preserving a clean, healthy and beautiful environment. Tibet will be a completely demilitarized nation. Although technological advancement has brought material prosperity to much of today's world, it has also resulted in the loss of respect for human beings. Human beings have also lost much of their freedom, so much so that they have become the slaves of machines. While a privileged few live in an island of plenty, the vast majority have to go without even the most basic necessities of life.

In international policy, Tibet will not align itself with the policy and ideology of any other nation. It will remain neutral in the true sense of the word. Tibet will maintain harmonious relations with its neighbours, based on equality and mutual benefit. It will renounce hostility and promote friendly relations with all nations.

REFERENCES

'Reported Uprising in Tibet' Keesing's Contemporary Archives, 23-30 June 1956.

'Tibetans on Tibet' Beijing: China Reconstructs Press, 1988.

Andrugtsang, Gompo Tashi: Four Rivers, Six Ranges: Reminiscences of the Resistance Movement in Tibet, Information and Publicity Office of His Holiness the Dalai Lama, 1973.

Avedon, John F.: In Exile from the Land of Snows, New York, HarperCollins, 1997.

Barnett, R. and Akiner, S.: Resistance and Reform in Tibet, London, Hurst and Co., 1994.

Brown, Judith M.: Modern India: The Origins of an Asian Democracy, Oxford, Oxford University Press, 1994.

Burman, Bina Roy: Religion and Politics in Tibet, New Delhi, Vikas Publishing1979

Carrasco, Pedro: Land and Polity in Tibet, Seattle, University of Washington Press, 1959.

Edin, Maria: Transition to Democracy in Exile - A Study of the Tibetan Government's Strategy for Self-Determination, University of Uppsala, Department of Government Minor Field Study, 1992.

Himachal Pradesh Tourist Department: Dharamsala, A Little Tibet in India, 1992.

Jones, Ken: The Social Face of Buddhism: An Approach to Social and Political Activism, London, Wisdom, 1989.

Klieger, P. Christiaan: Tibetan Nationalism: The Role of Patronage in the Accomplishment of a National Identity, Meerut, Archana Publications, 1992.

McCarthy, Roger E.: Tears of the Lotus: Accounts of Tibetan Resistance to the Chinese Invasion, 1950-1962, Jefferson, McFarland and Co., 1997

Mullin, Chris: 'Tibetan Conspiracy' in Far Eastern Economic Review, 1975.

Nehru, Jawaharlal: The Discovery of India, London, Meridian Books, 1956.

Queen, C.S. and King, S.B.: Engaged Buddhism: Buddhist Liberation Movements in Asia, Albany: State University of New York Press, 1996.

Richardson, H. E.: Tibet and its History, London, Oxford University Press, 1962. Seymour, James D. and Cao Changching: Tibet through Dissident Chinese Eyes: Essays on Self-Determination, Armonk, M. E. Sharpe, 1998.

Shakya, Tsering: 'Tibet and the Occident: The Myth of Shangri-La' in Lungta, 1991.

Wangyal, Phuntsog: 'The Revolt of 1959' in Tibetan Review, 1974.

Westerlund, David: Questioning the Secular State: The Worldwide Resurgence of Religion in Politics, London, Hurst and Co., 1996.

Bibliography

Adams, Vincanne: Tigers of the Snow and Other Virtual Sherpas. Princeton, Princeton University Press, 1996.

Agarwal, A.: "The fifth World Conservation Lecture: human-nature interactions in a Third World country". The Environmentalist: Republished as An Indian environmentalist's credo in Guha, R. 1998: Social ecology.Delhi, Oxford University Press, 346-84, 1986.

Agha, Z.: "Explosive fallout". India Today International, 1996.

Agnihotri, V. and Mittal, R.: Managing personal affairs. In Agnihotri, V., Skills for effective administrators. New Delhi, Vikas, 1995.

Agnihotri, V. and Ramachandran, H.: Dimensions of the new economic policy, Vol. I: economic sector, Vol. II: social sector. New Delhi: Concept Publishing, 1996.

Ahmad, A.: In the mirror of Urdu: recompositions of nation and community. In Lineages of the present: political essays. Chennai, Tulika, 1996.

Ahmad, Zahiruddin: A History of Tibet by the Fifth Dalai Lama of Tibet. Bloomington, Ind.: Research Institute for Inner Asian Studies, 1995.

Alastair Lamb: The China-India Border: The Origins of the Disputed Boundaries, 1964.

Alexander, Andre: The Old City of Lhasa: Report from a Conservation Project. Berlin, Tibet Heritage Fund, 1998.

Allan, Michael.: Anthropology of Nepal: Peoples, Problems, and Processes. Kathmandu, Mandala Book Point, 1994.

Amin, S.: Capitalism in the age of globalization: the management of contemporary society. London, Zed Books, 1997.

Anant, V.: "Indomania". Race and Class, 1991.

Anderson, Benedict: Imagined Communities: Reflections on the Origin and Spread of Nationalism, London, Verso, 1991.

Andrugtsang, Gompo Tashi: Four Rivers, Six Ranges: Reminiscences of the Resistance Movement in Tibet, Information and Publicity Office of His Holiness the Dalai Lama, 1973.

Appadurai, A.: "Disjuncture and difference in the global cultural economy". Theory Culture and Society, 1990.

Appadurai, A.: Global ethnoscapes: notes and queries for a transnational, 1991.

Ardley, Jane: Resistance, Religion and Politics: the Tibetan Independence Movement in Comparative Perspective, Keele University, 1999.

Aris, Michael: Bhutan: The Early History of a Himalayan Kingdom. Warminster, Eng.: Aris and Phillips, 1979.

Aris, Michael: Hidden Treasures and Secret Lives: A Study of Pemalingpa (1450–1521) and the Sixth Dalai Lama (1683–1706). Shimla, Indian Institute of Advanced Study, 1988.

Aris, Michael: Report on the University of California Expedition to Kutang and Nubri in Northern Nepal in Autumn 1973. Contributions to Nepalese Studies 2 (2): 45–87, 1975.

Aris, Michael: The Raven Crown: The Origins of Buddhist Monarchy in Bhutan. London, Serindia Publications, 1994.

Arnold, Edwin: Bhagavadgita, New York, Dover Publications, 1899/1993.

Ash R. F.: "Agricultural Policy Under the Impact of Reforms", in Y. Y. Kueh and R. F. Ash, Economic Trends in Chinese Agriculture, Oxford, Clarendon Press, 1993.

Atkinson, Robert: The Life Story Interview. Thousand Oaks, Calif. Sage, 1998.

Attenborough, R.: The Population of Stongde, Zangskar. In Himayalan Buddhist Villages, ed. J. Crook and H. Osmaston, Bristol, University of Bristol Press, 1994.

Avedon, John F.: In Exile from the Land of Snows, New York, HarperCollins, 1997.

Axinn, William G., Thomas E. Fricke, and Arland Thornton: The Microdemographic Community Study Approach. Sociological Methods and Research, 1991.

Aziz, Barbara: Tibetan Frontier Families. New Delhi, Vikas, 1978.

Aziz, Barbara: Tibetan Manuscript Maps of the Dingri Valley. Canadian Cartographer, 1975.

Baker, Ian A., and Romio Shrestha: The Tibetan Art of Healing. San Francisco, Chronicle Books, 1997.

Balasubramanyan V. N.: "Incentives and Disincentives for Foreign Direct Investment in Less Developed Countries", Weltwirtschaftliches Archiv, 1984.

Barnett A. Doak: Communist China and Asia: Challenge to American Policy, Random House Inc., New York, 1960.

Barnett, Robert and Shirin Akiner: Resistance and Reform in Tibet, London, Hurst and Company, 1994.

Basu, Alaka Malwade, and Peter Aaby: The Methods and Uses of Anthropological Demography. Oxford, Clarendon Press, 1998.

Batchelor, Stephen: The Awakening of the West: The Encounter of Buddhism and Western Culture. Berkeley, Parallax Press, 1994.

Baumol W. J.: "Productivity Growth, Convergence and Welfare: What the Long-Run Data Show", American Economic Review, 1986.

Beall, Cynthia M., and Melvyn C. Goldstein: Work, Aging, and Dependency in a Sherpa Population in Nepal. Social Science and

Medicine, 1982.

Beckwith, Christopher I.: Medieval Tibeto-Burman Languages. Leiden, E. J. Brill, 2002.

Beckwith, Christopher I.: The Tibetan Empire in Central Asia. Princeton, Princeton University Press, 1987.

Beer, Robert.: The Encyclopedia of Tibetan Symbols and Motifs. Boston, Shambhala, 1999.

Bei Duoguang: Zhonguo Zijin Liudong Fenshe (A Study of China's Financial Flow), Shanghai, Joint Publishing Co., 1989.

Bell M. W., Khor H. E., and Kochhar K.: China: At the Threshold of a Market Economy, Washington, DC: IMF, 1993.

Bell, Charles: The People of Tibet. Delhi, Motilal Banarsidass, 1992.

Bell, David V. J.: Resistance and Revolution, Boston, Houghton Mifflin Company, 1973.

Bellezza, John V.: Divine Dyads: Ancient Civilization in Tibet. Dharamsala, Library of Tibetan Works and Archives, 1997.

Benedict, Paul K.: Sino-Tibetan, a Conspectus. Cambridge, Cambridge University Press, 1972.

Benn, James A: 'Where text meets flesh - burning the body as an apocryphal practice' in History of Religions, 1998.

Bentor, Yael.: Tibetan Tourist Thankas in the Kathmandu Valley. Annals of Tourism Research 20: 107–137, 1993.

Bernbaum, E.: The Way to Shambhala. New York, Anchor Press, 1980.

Besant, Annie and Bhagavan Das: The Bhagavad Gita, Madras, Theosophical Publishing House, 1926.

Bhattacharjee, Arun: A History of Modern India, Liverpool, Lucas Publications, 1988.

Bishop, Naomi H.: Himalayan Herders. Fort Worth, Texas, Harcourt Brace, 1998.

Bishop, Peter D.: Dreams of Power: Tibetan Buddhism, Western Imagination. Rutherford, N. J., Fairleigh Dickinson University Press, 1993.

Bishop, Peter D.: Reading the Potala. In Sacred Spaces and Powerful Places in Tibetan Culture, Dharamsala, Library of Tibetan Works and Archives, 1999.

Bishop, Peter D.: The Myth of Shangri-La: Tibet, Travel Writing, and the Western Creation of Sacred Landscape. London, Athlone Press, 1989.

Bista, Dor Bahadur: People of Nepal. Kathmandu, Ratna Pustak Bhandar, 1967.

Blejer M., Burton D., Dunaway S., and Szapary G.: China: Economic Reform and Macroeconomic Management, Washington, DC: IMF, 1991.

Blommestein H., Marrese M., and Zecchini S.: "Centrally Planned Economies in Transition: An Introductory Review of Selected Issues and Strategies", in H. Blommestein and M. Marrese, Transformation of Planned Economies, Paris: OECD, 1991.

Bondurant, Joan V.: Conquest of Violence: The Gandhian Philosophy of Conflict, Princeton, N.J., Princeton University Press, 1958.

Brada J.: "The Microallocative Impact of the Hungarian Economic Reform of 1968: Some Evidence from the Export Sector", Economics of Planning, 1973.

Brainard L.: "Strategies for Economic Transformation in Central and Eastern Europe: Role of Financial Market Reform", in Blommestein and Marrese, 1991.

Brauen, Martin: The Mandala: Sacred Circle in Tibetan Buddhism. Boston, Shambhala, 1998.

Brettell, Caroline B.: Fieldwork in the Archives: Methods and Sources in Historical Anthropology. In Handbook of Methods in Cultural Anthropology, Walnut Creek, California, Alta Mira Press, 1998.

Brookfield H. and Byron Y. (eds.): South-East Asia's Environmental Future: The Search For Sustainability, Tokyo, UN University Press, 1993.

Brower, Barbara: Sherpa of Khumbu. Delhi, Oxford University Press, 1991.

Brown, Judith M.: Modern India: The Origins of an Asian Democracy, Oxford, Oxford University Press, 1994.

Bruno M.: "Stabilization and Reform in Eastern Europe: A Preliminary Evaluation", IMF Staff Papers, 1992.

Buck J. L.: Chinese Farm Economy, Chicago, University of Chicago Press, 1930.

Burman, Bina Roy: Religion and Politics in Tibet, New Delhi, Vikas Publishing, 1979.

Byrd W.: "Enterprise Level Reforms in Chinese State-owned Industry", American Economic Review, 1983.

Caldwell, John C., Allan G. Hill, and Valerie J. Hull: MicroApproaches to Demographic Research. London, Kegan Paul, 1988.

Calvin, James Barnard: The China-India Border War, 1988.

Campbell, June: Traveller in Space: In Search of Female Identity in Tibetan Buddhism. New York, George Braziller, 1996.

Cao, Changching, and James D. Seymour: Tibet through Dissident Chinese Eyes. Armonk, N. Y., M. E. Sharpe, 1998.

Carrasco, Pedro: Land and Polity in Tibet, Seattle, University of Washington Press, 1959.

Cassinelli, C. W. and Robert B. Ekvall: A Tibetan Principality: The Political System of Sakya. Ithaca, Cornell University Press, 1969.

Ch'en Yi yen-lun hsüan (Selected Speeches of Ch'en Yi), Tz'u-lien ch'u-pan she, Hong Kong, 1967.

Chandra, Bipan: India's Struggle for Independence 1857-1947, New Delhi, Penguin, 1989.

Chang, Garma C. C.: The Hundred Thousand Songs of Milarepa. Boulder, Colo., Shambhala, 1977.

Childs, Geoff: A Brief History of Nubri: Ethnic Interface, Sacred Geography, and Historical Migrations in a Himalayan Locality. Zentralasiatische Studien, 2001.

Childs, Geoff: Claiming the Frontier: A Note on the Incorporation of Nubri within the Borders of Nepal. Studies in Nepali History and Society, 2000.

Childs, Geoff: Demographic Dimensions of an Inter-Village Land Dispute in Nubri, Nepal. American Anthropologist, 2001.

Childs, Geoff: Householder Lamas and the Persistence of Tradition: Animal Sacrifice in Himalayan Buddhist Communities. In Tibetan Studies, Vienna, Verlag der Österreichischen Akademie der Wissenschaften, 1997.

Childs, Geoff: How to Fund a Ritual: The Social Usage of the Kanjur in a Tibetan Village. In Tibetan Studies, Bloomington, Indiana University Press, 2004.

Childs, Geoff: Refuge and Revitalization: Hidden Himalayan Sanctuaries and the Preservation of Tibet's Imperial Lineage. Acta Orientalia, 1999.

China and the Asian-African Conference (Documents), Foreign Language Press, Peking, 1955.

Clarke, Graham: A Helambu History. Journal of the Nepal Research Centre, 1980.

Clarke, Graham: Lama and Tamang in Yolmo. In Tibetan Studies in Honour of Hugh Richardson, England, Aris and Phillips, 1980.

Combe, G. A.: A Tibetan on Tibet. Berkeley, Snow Lion Graphics, 1989.

Conboy, Kenneth, and James Morrison: The CIA's Secret War in Tibet. Lawrence, University of Kansas Press, 2002.

Conner, Victoria and Robert Barnett: Leaders in Tibet: A Directory, London, Tibet Information Network, 1997.

Cornu, Philippe: Tibetan Astrology. Boston, Shambhala, 1997.

Craig, Mary: Tears of Blood: A Cry for Tibet, London, HarperCollins, 1992.

Crook, John, and Stamati Crook: Explaining Tibetan Polyandry: Sociocultural, Demographic, and Biological Perspectives. In Himayalan Buddhist Villages, Bristol, University of Bristol Press, 1994.

Cuevas, Bryan J.:The Hidden History of the Tibetan Book of the Dead. Oxford, Oxford University Press, 2003.

Dagyab Rinpoche: Buddhist Symbols in Tibetan Culture: An Investigation of the Nine Best-Known Groups of Symbols. Boston, Wisdom, 1995.

Dargyay, Eva.: The Rise of Esoteric Buddhism in Tibet. Delhi, Motilal Banarsidass, 1979.

Dargyay, Eva.: Tibetan Village Communities. New Delhi, Vikas, 1982.

Dawa Norbu: Tibet: The Road Ahead. New Delhi, Harper Collins, 1997.

Desjarlais, Robert R.: Body and Emotion: The Aesthetics of Illness and Healing in the Nepal Himalayas. Philadelphia, University of Pennsylvania Press, 1992.

Diehl, Keila: Echoes from Dharamsala: Music in the Life of a Tibetan Refugee Community. Berkeley, University of California Press, 2002.

Diemberger, Hildegard: Lhakama and Khandroma: The Sacred Ladies of Beyul Khenbalung,Consolidation, In Tibetan History and Language, Vienna, University of Vienna, 1991.

Dobremez, Jean-François, and Corneille Jest.: Manaslu: Hommes et milieux des vallées du Népal central. Paris, CNRS, 1976.

Dobremez, Jean-François: Les collines du Népal central: Écosystèmes, structures sociales et systèmes agraires. Paris, Institute National de la Recherche Agronomique, 1986.

Dodin, Thierry, and Heinz Räther: Imagining Tibet: Perceptions, Projections, and Fantasies. Boston, Wisdom, 2001.

Dommen Arthur J.: Conflict in Laos: The Politics of Neutralization, Pall Mall Press, London, 1964.

Donnet, Pierre-Antoine: Tibet: Survival in Question, London, Zed Books, 1994.

Dowman, Keith: The Legend of the Great Stupa. Berkeley, Dharma, 1973.

Downs, Hugh R.: Rhythms of a Himalayan Village. San Francisco, Harper and Row, 1980.

Dudjom Rinpoche: The Nyingma School of Tibetan Buddhism. Boston, Wisdom, 1991.

Duncan, Marion H.: Customs and Superstitions of Tibetans. London, Mitre Press, 1964.

Dunham, V. Carroll, Ian Baker, and Thomas L. Kelly: Tibet: Reflections from the Wheel of Life. New York, Abbeville Press, 2001.

Dutt Vidya Prakash: China and the World: An Analysis of Communist China's Foreign Policy, Frederick A. Praeger, Inc., New York, 1964.

Edgerton, Franklin: The Beginnings of Indian Philosophy: Selections from the Rig Veda, Atharva Veda, Upanishads and Mahabharata, London, George Allen and Unwin, 1965.

Edin, Maria: Transition to Democracy in Exile - A Study of the Tibetan Government's Strategy for Self-Determination, University of Uppsala, Department of Government Minor Field Study, 1992.

Ehrhard, Franz-Karl.: A "Hidden Land" in the Tibetan-Nepalese Borderlands. In Mandala and Landscape, New Delhi, D. K. Printworld, 1997.

Ekvall, Robert B.: Fields on the Hoof: Nexus of Tibetan Nomadic Pastoralism. New York, Holt, Rinehart and Winston, 1968.

Ekvall, Robert B.: Religious Observances in Tibet. Chicago, University of Chicago Press, 1964.

Ekvall, Robert B.: Tibetan Sky Lines. New York: Octagon, 1976.

Eppsteiner, F.: The Path of Compassion: Writings on Socially Engaged Buddhism, Berkeley, Parallax Press, 1988.

Epstein, Lawrence: A Comparative View of Tibetan and Western Near-Death Experiences. In Reflections on Tibetan Culture: Essays in Memory of Turrell V. Wylie, ed. L. Epstein and R. Sherburne, N. Y., Edwin Mellen Press, 1990.

Epstein, Lawrence: Khams pa Histories: Visions of People, Place, and Authority. Leiden, E. J. Brill, 2002.

Epstein, Lawrence: On the History and Psychology of the 'Das-log. Tibet Journal, 1982.

Ferrari, Alfonsa: Mk'yen Brtse's Guide to the Holy Places of Central Tibet. Rome, 1958.

Fields, Rick: How the Swans Came to the Lake: A Narrative History of Buddhism in America. Boston: Shambhala, 1992.

Filippi, Filippo de.: An Account of Tibet: The Travels of Ippolito Desideri, 1712–1727. New Delhi, Asian Educational Services, 1995.

Fischer, Louis: The Life of Mahatma Gandhi, London, Jonathan Cape, 1951.

Fisher, James F..: Himalayan Anthropology: The Indo-Tibetan Interface. The Hague, Mouton, 1978.

Fisher, James F.: Sherpas. Berkeley, University of California Press, 1990.

Fisher, James F.: Trans-Himalayan Traders. Delhi, Motilal Banarsidass, 1986.

Forbes, Ann A.: Settlements of Hope: An Account of Tibetan Refugees in Nepal. Cambridge, Cultural Survival, 1989.

French, Patrick: Liberty or Death: India's Journey to Independence and Division, London, Flamingo, 1997.

Gandhi, M.K.: An Autobiography, or The Story of My Experiments with Truth, Ahmedabad, Navajivan Trust, 1927.

Goldstein, Melvyn C., and Matthew T. Kapstein: Buddhism in Contemporary Tibet: Religious Revival and Cultural Identity. Berkeley, University of California Press, 1998.

Goldstein, Melvyn C.: William Siebenschuh, and Tashi Tsering.: The Struggle for Modern Tibet: The Autobiography of Tashi Tsering. Armonk, N. Y., M. E. Sharpe, 1997.

Government's Strategy for Self-Determination, University of Uppsala, Department of Government Minor Field Study, 1992.

Grunfeld, A. Tom: The Making of Modern Tibet. Armonk, N. Y., M. E. Sharpe. 1996.

Guenther, Herbert V.: The Teachings of Padmasambhava. Leiden, E. J. Brill, 1996.

Guillet, David W.: Toward a Cultural Ecology of Mountains: The Central Andes and the Himalayas Compared. Current Anthropology , 1983.

Gunnar Myrdal. Asian Drama; An Inquiry into the Poverty of Nations. New York, Random House, 1968.

Gurung, Nareswor J.: An Introduction to the Socio-Economic Structure of Manang District. Kailash, 1976.

Gutschow, Kim: Unfocussed Merit-Making in Zangskar: A Socio-economic Account of Karsha Nunnery. Tibet Journal, 1997.

Gyatso, Janet: Apparitions of the Self: The Secret Autobiographies of a Tibetan Visionary. Princeton, Princeton University Press 1999.

Haksar, Vinit: Civil Disobedience: Threats and Offers: Gandhi and Rawls, Delhi, Oxford University Press, 1986.

Hale, Austin: Research on Tibeto-Burman Languages. New York, Mouton, 1982.

Halpern A. M.: Policies Toward China: Views from Six Continents McGraw-Hill Book Co., for the Council on Foreign Relations, New York, 1965.

Harding Harry and Melvin Gurtov: The Purge of Lo Jui-ch'ing: The Politics of Chinese Strategic Planning, Report, The Rand Corporation, Santa Monica, California, February 1971.

Harris, Melissa, and Sidney Jones: Tibet since 1950: Silence, Prison, or Exile. New York: Aperture and Human Rights Watch. 2000.

Harrison, Paul: A Brief History of the Tibetan bKa' 'gyur. In Tibetan Literature, Ithaca, N. Y., Snow Lion, 1996.

Harvey, Peter: An Introduction to Buddhist Ethics: Foundations, Values, and Issues. Cambridge, Cambridge University Press, 2000.

Havnevik, Hanna: The Role of Nuns in Contemporary Tibet. In Resistance and Reform in Tibet, Delhi, Motilal Banarsidass, 1994.

Havnevik, Hanna: Tibetan Buddhist Nuns. Oslo, Norwegian University Press, 1989.

Himachal Pradesh Tourist Department: Dharamsala, A Little Tibet in India, 1992.

Hinton Harold C.: Communist China in World Politics, Houghton Mifflin Co., Boston, Massachusetts, 1966.

History of the Conflict with China, P.B. Sinha, A.A. Athale, with S.N. Prasad: Ministry of Defence, Government of India, 1992. — Official Indian history of the Sino-Indian War, 1962.

Hudson G. F., Richard Lowenthal, and Roderick MacFarquhar: The Sino-Soviet Dispute, Frederick A. Praeger, Inc., New York, 1961.

Humphreys, Christmas: Buddhism, London, Penguin, 1951/1990.

Huntington, Samuel P.: 'Will More Countries Become Democratic?' in Political Science Quarterly, 1984.

Hutchinson, J. and Smith, A.D.: Nationalism, Oxford, Oxford University Press, 1994.

Inoki Masamichi: Japan's Future in Southeast Asia, Symposium Series II, Kyoto University, Center for Southeast Asian Studies, Kyoto, 1966.

Insor D., Thailand: A Political, Social, and Economic Analysis, Frederick A. Praeger, Inc., New York, 1963.

International Commission of Jurists: The Question of Tibet and the Rule of Law, Geneva, ICJ, 1959.

Iyer, R. N.: The Moral and Political Thought of Mahatma Gandhi, New York, Oxford University Press, 1973.

Jan Yün-Hua: 'Buddhist Self-Immolation in Medieval China' in History of Religions, 1965.

Johnston Douglas M. and Hungdah Chiu: Agreements of the People's Republic of China, 1949-1967: A Calendar, Harvard University Press, Cambridge, Massachusetts, 1969.

Jones, Ken: The Social Face of Buddhism: An Approach to Social and Political Activism, London, Wisdom, 1989.

Kelly, Petra K., Gert Bastian, and Pat Aiello: The Anguish of Tibet, Berkeley, Parallax Press, 1991.

Keyes Charles F.: Isan: Regionalism in Northeastern Thailand, Cornell University, Dept. of Asian Studies, Ithaca, New York, 1967.

Khilnani, Sunil: The Idea of India, London, Hamish Hamilton, 1997.

Klatt Werner: The Chinese Model. A Political, Economic and Social Survey, Hong Kong University Press, Hong Kong, 1965.

Klieger, P. Christiaan: Tibetan Nationalism: The Role of Patronage in the Accomplishment of a National Identity, Meerut, Archana Publications, 1992.

Lamb Alastair: Asian Frontiers: Studies in a Continuing Problem, Frederick A. Praeger, Inc., New York, 1968.

Lazar, E.: Tibet: The Issue is Independence, Berkeley, Parallax Press, 1994.

Lee Chae-Jin, "Chinese Communist Policy in Laos, 1954-1965," unpublished Ph.D. dissertation, University of California, Los Angeles, 1966.

Lin Cyril: "China's Economic Reform 2: Western Perspective", Asian Pacific Economic Literature, 1988.

Lin Justin: "Rural Factor Markets in China after the Household Responsibility System Reform", Discussion Paper No. 535, Economic Growth Center, Yale University, 1987.

Ling Nai-Min: Tibetan Sourcebook, Hong Kong, Union Research Institute, 1964.

Lipton D., and Sachs J. D.: "Prospects for Russia's Economic Reforms", Brookings Paper on Economic Activity, 1992.

Liu Guoguang: Guomin Jingji Guanli Tizhi Gaige Di Ruo-guan Lilun Wenti (Theoretical Issues in National Economic System Reform), Beijing, China's Social Science Publishing House, 1980.

Liu Hongru: Shehuizhuyi Huobi Yu Yinhang Wenti (Issues in Socialist Money and Banking), Beijing, Finance and Economics Publishing House, 1980.

Liu Jieshan, Wang W., and He P.: Qiye Gongzhi Gaige Shiyong Shouce (Practical Handbook of Enterprise Wage Reform), Beijing, China's Municipal Economic and Social Publishing House, 1988.

Liu T. C.: "Quantitative Trends in the Economy", in Eckstein A., Galenson W., and Liu T. C., Economic Trends in Communist China, Edinburgh, Edinburgh University Press: 87-182, 1968.

Lloyd P. J.: 'Global Integration', Mimeo, 1993.

Lopez, Donald S.: Prisoners of Shangri-La: Tibetan Buddhism and the West, Chicago, University of Chicago Press, 1998.

Lyons T. P.: "China's Cellular Economy: A Test of the Fragmentation Hypothesis", Journal of Comparative Economics, 1985.

Ma Hong: Xiandai Zhongguo Jingji Shidan (Contemporary Chinese Economy: A Compendium), Beijing: China's Social Science Publishing House, 1982.

Mao Tse-tung: The Selected Works of Mao Tse-tung, 5 vols., International Publishers Co., Inc., New York, 1954.

Marshall, Steven D.: Hostile Elements: A Study of Political Imprisonment in Tibet, 1987-1998, London, Tibet Information Network, 1999.

McCabe Robert Karr: Storm Over Asia: China and Southeast Asia, Thrust and Response, New American Library of World Literature, Inc., New York, 1967.

McCarthy, Roger E.: Tears of the Lotus: Accounts of Tibetan Resistance to the Chinese Invasion, 1950-1962, Jefferson, McFarland and Co., 1997

McKay, Alex: Tibet and the British Raj: The Frontier Cadre, 1904-1947, Surrey, Curzon Press, 1997.

Merton, Thomas: Gandhi on Non-Violence, Boston, Shambhala, 1996.

Mitra, S. and Baweja, H.: "RSS on the rampage". India Today International, 1998.

Mitra, S. and Chakravarty, S.: "Hello from hell". India Today International, 1999.

Mitra, S. and Rekhi, S.: "The great disclosure". India Today International, 1998.

Mitra, S.: "Old parents: unlovingly yours". India Today International , 1998.

Modelski George: SEATO: Six Studies, University of British Columbia, for the Australian National University, Vancouver, 1962.

Mohan, S.: "The changing political scenario". The Hindu, 6 January, 1998.

Monteiro, A.: Official television and unofficial fabrications of the self: the spectator as subject. In Nandy, A., The secret politics of our desires: innocence, culpability and Indian popular cinema. Delhi: Oxford University Press, 1998.

Morris-Jones, W.: The government and politics of India. London: Hutchinson, 1971.

Mozingo David: China's Foreign Policy and the Cultural Revolution, Interim Report No. 1, IREA Project, Cornell University, Ithaca, New York, March 1970.

Mukherjee, R.: The Penguin Gandhi Reader, New Delhi, Penguin, 1993.

Mullin, Chris: 'Tibetan Conspiracy' in Far Eastern Economic Review, 1975.

Mullin, Chris: 'Tibetan Conspiracy' in Far Eastern Economic Review, 1975.

Muralidharan, S.: "Cover story: Who's afraid of Article 356?" Frontline, 1998.

Muralidharan, S.: "Food economy: a price to pay". Frontline, 1998.

Muralidharan, S.: "For four new States". Frontline, 1998.

Muralidharan, S.: A bitter aftermath. Frontline, 1999.

Nair, P.: "Return of overseas contract workers and their rehabilitation and development in Kerala (India): a critical account of policies, performance and prospects". International Migration 37 (1), 209-42, 1999.

Nandy, A.: An intelligent critic's guide to Indian cinema. In The savage Freud and other essays on possible and retrievable selves. Delhi, Oxford University Press, 1995.

Nandy, A.: The uncolonized mind: a post-colonial view of India and the West. In The intimate enemy: loss and recovery of self under colonialism. Delhi, Oxford University Press, 1983.

Narasimhan, R. and Sattiah, D.: Pudupalakshmi groups in Nellore (AP). In Mathew, A. S., Promoting livelihoods for the rural poor: a source book for development administrators and NGOs. Mussoorie, Soft rain, Lal Bahadur Shastri National Academy of Administration, 1997.

Nayyar, D.: Economic liberalization in India: analytics, experience and lessons. Calcutta, Orient Longman, 1996.

Nehru, Jawaharlal: The Discovery of India, London, Meridian Books, 1956.

Nhat Hanh: Vietnam: The Lotus in the Sea of Fire, New York, The Fellowship of Reconciliation, 1967.

Ninan, T.: "A year in purgatory". Seminar 473, 1999.

Norbu, Dawa: 'The 1959 Tibetan Rebellion: An Interpretation' in China Quarterly, 1979.

Norbu, Jamyang: Warriors of Tibet: The Story of Aten and the Khampas' Fight for the Freedom of their Country, London, Wisdom, 1986.

Olsen, W.: Rural Indian social relations: a study of southern Andhra Pradesh. Delhi, Oxford University Press, 1996.

Omvedt, G.: Dalit visions: the anti-caste movement and the construction of an Indian identity. Hyderabad, Orient Longman, 1995.

Ould-Mey, M.. "The new global command economy". Environment and Planning D: Society and Space 17 (2), 1999.

Pahl, R.: Divisions of labour. Oxford, Basil Blackwell, 1984.

Pandey, B.N.: The Indian Nationalist Movement: Select Documents, London, MacMillan, 1979.

Parekh, Bhikhu: Gandhi's Political Philosophy: A Critical Examination, London, Macmillan, 1989.

Parrinder, Geoffrey: The Bhagavad Gita, Oxford, Oneworld, 1996.

Patterson, George N.: Tibet in Revolt, London, Faber and Faber, 1960.

Peissel, Michel: Cavaliers of Kham: The Secret War in Tibet, London, Heinemann, 1972.

Philips, C.H. and Wainwright, M.D.: The Partition of India: Policies and Perspectives 1935-1947, London, George Allen and Unwin Ltd., 1970.

Powers, John: Introduction to Tibetan Buddhism, Ithaca, Snow Lion Publications, 1995.

Purcell Victor: The Chinese in Southeast Asia, 2nd ed., Oxford University Press, London, 1965.

Queen, C.S. and King, S.B.: Engaged Buddhism: Buddhist Liberation Movements in Asia, Albany: State University of New York Press, 1996.

Radhakrishnan, S.: The Principal Upanishads, London, Allen and Unwin, 1953.

Ray, S.: Gandhi, India and the World: An International Symposium, Melbourne, Hawthorn Press, 1970.

Richards, Glyn: The Philosophy of Gandhi, Surrey, Curzon Press, 1991.

Richardson, H. E.: Tibet and its History, London, Oxford University Press, 1962.

Robbins, Christopher: The Invisible Air Force: The True Story of the CIA's Secret Airlines, London, Pan, 1981.

Robinson Thomas W. et al.: The Cultural Revolution in China, University of California Press, Berkeley, 1971.

Sartori, Giovanni: The Theory of Democracy Revisited, Chatham, N.J., Chatham House, 1987.

Schurmann Franz: Ideology and Organization in Communist China, University of California Press, Berkeley, 1966.

Schwartz, Ronald D.: Circle of Protest: Political Ritual in the Tibetan Uprising, London, Hurst and Company, 1994.

Seymour, J. P. and Cao, C.: Tibet Through Dissident Chinese Eyes: Essays on Self-Determination, Armonk, M. E. Sharpe, 1992.

Shakabpa, Tsepon W.D.: Tibet: A Political History, New York, Potala Publications, 1984.

Shakya, Tsering: 'Tibet and the Occident: The Myth of Shangri-La' in Lungta, 1991.

Skinner G. William: Chinese Society in Thailand. An Analytical History, Cornell University Press, Ithaca, New York, 1957.

Smith, Warren W.: Tibetan Nation: A History of Tibetan Nationalism and Sino-Tibetan Relations, Boulder, Westview Press, 1996.

Snellgrove, David and H. E. Richardson: A Cultural History of Tibet, Boston, Shambhala, 1986.

Snow, Edgar: Red China Today: The Other Side of the River, Harmondsworth, Penguin, 1962.

Strong, Anna-Louise: When Serfs Stood Up in Tibet, Peking, New World Press, 1960.

Su Wenming: Tibet: Today and Yesterday, Beijing, Beijing Review, 1983.

Subba, T.A.: Flight and Adaptation: Tibetan Refugees in the Darjeeling - Sikkim Himalaya, Dharamsala, Library of Tibetan Works and Archives, 1990.

Ten Glorious Years, Foreign Language Press, Peking, 1960.

Text of speeches given by Professor Samdhong Rinpoche on his visit to Britain, October 1997.

The Dalai Lama: My Land and My People: Memoirs of the Dalai Lama of Tibet, New York, Potala Corporation, 1962.

Thompson Virginia and Richard Adloff, The Left Wing in Southeast Asia, Wm. Sloane Associates, under the auspices of the International Secretariat, Institute of Pacific Relations, New York, 1950.

Toye Hugh, Laos: Buffer State or Battleground, Oxford University Press, London, 1968.

Trager Frank N.: Marxism in Southeast Asia: A Study of Four Countries, Stanford University Press, Stanford, California, 1959.

Van Lyman P. Slyke: Enemies and Friends: The United Front in Chinese Communist History, Stanford University Press, Stanford, California, 1967.

Wangyal, Phuntsog: 'The Revolt of 1959' in Tibetan Review, 1974.

Westerlund, David: Questioning the Secular State: The Worldwide Resurgence of Religion in Politics, London, Hurst and Co., 1996.

Westerlund, David: Questioning the Secular State: The Worldwide Resurgence of Religion in Politics, London, Hurst and Co., 1996.

Williams Lea E.: The Future of the Overseas Chinese in Southeast Asia, McGraw-Hill Book Co., for the Council on Foreign Relations, New York, 1966.

Williams, Paul: Mahayana Buddhism: The Doctrinal Foundations, London, Routledge, 1989.

Wylie, Turrell: 'A Standard System of Tibetan Transcription' in Harvard Journal of Asiatic Studies, 1959.

Zaehner, R.C.: The Bhagavad-Gita, Oxford: Clarendon Press, 1969.

Index

D

E

F

G

H

I

J

K

L

M

N

O

P

Q

R

S

T

U

V

W

X

Y

Z